How to Prepare, Stage, and Deliver WINNING PRESENTATIONS

Third Edition

Thomas Leech

American Management Association

New York • Atlanta • Brussels • Chicago • Mexico City • San Francisco
Shanghai • Tokyo • Toronto • Washington, D.C.

Special discounts on bulk quantities of AMACOM books are
available to corporations, professional associations, and other
organizations. For details, contact Special Sales Department,
AMACOM, a division of American Management Association,
1601 Broadway, New York, NY 10019.
Tel.: 212-903-8316 Fax: 212-903-8083
E-mail: specialsls@amanet.org
Website: www.amacombooks.org/go/specialsales
To view all AMACOM titles go to: www.amacombooks.org

*This publication is designed to provide accurate and authoritative
information in regard to the subject matter covered. It is sold with the
understanding that the publisher is not engaged in rendering legal,
accounting, or other professional service. If legal advice or other expert
assistance is required, the services of a competent professional person
should be sought.*

Library of Congress Cataloging-in-Publication Data

Leech, Thomas.
   *How to prepare, stage, and deliver winning presentations / Thomas
Leech.—3rd ed.*
      p.   cm.
   *Rev. ed. of: How to prepare, stage, & deliver winning presentations. New
and updated ed. c1993.*
   Includes bibliographical references and index.
   ISBN-10: 0-8144-7231-1
   ISBN-13: 978-0-8144-7231-6
   *1. Business presentations.   I. Title: Winning presentations.   II.
Leech, Thomas. How to prepare, stage, & deliver winning presentations.
III. Title.*

HF5718.22.L43   2004
658.4'52—dc22   *2003019971*

Printing number

10   9   8   7   6   5   4   3

Contents

Part III
Stage   165

Part IV
Deliver and Follow Up   205

Part V
Special Presentation Situations   285

Acknowledgments

hanks to the current AMACOM editorial and production support team of Ellen Kadin, Mike Sivilli, Niels Buessem, and Lydia Lewis, for their diligent review, suggestions, and honing of this edition, continuing the Winning Presentations treatment into the third edition.

Also, much appreciation to Patsy Corlett for major administrative aid, and to my wife, Leslie, for her patience, professional feedback, and stress management during the research, writing, and tuning phases.

And finally, to the previous AMACOM editorial team, which, through two previous editions, provided guidance, encouragement, and friendship along the way.

Presentations: An Overview

CHAPTER 1

Presentations: Vital to Success in a Changing World

"You can have brilliant ideas, but if you can't get them across, your brains won't get you anywhere." So says Lee Iacocca, former chief executive officer (CEO) of Chrysler Corporation. "I've known a lot of engineers with terrific ideas who had trouble explaining them to other people. It's always a shame when a guy with great talent can't tell the board or a committee what's in his head."[1]

If you're a professional, whatever your specialty or level in the organization, you'll probably find that presentations come with your job. It is a rare individual who can conduct his or her career communicating with only test tubes or computers. As business becomes increasingly complex, the need to communicate in concise terms that a broad audience can understand becomes more critical. One of the most important tools for doing this is the face-to-face presentation.

Top executives, program managers, engineers, bankers, architects, trainers, union leaders, politicians—all frequently find themselves facing audiences and selling their ideas through speeches and presentations. These can be as simple as an informal talk to a half-dozen colleagues, using a few handmade viewgraphs, or as complex as a fully

3

developed presentation using a hundred computer-generated slides and involving a dozen speakers.

Presentations Play a Powerful Role

People have been giving presentations with visual aids since time began. Cave dwellers supplemented their tales with wall paintings; the Egyptians probably got progress reports on the pyramids' construction via hieroglyphics; and Moses relayed the rules of life with the Ten Commandments.

Presentations can open doors, win and sustain business, and communicate with management and colleagues. Here are eight important roles they play:

1. *Aiding in the Pursuit of New Business.* A company pursuing a competitive bid from government agencies or larger prime contractors, a civic economic development committee convincing industry to relocate, an advertising agency going after a new client.
2. *Getting Backing for Growth or Image.* An entrepreneur needing start-up money from venture capitalists, an expanding company floating a new financing program, the company president addressing the Chamber of Commerce.
3. *Reporting Status of Ongoing Projects to Customers or Management.* Design reviews, product updates, investigation reports.
4. *Helping Management Stay Informed for Astute Decision Making.* Status of employee morale, budget reviews, requests for new equipment, go-ahead to pursue a new business line.
5. *Keeping Employees Involved, Informed, and Current.* Motivation meetings, new employee orientation, training seminars.
6. *Communicating Among Peers.* Industry trade shows, professional society annual conferences, management meetings.
7. *Personal Interests.* Convincing the Council to spend money on a new library, encouraging high school freshmen to stay off drugs, getting elected.
8. *Getting Hired or Promoted.* Today many organizations are less interested in the resume, and more in how candidates present themselves.

Presentations Represent Opportunity: To Gain or Not to Gain

A presentation is an opportunity to convey ideas to a group of important people. During that time, and possibly only then, you have their attention focused. This opportunity should not be taken lightly, as a second chance may never come.

According to Michael Bayer, who has been a top official in many agencies in Washington, D.C., presentations in his business are life or death to ideas: "Here you are marketing to people overwhelmed with ideas. A bad presentation means the idea never connects, and in D.C. you rarely get a second chance."[2]

Presentations are more important than ever in many competitive situations today. RFPs (Requests for Proposals) often require presentations by the bidder's team before the Source Evaluation Board (SEB). Increasingly these replace written proposals—long the standard selling documents—and are significant parts of the evaluation and selection. Many winning teams have scored high and won because of their high-quality presentations.

It cuts both ways. You may not win it with a good presentation, but you sure can lose it with a poor one. Denny Krenz has been on many of those review boards for the Federal Government. He said one team absolutely lost because of the performance of the presenting team. "It was a seven-man team and one member's arrogance turned off the board. As we left the meeting, my deputy said to me 'How'd you like to work with that SOB for the next five years?' They scored zero."[3]

Presentations are also key when organizations sponsor connection meetings between entrepreneurs—the ones with the bright ideas—and venture capital firms—the ones with the money. For example, during a full morning, a series of CEOs deliver eight-minute presentations with the objective of enticing the VCs to meet with them for a more detailed discussion. The presentations largely determine which CEO gets the private meeting.

Computer Technology for Better Presentations—Maybe

Presentations technology has hugely changed the way presentations are prepared and delivered. It enables the content experts to prepare their own high quality graphics (with animation and video clips), fine-tune them on an airplane, and operate them from their laptop computers connected to high-quality five-pound projectors.

These options have changed the nature of meetings and presentations. Tele- and Internet-conferencing allow groups to communicate from different locations, cutting down on travel costs and lost time. Web seminars have changed the way people learn as they can hear from experts and take college courses online. Presentations can be sent via e-mail, with speakers displaying the same PowerPoint presentation on each side of the country.

As managing director of Global Partners, Inc., Paul Sullivan has worked with firms around the world. His firm is increasingly using the Internet for client and team communications. "It's helpful in working with clients in other countries. We find it is most productive to have an initial meeting in person. Then for follow-up we use the Web to get everybody online and review progress, eliminating the need for travel."[4]

These days school kids are getting early introductions to presentations. My niece recently showed me her PowerPoint presentation, which was as good as those of many corporate managers, and especially impressive considering that she was in the seventh grade.

Yet in this high-tech world, presentations are not necessarily better than those done with mostly slides or transparencies. Many computer-generated visuals are still hard to read, or they obscure, rather than clarify, a point. It is still the presenters themselves—the executives, engineers, sales reps, and others—who must come through with the knowledge, credibility, and persuasiveness to win over audiences.

Tools are only as good as the wisdom and skill of those who use them. A well-known acronym is GIGO: Garbage In, Garbage Out. (A difference is that today's garbage out is much prettier than in the past.) Having the tools and the ability to use them properly may lead to better presentations, yet without the fundamentals of public speaking and its related specialties, those tools are of marginal value.

It's tempting to get carried away with the many exciting options available in graphics programs. With slides (referring now to computer images, as distinct from 35mm slides) coming in from six directions, with animations or builds adding bullets and boxes one at a time, and with images sliding in or appearing in enticing ways, some of today's presentations resemble works by Salvador Dali.

And not all audiences are thrilled with the snazzy effects. Within the U.S. Department of Defense, this issue was addressed from the top, as the Chairman of the Joint Chiefs of Staff issued an order stating, "Enough with the bells and whistles—just get to the point. . . . We don't need Venetian-blind effects or fancy backdrops. All we need is the information."[5]

Presentation Skills Complement Professional Skills

According to Michael Cogburn, executive vice president of Anteon Corporation: "Two skills in life are needed to prepare for success: Develop (1) your ability in the field you're chosen and (2) your ability to communicate, being able to write well and speak well."[6]

In a 1980 survey of business leaders, 62 percent said the ability to write well was very important to their jobs, *but 90 percent said the ability to speak well was very important.*[7]

The most brilliant idea is worth little until it is expressed. How well it is expressed can be as significant to its acceptance and implementation as the idea itself. A person can carry around terrific insights, knowledge, and analytical capability, but none of these abilities do him or her, the organization, or the world any good until they are communicated—fundamentally through writing or speaking.

Winning Presentations Can Boost Careers (and Get You Hired)

A tip to college students: Pay attention to those speech teachers as well as the ones in the disciplines you're pursuing. According to Mary Mandeville, a professor of speech communication at Oklahoma State University, "One of the first things the employment interviewer checks is communication skills. Employers want people who can communicate first and foremost. So I advise students to stick up front on their qualifications the communication skill classes they've taken. That will get them the job over someone else."[8]

Regardless of your work experience, your communication ability or lack thereof can be a key factor in whether you get hired. Jeff Young, general manager of ATA, a small engineering services firm, says: "Communication is a major part of what we do as consulting engineers, with each other and with our customers. So when interviewing people, we look hard at not only their technical or managerial skills, but also how well they can present."[9]

In the Federal Government, it's common for people being considered for promotion to meet with an interview panel. William Reschke, who is plant general manager at Naval Air Depot, North Island, said that the candidates are asked five questions, given ten minutes to prepare, and then present their answers. "The reason we do this is because 70 percent of what we do is give presentations, formal or informal. So the most important attribute for managers is being able to communicate well. Some totally choke at the interview—this is the most common error. They get so tied up and stressed they're unable to communicate. It definitely hurts their promotional potential."[10]

Few other activities have more potential for attention—favorable or otherwise—than presentations. A person who has toiled unnoticed for years in the bureaucracies of large organizations can give one presentation to the right audience and suddenly be in the limelight.

During the President Clinton impeachment hearings, many heavy hitters pressed their arguments for and against impeachment. Dreary legal citations, lengthy statistical references, dry and lengthy arguments prevailed. Until a young black attorney, unknown to most people in the country, took her turn, defending the President. For the first time in days, here was a speaker most anyone could relate to. Articulate, speaking personally, making arguments in closer to everyday English, Cheryl Mills held the attention of audiences both in the chamber and watching on TVs across the nation.

Another example from politics is the governor who became Vice President of the United States as a result of his superb keynote speech at the Republican convention. It was Spiro Agnew, who became Richard Nixon's running mate in 1968. The decision makers were so dazzled that they picked him without really investigating him—a big mistake, as he later had to resign from office for malfeasance as governor.

Today's Presenters: A Mixed Bag

Every organization has outstanding employees whose technical or administrative skills are matched by their presentation skills. Much of the material in this book comes from the observations and experiences of many of these top presenters. In my experience, most of the people who rise to the top in organizations do so not only because they have demonstrated expertise in their specialties, but because they have good communication skills, particularly oral skills. (There are exceptions.)

Kevin Werner, president of the SAIC Venture Capital Group, said: "It is very important that people be able to present well, and occasionally we will see a spellbinder who holds our attention and addresses issues relevant to us. Gives them a big advantage over others who may have a good case but can't present it so well."[11]

As a presentations consultant, I've worked with teams that have developed winning presentations, as demonstrated during rehearsals and actual presentations, and through winning outcomes and debriefings from customers. I've also seen many professionals whose presentation skills are extremely poor. I have sat through high-level corporate presentations where the visual aids could not be read, where presenters mumbled their words, where the message defied understanding, and where equipment failed to work.

From the vice chief of staff of the U.S. Air Force: "I am increasingly concerned about the quality of presentations. They need streamlining. A large number of presenters talk at great length from busy and unreadable charts on issues that are not germane to the subject."[12]

In "Executives Can't Communicate," Robert Levinson, then vice president of American Standard, said: "I have come to a shocking conclusion about the American executive. He talks too much, expresses himself poorly, and has an uncanny ability for evading the point. . . . It is astonishing how many otherwise able executives lack either the tools or the techniques for delivering their messages briefly, yet comprehensively."[13]

Presentation Skills Take Work—and It's Worth It

Developing proficiency in oral communications doesn't occur automatically. The ability to speak may have come much as did walking and breathing, but speaking well to groups is another matter. Learning to organize thoughts and present them so people will listen and understand, determining what will win people over to your point of view, using visual and other nonverbal channels as well as the oral channel, developing sensitivity to what turns listeners on or off—these things may be assimilated by life experience, but to acquire a deeper knowledge of them requires attention.

Few things are more satisfying and confidence building than to experience important people intently listening to you as you make your case. Increasing your capability in oral communications will serve you well in many areas. Meetings, training, committees, personnel coaching and appraisal, leadership in professional societies, political or civic activities—all extensively involve oral skills. A person proficient in those skills is a valuable asset.

In Summary: Presentations Come with the Territory

Whatever your career direction, be aware that knowledge of your specialty is not enough. If you can't communicate it, how much is it worth? Developing this other important facet—oral communication skills—requires special attention and is an important investment for enhancing your business and career success. This book will help you do that.

By the way: in case you need a bit more motivation, consider these words from Gilbert and Sullivan (tuning a major line from Shakespeare):

> If you wish in the world to advance,
> And your merits you're bound to enhance,
> You must stir it and stump it,
> And blow your own trumpet,
> Or, trust me, you haven't a chance.

CHAPTER 2

Executive Summary

The Fundamental Fifteen Keys to Winning Presentations

While much goes into planning, preparing, and giving business presentations, fifteen concepts stand out as fundamental, based on my experience and observations from top executives and presenters (Figure 2–1). A speaker who applies the *Fundamental Fifteen* is well on the way to a successful presentation.

These basic keys will all be developed more fully in the pages to follow.

1. *Go in prepared.* One of the worst openings for a presentation is "I really didn't have much time to prepare." (Translation: "Yes, it's going to be lousy, but don't clobber me too much.") According to many top executives, one of the key messages they bring to seminar participants is to take the time to prepare. Many people do not do this, as is evident when they show up obviously inadequately prepared.

2. *Believe in yourself and your idea.* Denny Krenz, former top official in the Department of Energy, says that in going before re-

Figure 2-1. Back to basics: Fifteen fundamentals to keep in mind.

1. Go in prepared.
2. Believe it's important.
3. Know your purpose and communicate it.
4. Have a focused central theme and core points.
5. Know your audience—address their needs.
6. For busy executives, summarize early.
7. Help them get it with powerful reinforcement.
8. Make visuals add, not impede, communication.
9. Stage with care 'cause Murphy's there.
10. Practice, and get good feedback.
11. Make your delivery personal and passionate.
12. Keep alert and flexible.
13. Anticipate and manage questions well.
14. Keep your perspective—enjoy.
15. Remember you're selling.

view boards, "you have to convey sincerity and honesty." In rehearsals for major presentations, this is a common exchange:

> Reviewer/coach: "Do you really want to work on this job?"
> Presenter: "Well, of course."
> Reviewer: "Then why don't you show it?"

3. *Know your purpose.* According to Mike Cogburn, Anteon's former chief operating officer: "Number one in making presentations is to be really clear about your objective. Know that before you start to prepare."[1] I've been in many meetings where, after ten minutes, the VP says "Why am I hearing this?" Failing to establish a clear and realistic objective makes it difficult to (a) shape the presentation, (b) know what to ask for (a common failing), and (c) know that you've achieved the objective (so the boss can give you a raise).

4. *Have a focused central theme and core points.* The most important chart in a presentation is the summary. Develop this chart first to clarify and focus what the presentation boils down to. Many listeners look immediately for the summary chart, and if it's not there, will probe to find it. Far better to have done this in advance, rather than flail around in real time.

5. *Know your audience and tailor your presentation to them.* "The biggest deficiency in presenting," says Nick Vlahakis, Alliant Tech Systems' chief operating officer, "is not making it meaningful to the audience. Most people present from their own viewpoint and think the audience will connect."[2] The primary question in the minds of listeners is "What is this going to do for me?" Knowing and satisfactorily addressing audience priority needs is at the heart of successful attention and persuasion.

6. *For time-pressed audiences, summarize early.* In our major competitive presentations, we always open with the executive summary. Kevin Werner, president of SAIC Venture Capital Corporation, often hears from executives pursuing financing. "The biggest shortcoming is not being clear and crisp about your value proposition, what problem you'll solve. Do that up-front; otherwise it just gets bogged down."[3]

7. *Help them get it with powerful reinforcement.* The power of a story, example, or startling statistic has been demonstrated in business, political, and religious speeches. A common marketing maxim is that a claim must have substantiation, must be backed up. I've seen many instances where the speaker's personal success stories were the key factor in winning over the audience.

8. *Make sure visuals add, don't impede, communication.* A standard comment from speakers is "I know you can't read this, but. . . ." (Guess what—we already know that.) At a large conference the CEO of a major firm displayed a graphic on two large screens and asked rhetorically "Now what's wrong with this picture?" My colleague and I both agreed instantly on what was wrong—we couldn't read it, which was not quite the reaction the CEO was pursuing.

9. *Stage with care 'cause Murphy's there.* Take care of the mechanics—or they'll take care of you. Failure to follow this simple axiom has been the grief of many presenters who tried to wing it and forgot the perverse nature of Murphy's Law: "Whatever can go wrong, will." And, often despite diligent care, Murphy hits. Just ask Bill Gates or Bill Clinton, both victims of technology failures in high-profile situations: Gates during the Windows '98 introduction, and Clinton during a major congressional address.

10. *Practice, and get good feedback.* The value of practice in pre-
    paring for important presentations has been demonstrated repeat-
    edly. People whose confidence and presentations skills are weak
    can be transformed with good practice and coaching. And I've
    seen the disasters that have hit when speakers insist they need no
    practice. (Usually the ones who resist the most, need it the most.)
    Kobi Sethna, president of Nereus Pharmaceuticals, has conducted
    business all over the world: "Be able to articulate your business
    quickly and concisely in a way that other people can understand.
    Keep sharpening that message and it gets better every time. The
    key is practice."[4]

11. *Make your delivery personal and passionate.* Many people
    downplay the importance of delivery, noting "The data speaks for
    itself." How information is presented is clearly a major part of
    success. The person who projects enthusiasm, credibility, and con-
    fidence keeps audiences tuned in and often won over. Both as
    CEO and VC partner, Martha Dennis has observed many present-
    ers. "Listeners evaluate you both on what you know about your
    topic and on your comfort level as you tell us about it."[5]

12. *Keep alert and flexible.* Stay tuned to the audience and situation,
    then adjust your presentation rather than continue along in a di-
    rection that's no longer appropriate. "One thing that really tees
    me off, " said SAIC's Werner," is when presenters aren't prepared
    to deviate from their script when it's clear they're not focusing on
    issues the listener is interested in."[6]

13. *Anticipate and manage questions well.* The ability of the
    speaker to handle audience comments or questions is often more
    critical than the ability to make the formal presentation. In a major
    competitive presentation, one of the speakers had never done a
    formal presentation of this sort. However, he worked hard, in-
    cluding repeated rehearsals on Q&A. During the presentation, he
    became engaged in a dialogue with several of the review board
    members concerned about a key issue, and he came through admi-
    rably. Said our team's VP: "It was great to watch, like a meeting
    of like minds."

14. *Keep your perspective—enjoy.* Let yourself come through and
    even enjoy the presentation a little bit. Audiences relate well to

speakers who are genuine, enjoy what they're doing, and aren't uptight with fear about everything that can go wrong. Fun is contagious.

15. *Remember you're selling.* In my training seminars, I invite top executives to pass on some lessons-learned to the attendees. Consistently they say: "Above all, keep this in mind: When you're up before that audience, you're selling!" What are you selling? Yourself and your credibility above all, then your organization, your information, and your proposition.

In Summary: The Basic Stuff Will Serve You Well

Major presentations were significant to both of the U.S. Gulf Wars. The first took place in 1991, when General Norman Schwarzkopf summed up how the U.S.-led forces so quickly succeeded in defeating the Iraqi troops. Using poster charts, "Stormin' Norman" personified many of the Fundamental Fifteen: clear organization, good visual aids, energy and passion, and superb question-and-answer capability. This briefing caught international attention, became a hot-seller in video stores, and, after retirement, led to his demand on the lecture circuit at $25,000 a speech.

Twelve years later, General Colin Powell, who had been the other key Pentagon player in 1991, was now the Secretary of State in the George W. Bush Administration. In a critical presentation to the United Nations, Powell used various means of audiovisual support—photos, videos, maps, audios—to lay out the case that Iraq indeed had weapons of mass destruction (WMD, the most famous acronym of the war and post-war), thus providing the rationale for a U.S.-led invasion. While it was greeted with skepticism by some nations, it was a well-crafted and well-executed presentation.

Both presentations were outstanding and applied many of the fifteen elements contained in the Fundamental Fifteen.

CHAPTER 3

Becoming a
Winning Presenter

This chapter shows how you can improve your presentations capabilities and ensuing success, heading toward the objectives realized by the speaker in Figure 3-1.

Enhancing Presentation Skills and Knowledge

Presentations capabilities range widely, from outstanding to dreadful. Some people never test these capabilities because they avoid presentations entirely; maybe they don't like doing them, maybe they've had

Figure 3-1. Wouldn't you like your presentation to get these results?

bad experiences, or perhaps their pulse rate skyrockets at the mere thought.

Make a Self-Assessment

A starting place for improvement is to do a realistic check of your capability. How successful have you been in the conference room or on the podium?

To find out your capability, do a post-speaking assessment yourself. Having yourself audio- or videotaped and reviewing the tape later provides helpful insights, if sometimes a dreadful jolt. Discuss with your supervisors how they see your skills and needs. Get some friends to sit in on a dry run or actual presentation as observers and give their feedback.

Project Ahead to Where You'd Like to Be

Would being a better presenter help you achieve that new position or enable you to be a more effective contributor? It almost always does.

In pursuing new business, many customers today require that the assigned personnel deliver a presentation showing why their team should be selected. This means each person is expected to present, and sell themselves and their team. As a result, organizations not only have to consider who is their best person for each position, but how well each can make a winning presentation. Consequently, the person with the best professional talent may well miss out while the position goes to another team member who management believes can make a positive impression.

Perhaps you're already a good presenter, and you have a message you'd like to share with a broader audience. Or maybe you'd like to be more influential on a larger scale than your workplace. Your goal may be running for office, becoming a professional speaker, conducting university workshops, or starting your own company. Consider the level of presentation capability that will help you achieve those goals.

Commit to a Long-Term Plan to Improve

Because you've gotten this far, you've already made a major commitment. Keep it going. One way is to write down your plan, with specific objectives and milestones. Your supervisor can help by providing opportunities and guidance.

Don't Let Anxiety Dampen Your Pursuit

If you are someone who has been ducking presentations because you fear speaking before groups, you're far from alone. In one survey, researchers at Purdue University found that fear of public speaking was among the top ten fears (out of a list of 131).[1]

In the "knew it all along" category is the study done by Cedars-Sinai Medical Center, which found that many mental conditions can trigger the physical condition of heart stress. The worst of all was asking people to give five-minute talks about their personal faults and bad habits to two observers. Moral: Choose a different subject for your speeches.[2]

Leslie Johnson-Leech has helped many speakers and amateur actors to become both more comfortable and better. Her own presentations are noted for high spark, high-interest content, and enthusiastic audience response. Here's her advice: "Do something to help yourself deal with inevitable stress. Take meditation, yoga, Tai Chi, or Qi Gong classes. They really work! And don't be afraid to be yourself with a group. Have fun. Remember most audiences are very forgiving and want you to succeed—that benefits them and you. And no one expects 100 percent perfection. That's a restriction we put on ourselves."[3]

Six Myths That Stifle Presenters

1. *You need God-given talent to be a good speaker (and I don't have it).* This is the myth that good speakers are born, not made. Who hasn't heard the powerful voice and speaking style of James Earl Jones? God-given talent, you probably conclude. Yes, but Jones had to help a little. His teenage years were spent writing notes to teachers and chums instead of talking because he was a stutterer. "Whenever visitors came to the house," he recalls, "I was in terror of having to say hello." Fortunately, for his benefit and that of his many fans, Jones had a high school teacher who encouraged him to recite poetry, and he was able to do it fluently.

That started him on the road to becoming the acclaimed actor he now is.[4]

2. *Good speakers probably never had stage fright like mine.* In his autobiography, auto industry executive Lee Iacocca talks about learning to speak by joining his high school debating team. "At first I was scared to death. I had butterflies in my stomach— and to this day I still get a little nervous before giving a speech. But the experience of being on the debating team was crucial." Even with that background, Iacocca avoided speaking during his first few years on the job, describing himself as an introvert, a shrinking violet. He broke that pattern when the company sent him to a public speaking course. The rest is history.[5]

3. *Good speakers don't have to work at it (the way I do).* Phil Joanou, past president of ad agency Dailey & Associates, said: "Lots of people have the misconception that this is easy stuff. The best presenter I've ever seen is our creative director, and he really works at it just like the rest of us. When some fellow workers commented on how he had a gift for speaking, this is what he said, 'Gift, my ass! I've been working three nights on this pitch. These clowns think this just happens. Bull. You sweat!' "[6]

4. *Experienced people don't get nervous anymore (and I do, so I must not be meant for this stuff).* Andrew Young has been a long-time leader in many arenas, as a civil rights activist, a minister, congressman, and United Nations ambassador. Looking back at his college days he wrote, "The only course I got an A in was speech. I have never been afraid to talk or state my opinions. I could also organize my thoughts rather quickly and express them with some coherence. I still get butterflies when I have to make a speech."[7]

5. *I could never be a good speaker (so there's no sense trying).*

6. *I've tried all that and it didn't work (so it's futile).*

These last two are the most devastating misconceptions. Number 5 prevents action, and number 6 represents resignation to failure. The most important step is to break the mold that says "I can't do it." This is the hardest one as well.

Pam Lontos is president of her own firm, PR/PR, which provides publicity services to professional speakers. She's spoken to hundreds of groups about ways to improve sales results. A natural speaker, right? Not at all.

"I was always really shy," she says. "Even into my twenties at parties I was shy. I did take a speaking course, and was one of those who could hardly say their own name. I got into radio sales and then started training others. This was for small groups around a table. The company signed me on to speak at a national convention for, I thought, a small group. When I walked out there were 2,500 people. I said 'I'll never do this again.' But I got away from the lectern, used the techniques that had gotten people involved in small groups, and was a hit. It was written up in the trade magazines, and the company sent me off to do eighteen more groups around the country. Looking back, if anybody had told me when I was in my twenties that I'd be a professional speaker, I'd have said they were insane."[8]

In Chapter 11 we'll address specific techniques to help you reduce anxiety to at least manageable levels.

Follow the Winning Presentations Path to Success

The stars in any field know what they are doing and why and how. Executives, financial analysts, and techies have this characteristic in common with Tiger Woods and Michelle Kwan. They achieve results by applying proven techniques to whatever problem they tackle.

Roughly the same sequence of events occurs in producing any product, whether it is an automobile, a can opener, or a software system. You don't start to build a new automobile before you design one, and you don't start to design one before you figure out whether one seems needed and what kind.

One of the key factors that distinguishes the cool, efficient professional who gets results from the duffers who stumble around and rarely get anything done well is this knowledge of process. When given a tough problem, the duffer often doesn't know where to start. The professional knows precisely where to start and what has to be done to get to the desired result. (This lesson was reinforced the last time I tried to repair a faucet. Knowing little about the tools or the process, I soon had water running all over the floor. With an emergency call to a plumber, I watched him fix the problem in about ten minutes.)

Now a strange thing happens to many of those same professionals—executives, financial wizards, and scientists—when they are asked to prepare presentations about their specialties. They forget all the wisdom that separates them from the amateurs—the proved, rigorous approach—and instead tackle the presentation in a haphazard, casual manner.

The same proven procedure that professionals use in tackling any project can be applied beneficially to the development of presentations. This methodical, six-step approach can lead to better presentations, produced more efficiently (Figure 3-2).

1. *Plan.* This is the market analysis, fundamental thinking-through phase, asking, "What do I want to get out of this presentation? How might that best be done?" The audience is identified, its interests are examined, and themes and strategies are developed.

2. *Organize.* This develops the framework, the skeleton of the package. The key ideas are identified and arranged in a clear, concise, and convincing manner.

Figure 3-2. Apply the "Winning Presentations Six-Step Approach to Success."

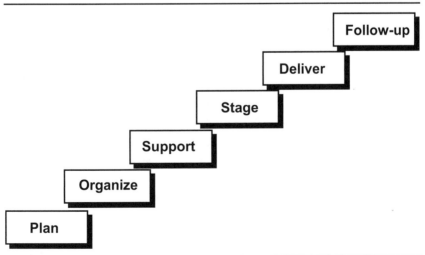

3. *Support.* This adds the meat to the organizational skeleton. Material is developed to back up, illustrate, and clarify the positions and claims set forth. Visuals aids—or today's common term, graphics—are shaped into punchy, effective tools of communication.

4. *Stage.* The goal is to head off the relentless power of Murphy's Law: Whatever can go wrong, will. Leaving nothing to chance, the presenter identifies facilities, equipment, and schedules. Before heading off to the actual event, the wise presenter tests the product.

5. *Deliver.* Show time: It is the presenter's opportunity to convey information, ideas, and propositions. It is the audience's time to sound out the speaker with friendly or nasty questions or comments, presumably aimed at clarifying information, resolving uncertainties, and sizing up the speaker's ideas and credibility.

6. *Follow-Up.* All is not over when the product is delivered. Now is the time to tally up the scorecard, take care of the loose ends, and apply the lessons learned toward a better job with less wasted effort the next time.

A department head related a sad result from not doing it the right way: "This was a program review on an existing contract. We were awfully busy and felt we were in good shape on the program, so we didn't spend much time getting ready. No dry runs, for example. We got into the presentation, and the customer tore us apart. It was clear we were not prepared for this meeting. One measure of our success can be seen in the number of action items we carried away. Typically we get twenty-five. This time we got 300. It's going to take us months to take care of them all!" What a painful way to get reminded of the importance of preparing well.

In Summary: Why Not Add to Your Presentations Capability?

Many people work hard to master the knowledge and skills of their profession. Developing the capability to present that expertise and their ideas in the best light is a valuable investment. Presentations growth comes from a determination to do it, followed by a program of knowledge sharpening and skill development through practice. And applying the proven six-step Winning Presentations approach helps you get the job done successfully.

As an example, at an early team meeting for a major competition we set all the milestones for speakers to prepare for the event. One of the key speakers, Jean, was a solid professional but with little experience at this level of presentation. She dug in however and met each milestone, meeting with the coaching team with her plan, outline, storyboard, rough graphics, etc. We gave her feedback, and after some give-and-take (O.K., grumbling), she went back to revise and move forward. Came time for rehearsal, she was the first one ready to practice. And came back for another one.

For the major rehearsal, a Red Team review, she spoke for twenty-eight minutes, with an allocation of thirty minutes. The reviewers were silent, as they had little to offer in the way of fixes (a very rare event for Red Teams). One said, in a bit of jest, "Why don't we have her do all the segments?" As the comments were few, she headed home. Others, who had not been so diligent about meeting the milestones, were engaged with the Red Team until midnight. Two days later there was another rehearsal. The reviewers said there was no need to review Jean as she had done so well on the earlier review. And she did fine in the actual event.

Prepare

CHAPTER 4

Plan

First Analyze and Strategize

A manager of an important new electronics program was asked to tell a group of visiting Explorer Scouts about the program. He pulled two dozen visuals used for working meetings, went into great detail about technical aspects, and spoke of FLMs and MOKFLTPAC. He was enthusiastic, knowledgeable, and totally ineffective, since his audience was lost for about forty-four of his forty-five minutes.

During the 1960s, one of the big three television networks gave a presentation to several potential sponsors for a new series, *Twelve O'Clock High,* based on experiences of Allied bomber pilots in World War II. Volkswagen was one of the prime client targets. Perhaps you can see some potential difficulties in that match up. The network led off with drama, rolling the opening scenes of the film, which showed terrific shots of American bombers unloading their payloads and blasting the targets below. Within two minutes a German-accented voice—that of the Volkswagen representative—was heard muttering, "There goes our factory in Stuttgart." Shortly thereafter, the network team packed up its film and silently left the room.[1]

Many speakers are sincere in their desires to impart a message and

27

Figure 4-1. Planning examines several interrelated factors to develop a sound approach.

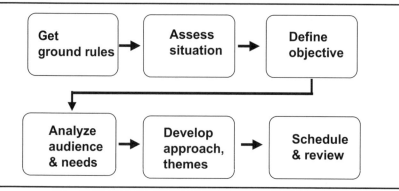

put forth great effort in preparation, but all their efforts are for naught because they are misdirected. The foundation is faulty because of failure to consider adequately or correctly the audience part of the communication process.

Planning addresses the strategic aspects of your presentation, as opposed to the tactics. It is doing the market research and analysis, needs assessment, and thinking. This is where the basic questions are asked:

◆ Who is going to be in the audience?

◆ How can we get them to accept our ideas?

◆ Do we even want to give a presentation?

The effective presenters almost always know the importance of planning, the process, and that it is a wise investment. The typical steps in the process are outlined in Figure 4-1. This is a neat, sequential process, for simple presentations. But for major ones, such as competitive marketing presentations by a team of speakers, the planning process can be involved and highly iterative. Figure 4-2 summarizes the key concepts of planning.

Get Ground Rules

Before racing off to order a hundred slides by Monday morning, gather, list, and clarify certain basic information. Ask questions now to head off wasted effort and dollars.

Figure 4-2. Apply these tips for effective planning.

◆ Establish requirements, constraints, and budget.

◆ Be aware of how situations and environment can shape your strategy.

◆ Define your primary objective in terms of what the audience will do or know.

◆ Identify key members of the audience and analyze the various factors of importance.

◆ Set the presentation at a level appropriate for the audience

◆ Consider audience attitudes in planning your approach.

◆ Consider both business and personal needs.

◆ Identify benefits your proposal will offer listeners.

◆ If you have a lemon in your package, see if you can convert it to lemonade.

◆ Incorporate all factors into your overall theme or central message.

◆ Keep rechecking planning assumptions and decisions through all phases of the presentation. Be an ever-listening speaker.

◆ Set key milestones for orderly presentation development.

The Five Ws

◆ *Who/ Audience.* Who makes up the audience? Identify the organization, number of participants, and key individuals.

◆ *What/ Subject of Specific Area of Interest.* What do they want to hear about? What specific topic do they want to focus on? This may be only loosely defined for some presentations but tightly targeted for others.

◆ *Why/ Function.* What is this presentation intended to do? How does it fit into the broader scheme? Is this tied in with something else, such as a group of visiting dignitaries or the annual meeting?

◆ *When/ Event and Occasion.* Is it tomorrow or next week? What time of day? Different considerations will be in order depending on whether the talk takes place first thing in the morning, over lunch, late in the afternoon, or after dinner. How firm are the date and time?

◆ *Where/Location.* Here, there, or elsewhere? Is the room already set, or is one to be scheduled? What kind of place is it? Is travel involved?

Receiver Requirements

For many presentations, the audience will explicitly request that certain items be addressed or procedures followed. It is vital that these be known, understood properly and clarified if needed, and integrated into the presentation. A presenter who doesn't heed this request will be deemed nonresponsive. Typical items include:

- ◆ Topics to be covered and order of presentation.
- ◆ Criteria for evaluating competing presentations established by potential customers, such as source selection boards; internal management reviewing research projects for future funding; or judges for speech contests. They may even have set evaluation forms; what's on those forms?
- ◆ Specific questions, given in advance or at the actual presentation.
- ◆ Detailed guidelines (How). This gets into the operational, nitty-gritty stuff that you must know from the start:
  - Type and length of presentation (formal, informal, on-site group, video/Internet).
  - Format and medium (computer-based, demonstrations, viewgraphs, slides).
  - Nature of meeting interaction (audience questions during or after, many likely or few).
  - Operational constraints (related to event, program, location, shipping, travel).
  - Budget and priority.
  - Available help (resources and people, decision makers, reviewers, presentations support, content contributors).
  - Anything else to be aware of.

Assess Situation

A human resources manager was to be one of many speakers at a three-day management retreat. His slot was at 4 P.M. on day two. His job was to renew interest in the employee suggestion program, not a high-interest topic. After reviewing his planned presentation and finding it to be dry, information heavy, and weighty with busy charts, the review team predicted severe Slumbersville and headed him back to the drawing board to liven it up. ("You mean it's O.K. to have fun?") He came back with a totally transformed presentation: a much snappier opening, simpler content, punchier visuals, and a more spirited delivery. His presentation was rated one of the best at the conference.

For the finale of a three-day national conference, we all gathered for an extended happy hour, then filed in for dinner, with wine at every table. The emcee started the program about 8 P.M. First came all the attaboys for the hard work done by each of the committees, then a series of sectional leaders all told about their activities, then a couple of awards were given out. He introduced the keynote speaker at 10:30 P.M. He launched into a talk that went on for 45 minutes, with lots of details. The audience soon started fading, some sneaking out of the room, others with glazed eyes, a few actually snoring. The speaker seemed totally oblivious of what was happening. The only people listening after the first five minutes were the emcee, the speaker's spouse, and me, taking notes incredulously. He finally called for support of an important cause, but alas, only a few heard it.

Knowing the meeting environment or circumstances surrounding the event can help a presenter do the right thing or avoid doing the wrong one. Probably every experienced speaker has realized upon leaving the podium that he or she has just done something stupid. Several questions are worth asking to avoid problems:

◆ *Does the occasion have any special requirements that may be peripheral to the presentation?* For example, protocol can define rigorously specific procedures or rituals that must be observed. Is there anything I must absolutely not forget to say or do? You can talk wonderfully for an hour and then blow the whole situation by neglecting some required statement or task.

A painful personal experience serves as an example. In an early political campaign, we had a fund-raiser at a popular restaurant/ dance venue. Good, lively crowd. After a half hour of dancing, I took the floor for the political talk. I spoke for two minutes and then said something like "O.K. let's get back to the music." Shortly thereafter some people came over to ask about my position on an issue. I realized I'd made a big mistake, by just talking and not having a dialogue, far more important in winning over supporters than more dancing.

◆ *Is there anything I must clearly avoid?* During the 2003 California Governor recall campaign, candidate (and actor) Arnold Schwarzenegger brought on some high-profile economic advisors. One of those, Warren Buffet, said the first need was to raise property taxes (by modifying the voter-approved Proposition 13). The outcry in opposition was instant and loud as this was regarded as a no-touch issue. The candidate immediately distanced himself from the Buffet position.

◆ *Is there a vital issue—something the audience specifically wants to hear about?* If the audience is hungry for news about the new contract, failing to mention it can leave them dissatisfied. Even saying "I can't say anything about that yet" is generally better than skipping the subject entirely.

◆ *Is anything else occurring that is likely to affect my presentation?* If the presentation follows a two-hour hospitality period, your audience may not be in a proper mood to assimilate a forty-five-minute talk on the needs of higher education.

◆ *Is anyone else involved that I should know about?* If you are scheduled to follow Robin Williams (or vice-versa), you may want to reschedule.

◆ *Is the present audience the real audience?* An example where this is not the case is a televised talk. Focusing on the immediate audience may prove detrimental to communicating with the real audience: the television audience. During the 1960 presidential debates, Richard Nixon was credited with winning the debate inside the television studio; John Kennedy won it where it counted, in the homes of millions of viewers. As seen on TV, Nixon's five-o'clock shadow overshadowed what he had to say, and made him look tired and old, whereas Kennedy looked young and vigorous.

Situation analysis is not something done once and forgotten. Events may occur right before or during the meeting that can seriously affect attendees' spirit or attention. I was conducting a seminar the morning the space shuttle Challenger blew up during launch. The company was a shuttle subcontractor. As we watched the event on television, I knew the relaxed, learning mood was no longer there and suspended the planned activity.

Define Goal and Message

As a speaker, what is your purpose? What do you hope to achieve? What message do you want to get across? This is the raison d'être, the basic object, of the presentation, and yet it is frequently unrealistic, or not clearly understood.

Three steps are involved: defining the basic purpose, end product, and main message or theme.

1. Basic Purpose

Frequently presenters either lose sight of their purpose or have not thought through clearly enough what their purpose should be. The result is often an inappropriate presentation or a confused audience. With the proviso that a presentation may have multiple purposes, the primary one is likely one of these:

◆ *Persuade/Convince.* Marketing presentations are almost always of this type, as are presentations seeking approval and support for new programs or facilities or ideas.

◆ *Inform/Explain.* Program review, professional paper, orientation (new hire, product, or procedure), all-hands meeting, training session).

◆ *Inspire.* Many authorities regard this as a subset of persuasion. Its primary purpose is to fire up or move the troops, such as a coach's send-off of the team

◆ *Entertain or Preside.* Welcoming new employees, presiding at a retirement or change of command, contributing at a "roast" are in this category.

2. End Product

The end product is the outcome you desire from your audience in specific terms that help you know, not guess, whether you succeeded. It is what they will do, believe, and know. Writing down your end product helps clarify and focus your presentation. Here are some criteria to help you do that:

◆ *Is it achievable?* Getting the audience to give blood to the blood bank is a worthy objective, but how likely is success if the audience is composed of hemophiliacs? If you need approval of a $50,000 budget item and the principal listener can approve only $10,000, you need to rethink your plan.

◆ *Is it a present or ultimate objective?* Ask an eager marketer what the objective is, and the answer may be, "To win the contract, of course!" Is that likely to occur as a result of this specific presentation? "Well, not really. We have a long way to go before that can occur." Then what is possible with this presentation? "We'd like to get them to put us on the bidders list." A series of hurdles may be involved; are you focusing on the current one?

◆ *Is it measurable?* When you ask yourself or the boss asks, "Was it a winner?" a well-defined end product gives you a yes or no. "How do you know that?" may be met with silence unless it's measurable. "Get four sign-ups" is measurable; "sell the idea" may or may not be. This criterion may not be easy to define for some presentations.

◆ *Is it sound business?* "I convinced them to invest," said the salesperson from Investments-R-Us. "They're putting all their money into no-load mutual funds." Nice job, except IRU isn't in that business and won't make any money themselves.

Now for some specific end products. A helpful way to write these is to state "As a result of my presentation, the audience will _____," and fill in the blank. Some examples are shown in Figure 4-3.

3. Main Message (First Look)

If you could say only one sentence to your audience, what would it be? This may seem trivial and obvious. Let me assure that it is not. Many presenters are vague about their main messages (or even their purpose) in speaking.

Where this occurs in the planning process depends on the situation. Sometimes you may know early on what the nature of your core message is. At other times you may not have a good grasp on it until you dig deeper into planning.

Figure 4-3. Make sure you know your objective.

Specific Purpose	To Achieve	End Product: The Audience Will:
Persuade	Action or attitude change	Approve $10,000 for new computer. Write Congress and ask support of Bill 205. Buy off on the estimate.
Inform	Change in audience knowledge or ability (behavioral objective)	Know three main problem areas of program (upper management). Complete new form correctly in ten minutes.
Inspire	Emotional impact, enthusiasm	Be eager to do a great job on new promotion (sales force). Be aroused for the final push (proposal team).
Entertain or preside	Warm feeling suitable for the occasion	Give Charley an appreciative and jolly send-off for his retirement. Greet the new leader with respect.

Distinguish between the "subject" and the main message. A frequent comment by presenters when they're asked to state their main message is: "Well, I'm talking about safety." That's the subject, not the message. The message would be, perhaps, "Knowing and following safety procedures saves lives," or "Wear your safety glasses at all times when operating machinery."

Why is identifying a main message so important? For one thing, it may be the wrong message for your audience or not the best one for your purpose. Writing it down as a complete sentence serves as an early check on where your presentation is going. In addition, having a clear main message will help ensure that it gets said, emphatically and often. Finally, your main message is the focal point for all other parts of your presentation. Don't include or generate anything that does not support or tie directly to that single statement. If your main message is poorly stated or faulty, to a large degree your efforts to follow will be misdirected.

Beveridge and Velton apply this concept to proposals: "A good proposal opens with a message. It closes with a message. And in between you keep socking home the message. . . . You dare not start any proposal effort without knowing just what your message will be."[2] This advice is equally valid for presentations.

Another way to think about the main message is to ask, "What is the main theme, idea, or point I want the audience to take away with them?" Gerald Phillips and Jerome Zolten, in *Structuring Speech*, call this the "residual message—the idea that breaks through the resistance, that stays in the listener's mind when everything else is forgotten."[3]

In addition to writing out your main message or theme, identify the three or four key points of your main message. A practical way of uncovering those is to assume you are writing the summary visual aid for your talk, and that it is all you will be able to show the audience. What would you put on it? These preliminary points may be changed as the presentation structure takes shape, but they provide useful early clarity and guidance.

Here are some examples of a main theme and key points.

♦ *Wear your safety glasses at all times when operating machinery* (main theme to persuade).
   • Several serious accidents have occurred recently.
   • Safety glasses could have prevented the injuries.
♦ *XBC Corporation has three major product lines* (main theme to inform).
   • We make and sell food products.
   • We supply medical products.
   • We design and build shopping centers.

Conduct Audience Analysis

In the audience were a dozen high-level, extremely knowledgeable people. The speaker was describing the procedures used for financial analysis and resource allocation. Said one attendee: "It was awful. The speaker went into every detail of every procedure and covered the full background of how each system evolved. No one cared, but he never caught on. We kept waiting for him to get to the heart of it, but he was enamored with all this history and background. If you asked him a simple question, he went off again into every minute detail. I couldn't wait to get out of there."

This presenter failed to ask some basic questions about the audience, a crucial and often neglected part of presentation development. It can encompass many parts and levels, including psychological drives, learning theory, and resistance to change. What baggage—impressions, experiences, and agendas—do listeners bring to a presentation, and how did they come by it? To boil all that down to something manageable, we're going to look at five composite audience characteristics (see Figure 4-4).

- What are they capable of doing?
- What do they already know?
- How interested are they in what I have to say?
- What are their needs?
- What are their attitudes toward my proposition, my organization, me?
- What is their meeting or listening style?

Audience analysis is not a one-shot activity but continues through phases of preparation and during the presentation itself. This continuous sensitivity to the audience results in a "listening speaker," a term coined by Paul Holtzman: "The listening speaker, throughout his preparation, engages in an imagined transaction with his audience-

Figure 4-4. Audience analysis attempts to discover what "baggage" principal listeners will bring to the conference room.

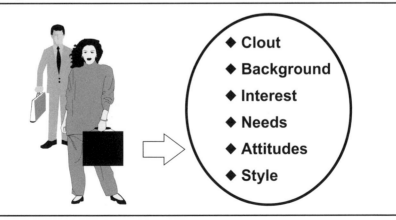

- Clout
- Background
- Interest
- Needs
- Attitudes
- Style

image. He tests ideas and material, and ways of stating them to see if they evoke the desired responses. On the basis of his tests, he organizes or programs his ideas and materials and his ways of stating them. Then, while in the actual speaking situation, he continues to test for response and continues the process of seeking causes for the desired effects."[4]

Audience Capability

Many speakers do not adequately define the action they expect to achieve and, consequently, do not match that action against the audience's ability to achieve it. Gaining a favorable attitude toward your goal is nonproductive without the power to implement it.

Making sure you are speaking to the right audience is at the very core of presentation planning. Your first task is to identify the decision makers or influencers. The second is getting them to listen to your presentation. If you can't do that, any further work you do on the planned presentation will be worthless, and you need to redefine the objective of the presentation or rethink the whole approach.

Assessing audience characteristics is complicated by the heterogeneous nature of many business audiences. In one group may be the company controller, the quality director, and a human resources manager. How do you tailor a message to fit all these people?

Consider whether this group contains key or primary listeners at whom the talk is mainly aimed. For a talk to a professional society, probably all listeners are roughly equivalent in importance. For a marketing presentation or program review, one or several listeners generally carry the greatest clout. In that case, thorough audience analysis should be done for each primary listener.

Occasionally speakers concentrate exclusively on those individuals they determine to be the key decision makers. They prepare a talk with only the leaders in mind and during the talk direct the message almost entirely to those few people. This can be a serious mistake, as other so-called lesser individuals may be more influential than is assumed and may be irritated at receiving cavalier treatment.

For other situations, every member of the audience may be key. A typical proposal review team comprises members from many specialties, levels, and areas of responsibility, and each member has a vote.

Within the bounds of practicality, an audience analysis should be done for each member. The approach to the presentation may be to give the full audience a summary, then address specific topics while being ready to go into more detail should audience members ask questions.

Audience Knowledge

Correctly gauging the knowledge level of the audience is a constant problem in business, with highly diverse audience members and many presentations for a specific program. How much do they know? How much background should you go into? Can you assume they know all the program terminology? These are serious questions that need to be asked and for which answers are often hard to come by.

"People don't do much homework regarding the sophistication of audiences," noted Brook Byers, principal partner of Kleiner, Perkins, Caulfield, Byers. "They usually underestimate the level; for example, all of our partners have backgrounds in managing technology. You want to present at or slightly above the knowledge level of people in the room." Knowing that level in advance can be a problem. Byers says, "If I don't know, the first thing when I get the floor is to ask, 'What level of technical detail should I go to?'"[5]

If audience members can't understand your language, don't relate to your references, or can't follow your line of discussion, it is highly unlikely that they will grasp your message. On rare occasions they may go away impressed at the knowledge you seem to have, but more often they will be baffled and irritated. The standard comment is, "I don't know what he said. It was over my head."

Jargon and acronyms are among the worst culprits (Figure 4-5). Speakers tend to assume everyone will know what the terms mean, and often that is a bad assumption. Or they say it's no big deal because if people don't understand, all they have to do is ask. However, often they won't ask, so you won't know you're on two different wavelengths. I was in a top level group meeting with directors and VPs. One exec was giving a report on union negotiations and used the term COLA several times. The person next to me leaned to the VP on his left and whispered "What's COLA?" "Beats me," came the answer, whispered back. The speaker was not clued in.

Figure 4-5. Set your presentation at a level that the audience can understand.

Here's a short list of common acronyms. What do they mean?

COLA	NATO
FICA	CIA
PC	TWAIN

(Maybe these, maybe not: Cost of Living Adjustment? Allowance?; Federal ????, oh, heck, Social Security; Politically Correct?; National Alliance of Theater Owners?; Culinary Institute of America?; TWAIN . . . hmmm)

Audience Interest

Are they highly enthusiastic about hearing what you have to say? Or are they lukewarm, or even apathetic about it, inspiring and significant as you might be? What about the mandatory weekly safety lecture? The annual time cards update?

Talk to the local 10th-grade class about your area of expertise if you want to have a taste of mixed audience attention, and possibly a shaky experience. It will give you a much greater appreciation of what talent it takes to be a successful teacher.

When given an assignment to a low-interest group, consider delegating that to an associate as a valuable learning experience. Put in an order for donuts to give the group at least one positive reason for showing up. Or recognize this as a challenge and work to understand ways to make this a useful experience for audience and speaker.

Audience Needs

At a success seminar, a dozen top speakers offered inspiration and ideas. They were flamboyant, told great stories, and employed sensational visual effects. One speaker opened his talk by flatly stating he had none of those—he was not a spectacular speaker. What he did have was a message that hit home with his audience and powerful credentials to verify that his words were worth heeding. He was the most spell-binding speaker of all. Audience members hung on his every word and feverishly scribbled notes to capture as much of his message as they could. They also cleaned out the supply of books he offered for sale afterward.

Identifying what aspects of the subject the audience might be interested in hearing about is essential. This is generally more difficult to assess than the knowledge level, but also more critical to presentation success.

An equally important reason to explore your audience's interests and concerns is that they provide the principal avenues for reaching and moving an audience. The heart of successful persuasion is showing people that adopting your proposition will serve them well. Venture Capitalist Partner Martha Dennis: "When approaching us for financing you have to convince us there is a need. If you can't do that you shouldn't be presenting."[6]

Needs Analysis: Business

Targeting the right needs is the difference between gaining an interested ear (and perhaps the contract) or a bland reception, followed by the hated phrase, "Don't call us—we'll call you."

In the early 1990s the U.S. government sought proposals for a new unmanned air vehicle (UAV). The winner was none of the well-known players, but a San Diego firm, General Atomics, known for energy research, not for making aircraft. How could they have won against the heavyweights? The answer lay in identifying and targeting the government's most critical need, which was to have the specified UAV flying in six months. GA brought on a partner firm, which already had a working model in the air. They thus became the only team that could meet the requirement. Years later that product is still going strong, with new models in the works.[7]

Locating key audience members' most pressing single need, or group of needs, is thus critical to success. Knowing your audience well and sounding out ideas in informal advance discussions is paramount. One of the values of presentations is that they give you an opportunity to test if you have guessed right and are emphasizing the right points. If the real customer "hot buttons" are identified early enough in the marketing program, later efforts, such as formal proposals, can reflect these.

Needs can be highly flexible. A change in job or charter, an emergency at home or work, a dragged-out meeting can all cause people suddenly to lose interest in a topic they would normally respond well to. After the September 11 terrorist attacks, interest in almost any other subject dropped for several days.

Frequently, shifts in need can be identified well before the presentation—early enough so that appropriate changes in the approach can be made. Other changes may be so recent that only last-minute adjustments are possible.

It is a rare situation where appealing to a single need will be successful. Audiences are made up of many individuals, each with his or her own internal set of hot buttons. Each individual has multiple needs, some stronger than others, but several possibly related to your topic or proposition. The successful speaker will address the several audience needs that seem most pertinent.

Needs Analysis: Personal

Houston contractor Brown & Root won a major contract for a multibillion dollar resort in Japan. The president of the firm developing the resort said he wanted a U.S. prime contract for partly personal reasons. A U.S. military officer had been kind to his older brother during the occupation of Japan after World War II.[8]

The Society for Marketing Professional Services asked 150 firms what attributes they valued in choosing among competitors for design and construction projects. Respondents said "personal chemistry," a hard-to-define term, frequently was the winning difference. Per one respondent, "Honesty, responsiveness and *good listening skills* won out over 'overt sucking up.'"[9]

This suggests that another set of needs may be at work: the personal needs that individual listeners carry within them. These deal with such mundane matters as personal prestige, career opportunities, recognition, external or internal pressures, memory, and comfort. These needs almost never get put into writing. They may not ever be spoken or be recognized as existing. Yet they are powerful baggage that each listener has brought to the conference room.

The following illustrates these two types of audience needs:

Business Needs	*Personal Needs*
Cost	Political
Schedule	Power
Performance	Chemistry
Quality	Relationships
Support	Culture

In *Strategic Selling,* Miller and Heiman say that "the reason that people really buy is only indirectly related to product or service performance. That's why we don't focus on the product. Instead, we show you how to use your product knowledge to give each of your buyers personal reasons for buying. You can't just meet their business needs. You have to serve their individual, subjective needs as well."[10]

According to Jim Dollard, former MACTEC president, who has been involved in many business presentations, "When you are presenting to an evaluation board, it's important to remember those gut level issues which may not be in the evaluation criteria or on a list. A friend used to say, 'There are the issues and then there are the real issues.'" Dollard offered some possibilities:

◆ A suspicion that some of the key players may not be truly available.

◆ Political issues, such as what would be good for the procuring agency or some of the decision makers.

◆ Having a foreign team member. It may be acceptable on the surface but at the gut level may be troubling to the board reviewer.[11]

Audience Attitudes

Having given careful thought to all the considerations thus far discussed the presenter should have a reasonably good picture of the audience. Glimmers of an important audience characteristic—attitude toward the subject, proposition, speaker, or organization—may have already been seen. Understanding the audience's predispositions on these matters is vital to establishing the presentation approach.

Attitudes can vary from totally enthusiastic and supportive to uncommitted but willing-to-listen to tomato throwers (Figure 4-6). Complicating the process is the fact that all of them may be in the same audience. Speaker style, arguments used, order of presentation, type of support, and recommendation all are influenced by audience attitudes.

Ferreting those out may be difficult. People may not be willing to state publicly the attitudes they hold. A decision may have been reached but may not yet be ready for release. Showing bias either for or against may not be appropriate. Listeners may hold down their

Figure 4-6. Are they with you? Neutral? Against you? Your approach differs for each audience attitude.

own preferences in favor of those of higher-level listeners or group influences. People also may not be aware of the attitudes they hold.

Group Influences

Identification of group influences that will affect the responsiveness and actions of individuals is essential. Holtzman describes those as factors that do not generally account for success but can be the source of failure or of boomerang effects.[12] Groups themselves have interests and values that they hold dear, and ignoring or flaunting them is a likely source of trouble that may override all the other wondrous features of your case. A presenter hoping to win Army support for a program spoke with great admiration about how well the Marines had managed a similar program. He shot himself down in spite of a good proposal. Praising the Marines is not the way to win friends in the Army, he now knows.

How heavily individuals are influenced by the group depends on how firmly the individual is wedded to the group's values and how strongly the presenter's ideas touch or affect those pertinent values. A member of the Chamber of Commerce who strongly supports the Chamber is not likely to go for a proposal that runs counter to the Chamber's philosophy and positions. If the individual is loosely linked to the Chamber, he may be receptive to such ideas, especially if he belongs to other organizations that are more important to him and whose philosophy is compatible with the presenter's ideas. Clearly this information is of great importance to the presenter.

Individual Backgrounds

Tied closely to listeners' values and needs are the experiences, training, and environment to which they have been exposed. Awareness of these can offer valuable insight into what they are concerned about, what they might focus on, what they are prejudiced for or against, what level of discussion they are comfortable with, and what style of operation they are likely to employ.

A presenter from Company X spoke to an audience from a company considering X for a subcontract. To provide credibility for his cause, he spoke in glowing terms about several contracts X had undertaken in earlier years. An executive in the audience had been assigned to monitor one of those programs, and for him it had been a wretched experience. He reacted derisively to the speaker's comment and blasted the speaker several other times thereafter. No one had told the presenter (or, better stated, he had not found out) that the executive had had such a negative experience with the program. Inadvertently he had opened the legendary Pandora's box, much to his regret.

Cultural and Generation Gaps

A common error in assessing needs and attitudes of listeners is to assume that they see things the same way as the presenter and that they will respond to appeals in the same manner as the presenter—that is, to equate the speaker's way with the "logical" and "reasonable" way. A speaker who is disappointed because her terrific ideas have been rejected may have fallen victim to a cultural or generation gap. She may then question the intelligence or ambition of her audience as she puzzles over her lack of success: "Those people just don't know what's good for them. I just don't understand people like that."

Audience Style

Knowing how receivers behave or like to get information is crucial to communicating with them. Some people are information sponges; others go on overload after the third statistic. One of the first rules for success is "Know thy boss," the second is to provide information to her in whatever manner she prefers it.

The company's CTO (chief technical officer) was a detail person. All presenters knew to be successful you had to provide many detailed graphs, tables, and background info. Then a new CTO came onboard, definitely a big picture person, as several presenters realized when he made it clear he had no interest in seeing all those detailed charts. It was evident after about the third busy slide when the dreaded MEGO (My Eyes Glaze Over) effect appeared. Change the mode of presentation fast.

Figure 4-7 illustrates four very different receiver styles. None are good nor bad, they just are. Can you place two prominent speakers, President George W. Bush and his 2000 Democratic challenger Al Gore, on the style chart? Would you present in the same way to both of them? No way.

Presenters commonly err by speaking in their own style. In fact, the key style is the receiver's, not the presenter's. Consider the problem just discussed. If a detail-loving analyst presents detail to the big picture CTO: "Hook. Who's next?"

Figure 4-7. Different strokes for different folks. Know the style of your principal receiver.

Thus following the biblical Golden Rule—Do unto others as you would have them do unto you—can lead to trouble for speakers. A better rule is: Do unto others as they would like to be done unto— what the former president of the National Speakers Association, Jim Cathcart, calls the Platinum Rule. (Some apply a third rule—Do unto them before they do unto you—but I don't recommend that.)

Develop the Approach and Strategies

Now that you've gathered all that useful information, what will you do with it? All the factors analyzed must be deliberately weighed to determine how best to plan and shape your presentation. You will have made many preliminary judgments during the course of data gathering and analysis. Now is the time to review these and revise them as indicated by all the information at hand. Here are some suggestions for developing specific strategies for success.

Listen to and Heed the Input

Whether in business, government, or international relations, having information can be valuable if it is given proper attention. Examples abound where information was available about situations or people but was either blocked or ignored. Evidence is clear that pertinent information was missed for (a) the September 11, 2001 deliberate plane crashes into New York's World Trade Center and the Pentagon, (b) the failure of the Shuttle Columbia, and (c) the collapse of corporate giant Enron.

Similar outcomes can result when a presentation plan fails to adapt to the available information. For example, a customer invited five teams to bid on a large contract. They all had previously worked for the customer. Team Cyclone put forth their proposed team and the customer quietly told several of Cyclone's partners that, because of an earlier contract with Cyclone, they thoroughly disliked Oswald, a designated key player. The partners passed the info on, except Cyclone said "Phooey, we like him," and kept Oswald on the team. They lost.

Adapt to Audience Knowledge

Decisions stemming from the audience assessment include: the level of information presented, terminology, how much background to provide, form of reinforcement material, form of graphics, and style of delivery. The objective is to ensure that the audience (as an entity or key players) can follow the talk adequately without being bored or wiped out.

Suggestions for doing that for three levels of audience familiarity are summarized in Figure 4-8.

Assess Audience Attitude and Interest Level

Combining both of these important audience characteristics offers valuable insights not obvious from considering them separately. Three presenters, all real, planned their talks carefully, yet all were unsuccessful.

1. A military recruiter visited a high-school senior class to try to interest the students in a military career. The speaker gave a totally factual, dry presentation. Result: Most of the listeners went to sleep or wrote notes to each other.

Figure 4-8. Adjust your approach to fit audience knowledge.

Knowledge Level	Suggested Approach
Low	Be realistic about objective and points that can be covered. Stress use over how something is done. Lay the groundwork—background, basics—carefully without insulting your listeners. Speak lay English, avoid acronyms and jargon. Use stories, analogies, relevant examples; big picture versus detail; keep visuals simple, punchy, and pictorial. Build in checkpoints. Restate, summarize, and promote questions.
Medium	Set the level slightly above audience level. Be ready to shift into more detail. Give a big-picture overview. Check, by asking if necessary, if what you're covering is useful to them. Clarify and interpret information. Use jargon with awareness; explain acronyms the first time used if necessary.
High	Check your assumptions, especially if you have a mixed audience or one you don't know. Move through the groundwork quickly. Supply ample and detailed information, but cull to provide the most pertinent. Use trade terminology, but be alert for signs of uncertainty.

2. A task force from division Alpha of a large corporation investigated why sister division Bravo had botched a large contract. The Alpha team, presenting to the disgruntled Bravo managers, immediately set about showing how much smarter they were than Bravo had been. The speakers were aloof, gave abrupt answers, and deferred most questions. Result: The Bravo audience became hostile toward the presenters.

3. At his political party convention, the keynote speaker gave a highly informative presentation, presented the pros and cons of the issues, stepped through all the key points to prove his case—that the other party was incompetent. Result: An initially enthusiastic crowd soon settled down and then ignored the speaker. The end was met with polite applause, mostly in appreciation that he had stopped beating the dead horse.

The presenters could have averted these dismal outcomes by examining their planned approaches on an audience interest/attitude

50 *Prepare*

graph (Figure 4-9). This graph and the related strategies provide a quick look at approaches likely to be successful or unsuccessful.

Before reading further, size up each of the above three examples by locating them on the graph in Figure 4-9 based on their audience's interest and attitude. Now check the accuracy of your placements for the three situations:

1—The senior class was position B

2—Bravo division was position F

3—The political audience was position D

In each case the presenter applied the wrong strategy, with poor results. What could each have done? Figure 4-10 sums up general strategies for each of the six positions noted on the matrix.

Address Audience Attitudes Specifically

Here are more strategies for considering attitudes of your receivers.

◆ *Rank potential objections.* List the possible topics the audience may have concerns about and rank them in importance to the lis-

Figure 4-9. The audience attitude/interest graph provides a basis for first-cut strategies.

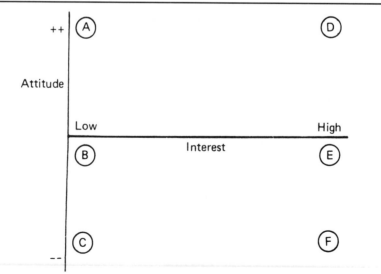

Figure 4-10. The attitude/interest matrix quickly shows basic strategies.

	Low Interest	*High Interest*
Positive attitude	They're pleasant but lethargic, convinced but not moving. Address value to them; visualize results and benefits with emotion. Make action easy and immediate.	They're sold, so don't bother with elaborate proofs or motivation. Go light on information, and heavy on catchy themes, color, and emotion. Move toward specific action.
Neutral	Get them to listen. Here's the place for a punchy dog-and-pony show, delivered with spirit. Get them into it quickly-mentally or physically. Get on their wavelength and tuned in. Then convert them.	Prove your case clearly and thoroughly. Show benefits and have facts well backed. Be prepared to discuss all options and defend your positions. Stress logic over emotion.
Opposed or hostile	Assess why they're so hostile and what you can do to rectify the situation, or at least show you are aware of that. Try a challenge, unusual approach, or self-effacing humor to lighten them up and maybe get them to listen.	Approach carefully. Set modest objectives. Look for common concerns or positions. Show you understand and respect their position. Stay cool and firm but not arrogant.

teners. This seemingly simple exercise is often treated lightly or ignored by presenters. These topics may be fetishes, high-risk areas, or parts of your proposition that you've done a mediocre job of explaining. If you're advising someone to include annuities in their financial plan, and a listener had a previous negative experience with annuities, be ready to answer detailed questions. If you have good answers, surfacing and addressing these issues can be beneficial (and potentially crucial) to your cause. Failing to anticipate objections can leave you with the proverbial egg on your face.

◆ *Develop counters for each major objection.* There may be some legitimate black marks or "lemons" on your record. If they're likely to be a major point of concern for the listener you can't ignore them, much as you would like to. Look for ways to make lemonade from the lemon—that is, turn the negative into a positive. One company did this with a manufacturing disaster it had on its record, a clear lemon. It was bidding to get a new contract in the same product area. What to do about the lemon? The initial plan was to ignore it, "to sweep it under the rug." The problem was audience members knew about the previous problems.

The company finally chose to face it head on and acknowledge that it had real difficulty with the earlier contract. "But," the company said, "we learned a great deal from that job, and we have made the changes necessary to do it right now. We've made our mistakes and learned from them." Unspoken was the hint that the main competitor, who had no experience of that type, was still learning and probably would run into the same problems, on the customer's money. They won the contract.

◆ *Trigger negative attitudes toward competing ideas or teams.* In proposal parlance this is called laying on a "ghost story," as demonstrated in the previous example. Suppose safety is an important factor, your team has an excellent safety record, and Brand X has recently had some serious accidents. It might be regarded as using a negative approach, even perhaps uncouth, if you flagged out this fact directly. You tout your own good record, so that the listeners can't help but contrast that with Brand X's, thus creating a problem for them. That's a ghost story.

Address Audience Priority Needs

One of the most common causes for the demise of presentations is the failure to (a) consider that the messages must be focused on the needs and interests of the audience, not the presenter, and (b) tailor the presentation accordingly. Here are five ways to help you direct your focus appropriately.

◆ *Rank audience needs—business and personal.* If you are not addressing audience key issues, the audience will be only mildly interested in your presentation. If you have accurately determined what issues are most pressing or foremost in their problem-solving/decision-making process and you address those issues, they will be attentive. Suppose you've identified the major issues:

Business	*Personal/Subsurface*
Reduction of inventory	Under fire from boss
Early delivery date, with confidence	Political "who controls"
Improved product quality	Competitor is reviewer's cousin

Further probing reveals that three issues are most pertinent and should be given priority treatment in the presentation with this ranking:

1. Political struggle
2. Confidence in delivery date
3. Improved product quality

◆ *Fill the need better than the competition.* By matching each of these identified priority needs with your solutions, you are stating "why our proposal is best." Addressing the personal issue (political power struggle) may need to be done subtly or even privately. What are your approaches to ensuring delivery date confidence and a high-quality product? If you've got the most credible answers (your discriminators) to all these versus the audience's other options, you probably will win out.

◆ *Stress benefits, not just features.* This is the old axiom: "Sell the sizzle, not the steak." A computer manufacturer may have a terrific product, an upgraded design, and a fine service network, none of which by themselves mean anything to a customer (Figure 4-11). This is a very important point: Don't emphasize how wonderful your product is but what it can do for the specific people who are listening to you. Excessively talking about features is a common mistake and generally leads to yawns and the predictable question: "O.K., I believe you have the greatest product since sliced bread, but what is it going to do for me?"

The astute presenter ensures that both benefits and features are addressed:

• Our Model Q will save you 35 percent over your present system (benefit) through improved design and production innovations (features).

Figure 4-11. Focus less on features, more on benefits.

- Our large service network (feature) means your downtime is minimal (benefit).

◆ *Stress results over process.* Technically oriented people frequently lose their audiences because they spend too much time talking about how something was done. Busy listeners rarely have the luxury of listening to all the analyses, trial and errors, and statistical methods used, and most of them don't care anyway. What they do care about is the "what" and the "so what"—the results, implications, and significance.

◆ *Adjust to current needs.* Joan has prepared a terrific forty-slide presentation as part of an all-day conference. Her talk is scheduled for 2 P.M. At 5:30 she finally gets the word: "You're on." Joan gives her full presentation, failing to notice that most of her listeners, having fidgeted for ten to fifteen minutes, were no longer around to see those lovely graphics.

What happened to Joan has happened to many other presenters who have failed to sense the mood of the audience. The group that would have sat intently for an hour at 2 P.M. was exhausted by 5:30 P.M. Their immediate needs—a quick summary and then relief—had superseded their long-term needs—to receive information and arguments contained in Joan's briefing.

Tailor to Individual Needs and Motivations

Personal needs often operate at a subsurface level, making them easy to miss. One way of assessing these is through Maslow's hierarchy of needs (Figure 4-12).[13] The key to reaching and moving a person is to find out the level with which he or she is primarily concerned. If your attention is given to a level either below or above the one at which the individual is operating, you are not addressing the need to which he or she will respond. A person operating at the ego/esteem level, for example, theoretically is little concerned about social, safety/security, and physiological needs, because all those needs (lower on the order) are taken care of. Thus, an appeal based on fitting into the group better (social) or getting more to eat (physiological) will receive little attention by that person, but stressing the increased recognition or leadership position (ego/esteem) possible through your proposal

Figure 4-12. The hierarchy of needs offers insight into listeners' personal areas of response.

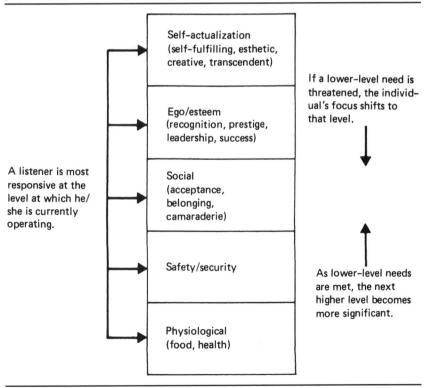

will be listened to. Whether you then move the person to accept your ideas or to act in the direction you desire depends on how strong those needs are, how believable your case is, and how well it meets those needs. Locating the correct level of interest is no guarantee for success, but talking at the wrong level generally ensures failure.

Lower-level needs certainly should not be ignored. According to Maslow's theory, if a lower-level need is threatened or becomes shaky, it becomes the overriding need. If accepting your proposition strengthens the listener's lower level needs or if not accepting it may lead to decreased fulfillment of those needs, it may be fruitful to address that.

Suppose your presentation is to persuade a group of smokers to quit smoking, and you determine that three types of smokers make up the audience:

◆ *Physiologically Concerned.* These people are sensitive to the need for good health but apparently haven't been adequately convinced that smoking is unhealthy. A factual presentation—or new findings, well substantiated—may have some success.

◆ *Socially Oriented.* Health is secondary to this group. People in this category want to be part of the gang, so if smoking is "in," they're likely to do it. Facts about cancer rates mean little, but if smoking can be seen to have strong social liabilities, they may respond.

◆ *Ego Oriented.* The slogan for this group is: "I am the master of my fate. I can do anything." Facts and social arguments are worthless for these people. But pointing out that nicotine seems to be the master, not they, may challenge them to straighten out that situation.

P.S. I know each of these three people and why they all quit.

Refine the Message

The theme is like an ad slogan. It captures the essence of the presentation or product in one line. It serves as the take-away that people might identify with the product and recall in a positive manner. Can you identify what these themes are associated with:

A. When you care enough to send the very best.

B. It takes a licking and (you finish it) _____.

C. If it doesn't fit you must _____.

Earlier we developed the concept of the theme and main points. In practice, the theme may not become clear until after audience analysis. Or the "obvious" theme may be seen on further review as not the best one, especially for persuasive presentations. Fine-tuning the theme takes into consideration the audience "hot buttons," such as priority needs and potential objections, and your strongest attributes, which enable you to meet those needs better than the audience's other options. The theme thus captures the essence of the overt selling message. (Addressing personal needs may require a subtle approach.) Some examples:

◆ Increased productivity achieved through better computer graphics capability

◆ System VI: Proven turnkey approach for assured delivery

◆ There's no fat in our system, so there's none in our prices (UPS ad slogan)

This is a good time to review not only the main theme but also the main points you identified back in the "define goal and message" stage, and to crystallize these into a set of core messages.

Back to those opening themes:

A. Hallmark Cards

B. "... keeps on ticking": Timex watches, showing the power of a slogan (not used for a couple of decades)

C. "... acquit": Defense attorney Johnny Cochran repeated this many times during the summation at the O.J. Simpson trial. (Remember what it was that didn't fit? A prop used by the prosecution that didn't work as intended.)

Lay Out a Realistic Operational Plan

The culmination of planning is to provide a basis for making smart decisions about how to proceed with this presentation. Here are some of those decisions you will make.

- ◆ Should a presentation be made? If so, when, where, and to whom? Test the assumption that a formal group presentation is needed; often an informal, one-to-one discussion will be better. Perhaps a series of presentations is needed because of different targets and themes.

- ◆ What media should be used? The purpose, situation, environment, audience, and budget affect media selection.

- ◆ What's the slant of the message? A soft-sell or no-sell approach may be wiser than a strongly partisan one. The extent of background and motivational material needed varies widely for different audiences.

- ◆ What type and depth of supporting material is suggested or readily available? For some audiences, fewer numbers and more stories or humor may be indicated.

- ◆ Who will be, or should be, the speakers? How should they dress and act? Does this call for a conservative business style or a more casual approach?

- ◆ What else needs to be considered besides the presentation itself? Hospitality, field trips, separate meetings, and distributions of materials should all be considered early.

Schedule Key Events

The final step in laying out the plan is to establish how all this work will get done. What specific steps will it take to get the presentation developed to meet the delivery date while making efficient use of available resources? For a one-person presentation of modest priority and due in two days, this plan may have only a few items. For a major presentation involving many speakers and support staff, the plan can he highly detailed. Whatever the level of presentation, it pays to lay out a milestone schedule, such as:

Event	*Target Date*
Kickoff meeting with team	_____
Plan details reviewed	_____
Outlines and storyboards done	_____
Visual aids/graphics ready	_____
Rehearsal	_____

Production   _____

Travel   _____

Presentation   _____

Before charging farther down the presentations development road, it's a good idea to bounce your analysis off someone else. An astute observer, such as your boss, someone more familiar with the audience and situation, or even a colleague can review your analysis from a perspective different from yours. A brief review (or sometimes not so brief, for major presentations) can provide insights you are missing, add information, and steer the presentation in a wiser direction.

In Summary: Planning Is a Sound Investment

This is the most important chapter in this book since it covers the most important activity you will do as you develop your presentation. The analyses and decisions made in planning set the direction and focus of all other phases to follow. Wise up-front thinking leads to good resource use and a successful presentation. The trails of many poor presentations and inefficient uses of resources often lead all the way back to slipshod or faulty planning.

In one of my seminars, the speaker tackled a real and often difficult presentation he often gave. It was the annual time card update, mandatory for all supervisors. Sounds like a tough audience? Applying many of the seminar concepts, he redid that same presentation. The first change was deleting most of the laborious detailed time card information, instead focusing each required topic with a stick figure cartoon character who pointed at the specific spot on the timecard, e.g., "Sick leave—what to do." Following this seven-minute presentation, several of the receivers praised him highly, one saying "I've sat in on your presentation for the last dozen years. This is the first time I paid any attention."

CHAPTER 5

Organize

Sort Out Your Ideas to Clarify and Convince

The event was an interchange between teams of entrepreneurs and venture capitalists. Each team had fifteen minutes to make their case. Speakers were consistently enthusiastic, had ideas that were interesting to hear about. Half the teams had serious trouble with the structure of their presentations, talking at length about their wonderful product. With the finish time closing fast, they dashed through marketing and financial segments, both of high interest to this audience, and through the summaries that tied it all together. It was good information, but it needed better structuring.

Audiences tend to be tolerant. They can put up with many characteristics of speakers that are normally regarded as weaknesses in public speaking. Unusual dress, poor grammar, "funny" accents, even loosely backed propositions may be readily tolerated or overlooked by listeners. One of only a few things that can cause them to become downright hostile to the speaker is poor organization.

The effectiveness of the message can be significantly increased by clear and logical organization. This is not only intuitively obvious; it has been demonstrated by behavioral studies in which audience members' receptiveness to ideas was measurably increased when ideas were organized as compared with random presentation of the same ideas.

Organization offers a powerful way to keep the attention of the audience focused. One of the most memorable speeches in recent history was Dr. Martin Luther King's "I have a dream!" speech before a quarter-million people at a rally in Washington, D.C., in 1963. King used this repeated theme dramatically with powerful results: "I have a dream that one day this nation will rise up and live out the true meaning of its creeds. . . . I have a dream that one day on the red hills of Georgia. . . . I have a dream that one day every valley shall be exalted."[1]

Another example of a politician's careful attention to organization appeared centuries earlier in Shakespeare's *Julius Caesar.* Brutus, fresh from putting a knife into Caesar, had just spoken to the alarmed Roman mob and convinced them that the assassination was admirable. He turned the platform over to Mark Antony, who was supposed to say much the same thing. Antony's true intent was to convince the mob of exactly the opposite viewpoint: that Brutus was a traitor who ought to be punished for this heinous crime. By presenting his ideas in an order that allowed him to conceal his true opinion until after he had conditioned the mob to hear it, Antony was able to reverse the mob from the position it had so enthusiastically applauded only minutes earlier.

Consider the organizing phase as a disciplining program, in which you take a jumble of ideas and set down the ones that are most vital and valuable, then order and prioritize them so the message can be readily digested in the time allocated. Key points are shown in Figure 5-1.

Principles for Sound Organization

◆ *The criteria for presentations are different from those for a written report.* Audiences commonly lament being subjected to boring, seemingly endless presentations. Too many people develop presentations that resemble technical or financial reports: thorough to minute detail, carefully rigorous in development, nothing pertinent left out. The trouble with this approach is that

Figure 5-1. Key how-to's for organizing a presentation.

◆ Start with an outline. Don't write out a presentation: write an outline instead.

◆ Set your theme and major points. Make this the first graphic you prepare—your "elevator" speech.

◆ Follow the "tell 'em" approach in introduction, body, and summary for most business presentations.

◆ Open with a "zinger"—catch their attention.

◆ For high level, busy audiences tell em up-front what's coming.

◆ Lay out your main points to be clear, concise, cohesive, and convincing.

◆ Apply tracking devices to help them stay on course.

◆ Set your time targets to cover key topics.

◆ Have a concise summary, reiterating the major points, and end with a strong send-off.

◆ To expedite the process apply organizational tools, both manual and computer.

---

it won't work with busy audiences who are unwilling or unable to absorb all that information.

◆ *Presentations illuminate the essential.* Presentations seldom cover the whole territory; they cover the key issues that will do the job to the audience's satisfaction and in the specific time allowed.

◆ *Simplicity is utmost.* In a world of complexity, achieving simplicity may seem an impossible task. Yet it is vital in presenting to people with possibly mixed backgrounds and in an environment loaded with hazards to communication. Structuring it so a fourth-grader can track it is not a bad policy.

◆ *The clock rules.* Ignoring this is a common failing. I recall a presenter showing up for a meeting with a stack of fifty transparencies for his twenty-minute time slot, a complete mismatch. In major presentations, time is tightly allocated and controlled, with a standard speaker's lament, "Impossible, I need more time." Sorry, you get ten minutes, so tailor the topics for highest priority. Remember that during Presidential debates each candidate gets one minute to sum up their entire story. Also, CEOs in meetings with venture capitalists have to do the job in eight minutes.

◆ *Less may be more.* "Brevity is the soul of wit," said Polonius in Shakespeare's *Hamlet*, and this is a key maxim in today's time-pressed world (Figure 5-2). This concept was well demonstrated by two headlines following President Gerald Ford's rejection of a federal grant to New York City.

From the *New York Times*:

Ford, Castigating City, Asserts He'd Veto Fund Guarantee; Offers Bankruptcy

From the *New York Daily News*:

Ford to City: Drop Dead[2]

Government executive Michael Bayer said: "The first-pass, door-opener presentation has got to be simple. Most are far too detailed.

Figure 5-2. Communicators old and new often need to tighten their topic organization.

"OK...I AGREE THESE 100 COMMANDMENTS CLARIFY YOUR POINT OF VIEW, BUT I'M GOING TO HAVE CIRCULATION PROBLEMS, NOT TO MENTION THE PUBLIC'S SHORT ATTENTION SPAN, SO WE'LL HAVE TO CONDENSE THEM *WA-A-AY* DOWN".

We're usually overwhelmed with information, as presenters ignore the fact that we've probably already been subjected to eight hours of presentations today. Most do a good job with a second presentation where detail is O.K., except they constantly do that on the first presentation."[3]

◆ *A journalist's approach may win points.* "Tell them the ending first," advises Alliant Tech Systems' chief operating officer Nick Vlahakis. "Many people make it like an Agatha Christie mystery novel. It's important to tell them the 'So what' first."[4]

◆ *Don't let the trees obscure the forest.* One of the things that hurts presentations is that people often go "into the weeds," according to Captain James Woolway, commanding officer of the U.S. Naval Air Depot North Island. "They get bogged down into the minutiae, spending so much extraordinary time on the details that the main point of the presentation is lost."[5]

◆ *Talk the issues that count.* An audience of financial specialists was gathered to hear about a new software package. For the first forty minutes of the forty-five-minute presentation they heard the sales rep cover all sorts of information about his company, its facilities and its many operations, the organization chart, the elegant analytical architecture that went into the software—information of apparently great importance to the speaker but only of mild interest to the audience. What did they need to hear to help them decide whether to buy the product? "What will it do for me?" They didn't hear it—and they didn't buy.

◆ *Change is likely, so plan for it.* According to SAIC Venture Capital Corporation's president Kevin Werner, "You need to be prepared for deviations from your script when it's clear you're not focusing on issues the listener is interested in. Many presenters aren't prepared to do that."[6]

◆ *Audiences like road maps.* They appreciate and need periodic guideposts to be clear about the route being taken and the territory already covered. Direction or transition statements are like road signs; they let the audience know what's coming and give assurance that progress is being made.

With that foundation of core principles, here are specific techniques that can lead to a presentation that is concise, clear, cohesive, and convincing.

Practical Tips for Sound Organization

Dottie Walters, head of Walters International Speakers Bureau, has spoken all around the world and worked with hundreds of speakers. She advises speakers to "start with humor and end with heart. Either a story from your own life or about someone else. People love it when someone gets knocked down and gets back up."[7]

◆ *Check the clock, process, and other ground rules.* How long is the presentation supposed to be? What specifically has been requested or specified? Is this likely to be a silent audience, or will it be highly interactive? These questions should have been addressed in planning but are often overlooked.

◆ *Answer the mail.* Follow the dictated agenda and topics. If the customer specifies the order of topics, and the amount of time to give them, that's what you do, unless further dialogue leads to a change.

◆ *Set a realistic presentation scope.* Knowing that the expected time is thirty minutes and that plenty of questions are likely is vital to the topic, coverage, and method.

◆ *Capture the essence of the talk in one complete statement.* That is the same message discussed in planning: the single statement you would make if that's all you could say. All ideas and support material are directed toward supporting that single theme, which may be as simple as "Buy our product" or "Our new Model M Computer is ready for delivery." Make it a simple declarative statement.

◆ *Boil down the dozen or so ideas you'd like to talk about to the three or four you must talk about.* This gets to the key points that can be presented in the time allotted. If you can get three clear ideas across, that's about as much as an audience can absorb. The high-end number has been experimentally shown to be about seven. Any listing above seven will be trouble.[8]

Suppose your task is to persuade the operations vice president to approve the purchase of a $5 million milling machine. You list all the benefits: faster turnaround, increased capability, reduced labor costs, fewer errors. You've done analyses to prove each point and need about five minutes to cover each, so you ask for a thirty-minute presentation. He gives you ten. Do you (1) cut the detail, (2) cut the number of points to cover, (3) arrive with a thirty-minute presentation anyway? If you choose option 3, start sharpening your resume.

◆ *Build in flexibility.* In presentations, plans often change. You're asked to give a thirty-minute presentation to the VP on the sixth floor. You get there and find that the meeting is running long; the VP asks if you can streamline your presentation. The wise presenter says, "Absolutely, how about the ten-minute version?" Or as often happens, the VP may say, "I'm heading for the airport. Ride down with me on the elevator and tell me your story." And you once more are ready and give her the essence of your presentation as you ride down on the *elevator* (which is why this is called the E_____ Speech). Message: In advance consider what you will do if the rules change.

Here are two masters of the brief summation:

◆ During the U.S. economy downtrend in 2001, the CEO of Advanced Micro Circuits Corporation, Dave Rickey, met with the press. Summarizing his company's situation, he said "We're sucking wind. Any questions?"[9]

◆ Moderator (and primary head chopper) for the TV series, *The Weakest Link*, Anne Robinson would retire contestants with her withering summary statement: "You are the weakest link. Goodbye."

◆ *Put the key points on one page as your summary chart.* Make this the first visual aid you prepare. Modify as needed, but keep it highly visible as you continue to develop the presentation.

◆ *Write out these core ideas as full statements.* This sounds simple, but it's often hard to do. Writing out ideas in full forces typical idea fragments to be crystallized into clearer points, and concepts to be cut because they're not clear.

For example, here's a basic presentation structure in topic form:

Main message: How great is the Model M
Key points: Cost, service, and features

Fleshing out the ideas into full sentences leads to this set:

Main message: Buying the Model M is a wise investment for your company.
Key points: 1. Our model is cheaper than that of our competitors.
                  2. Downtime is reduced with our extensive service network.
                  3. Faster speed increases production.

The second set is much clearer than the first. Both speaker and receiver understand clearly just what message the presenter intends to get across. Use this technique of writing out full sentences whenever you find yourself struggling to get your ideas to coalesce.

◆ *Prioritize topics.* Examine adequacy from two perspectives: the presenter's and the audience's. The listeners may have certain topics they specifically want addressed and some they don't care about. The presenter may feel specific topics must be covered to prove or demonstrate the case. Listing topics by priority can sort these out—for example:

Must	*Maybe*	*Low Priority*
Total sales	Sales by product line	Market share
	Sales by geographic area	Competitor sales
Sales trend	Trends by division	Competitor trends

◆ *Develop primary and backup materials.* Once you've settled on the primary, workable topics, don't discard the secondary ones. Remember the value of flexibility and the interactive nature of presentations. One common technique for contingency insurance is to be ready with a dozen backup (or JIC—Just In Case) charts. If detail is requested, having a backup chart can get that information across quickly and leave a strong impression of a prepared speaker.

◆ *Continue to follow these same concepts as the remaining details of the presentation are added.* Each key point becomes an entirely new main theme. Subpoints can then be tested for their relevance, independence, and adequacy.

The Standard Presentation Formula

Most business presentations follow the same organizational design, which is the old "tell 'em" formula:

◆ Tell 'em what you're going to tell 'em.
◆ Tell 'em.
◆ Tell 'em what you told 'em.

This is a straightforward approach, with the audience knowing upfront what the presentation is about and where it's headed, and with few surprises.

Introduction: Get Them on Board

The introduction is the most important part of the presentation and one shortchanged by many speakers. Often the presentation is won or lost in the first minute, or its direction may be completely shifted depending on how the speaker handles this phase. This is when attention is focused on the speaker, the stage is set, and the audience is conditioned to being receptive to all that will follow. Giving casual treatment to this phase or even ignoring it is like starting a car in third gear—you need to go through first and second gears first.

According to William Reschke, plant general manager at the U.S. Navy's Navair Air Depot facility: "The most important thing is to be concise. No one has enough time these days. Start with a very high level. Set the problem and methodology, then get feedback to establish if you're heading in the right direction."[10]

The items set out in Figure 5-3 are the key elements of an introduction. Tailor them to your presentation as all elements may not
apply.

1. *Establish rapport.* This item deals with the audience-speaker relationship. It may consist of comments about the occasion, the
   group, or the community to show that the speaker has some sensitivity to or kinship with the group. If appropriate and not done by
   someone else, the speaker should introduce herself and provide
   enough of her background to establish credibility.

2. *Catch attention.* Almost any presentation can benefit greatly
   from a snappy opening—a "grabber" or a "hook." Consider the
   difference between these two opening statements:
   "My subject today is printed circuit boards. We use these in
   many of our electronic packages and they're pretty expensive. I'm
   going to talk about three facets of this problem . . ." [dull, dreary]
   [Presenter holds up a printed circuit board.] "How many of
   you know what this is? It's a printed circuit board from our Q10
   robot. How much do you think it costs? $500. What if I told you
   of a way we could produce this same board for three dollars?" [a
   grabber]

Figure 5-3. What order and parts of the introduction's key elements
will be used depends on the presentation.

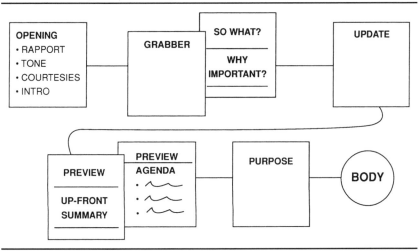

One of the most attention-getting introductions I've seen was delivered by a deputy sheriff. While making his opening comments, he deliberately pulled two rubber gloves onto his hands. At precisely the right moment, he reached into a box and pulled out a grimy motorcycle gang jacket and gingerly held it up for all to see. As he introduced more of the topic—violence among gangs—he pulled brass knuckles, chains, leaded belts, and other dangerous paraphernalia out of the box. He had our attention, and he never lost it.

That is the key concept: To overcome that "Ho-hum" tendency, you must first get the audience to listen to you. A presenter has a wide array of options from which to choose a punchy opener, such as:

- ◆ *Vivid Example.* A presentation on safety started with a story about a fellow employee and how an accident would have cost him an eye if he hadn't been wearing safety glasses. This often works well with a graphic.

- ◆ *Dramatic Demonstration.* An investment counselor opened a retirement planning presentation by holding up a $5,000 bill (a pretend one in case you're wondering), representing starting retirement income. Seemed pretty good, until he started tearing pieces off it, each one illustrating how a tax, inflation, medical need, etc. would reduce that as we grew older in retirement. Scary when he showed us the remnant of the bill, the amount we'd likely have to live on within ten years. We listened now with eager ears.

- ◆ *Testimonial or Quotation.* On the topic of discrimination to a lukewarm supervisory group, the speaker opened with a policy quote from the CEO, saying in essence, "We will not put up with it." They sat up a bit straighter after that.

- ◆ *Intriguing Statistic.* The method used by both the circuit board presenter and the investment guru.

- ◆ *Strong Opinion or Interesting Observation.* A proposal leader began his motivational talk this way: "Folks, at the rate we're going, we haven't the slightest chance of winning this proposal." From there he went into what the team had to do to win.

- ◆ *Event Tie-In.* Start perhaps with something intriguing or entertaining about a recent event, the honored guest, others on the platform or in the audience, the occasion or group, comments of previous speakers, or preceding activities. For example, "Yesterday the president of this company proposed a major policy change that will affect all of us." Former Vice President Dan Quayle spoke to a civic group and opened with a humorous exchange he'd just had, and asked that person to stand. I did and he described our dialogue and parlayed that into a funny message. The crowd roared and he was instantly linked with the audience (and we're still talking).

3. *Provide motivation.* This is a vital step that tells the listeners why the information to follow will be of interest to them. It answers the fundamental and unspoken question, "Why should I listen to you? What am 1 going to get out of this?" or, "Why bring that up?" The motivation step also provides a bridge into the topic. The speaker on safety who opened with the story about the worker who almost lost an eye, might continue with: "So what?, you might ask. The next almost-lost eye might be yours, if you ignore the safety procedures. That's what I'm here to talk about."

4. *Background: Bring them up to speed.* This is often helpful to your audience. They may be tracking a half-dozen programs like yours, and a quick update, perhaps with a visual aid, will be appreciated. For example: "This report covers the Amiga program. Our customer is the city of Chicago, contract value $6 million, first delivery June 1 . . . or "At our last meeting, you asked us to prepare a cost comparison of three options. We've done that and are here today with that report."

5. *Preview the message with a concise up-front summary.* "Tell 'em what you're going to tell 'em." Many executives stress the importance of this, with a guideline that the higher the audience level, the stronger the need for the preview. Recall Alliant Tech's Nick Vlahakis advice about avoiding the Agatha Christie approach. For presentations seeking financial backing, Brook Byers, principal partner of the venture capital firm Kleiner, Perkins, Caulfield, Byers, recommended "opening with the strongest thing you have to say. Senior people are busy, and you have about two or three minutes to capture their attention. Open with a bold,

sweeping, almost controversial statement, such as what goal or accomplishment you expect."[11]

6. *State or show the agenda.* Present the topics to be covered, the speakers (with full names, not initials) and other process information.

7. *Clarify the purpose.* Let the audience know early the reason for the presentation. I've been in meetings where about five minutes into it, a key VP asks, "Why am I hearing this?" He was expressing frustration at not being given the purpose, such as "At the conclusion of my presentation, I will be asking for your approval to purchase this new system." People listen with different ears if they know something is expected of them at the end. An exception to the rule of using an early purpose statement is when doing that may kill off success, as when the audience's starting position is negative (e.g., Mark Antony's speech after Caesar's assassination, in which he was careful not to state his true purpose at the start).

   In case you think I'm making too big a deal of this, here's what Captain James Woolway, commanding officer of the U.S. Naval Air Depot North Island, says about opening a presentation: "As a left-brained person, I look for a very organized presentation. I want to see the outline early. Then I want to know what's the purpose of the briefing. Is it to inform, get a decision, request some action? Knowing what to expect frames how I'll listen." He advises to send the meeting agenda, attendee list, and the briefing to attendees in advance, "So I can look at it, get prepared, and ensure we have the right people there. This allows me also to formulate my questions in advance. These add up to a more productive meeting."[12]

Body: Present the Main Sections

In the body, the presenter states each key point, amplifies with subpoints, and provides material to support or illustrate the points (Figure 5-4).

General Organizing Methods

Speakers have long used organizing formulas to lay out their thoughts in a clear and often dramatic manner. Here are some examples:

Figure 5-4. In the body, lay out topic segments in the best order.

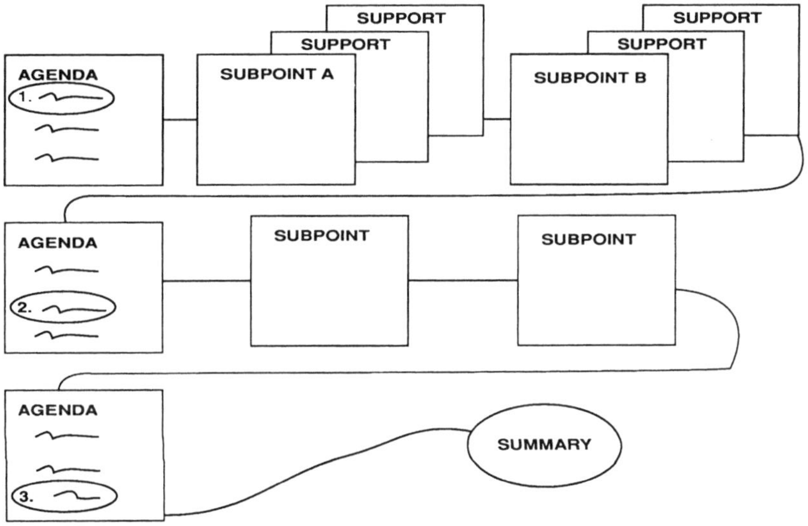

Enumeration	"Five factors . . . "Point 1. Point 2. Point 3."
Enumeration combined with alliteration	"Five C's of Marketing" "Four P's of Winning Presentations"
Repeated theme (politicians' standby)	"I have a dream that . . . I have a dream . . . "Jaime brought prosperity and so will Diana (our current heroine]. . . . He brought peace and so will Diana . . ."
Plays on popular themes	"The Good, the Bad, and the Ugly"

A team used the concepts *Good* and *Bad* and kept us intrigued as to which would be the *Ugly* for each topic. Others grabbed this idea as well, such as a university Web site's "The Good, the Bad, and the Tenured" or *Harvard Gazette's* "The Good, the Bad, and the Smelly."[13]

Specific Organizational Patterns

A variety of idea arrangements are possible. Which one is best for a given presentation depends on the nature of the subject, the purpose of the presentation, the time allotted, and the audience orientation (See Figure 5-5).

A proposal to acquire a new facility might be best presented by first describing the need and showing what's wrong with the existing facility; then presenting options to correct the problems identified;

Figure 5-5. The common organization patterns are applied here to a military/civil aircraft.

Pattern	Application Examples	Organizational Sections (Typical Key Points)
By subject affiliation Nature, features	Product description, system readiness review	Propulsion Electrical Hydraulic
Process/operation (may be chrono-logical as well)	Manufacturing se-quence, mission briefing	Fabrication Subassembly Assembly
Discipline	Total program review	Financial Engineering Production
Characteristics, qualities	Marketing presentation	Performance Cost Safety
By professional standard	Financial review	Sales Earnings Financial analysis
By time (chronology) or sequence	Program history, sequence of events	Phase A study (2001–2002) Full-scale development (2002–2003) Production (2004–)
By location	Supplier review, organizational responsibilities	Engine—Michigan Guidance—New York Air frame—California
By logical development	Change proposal, fail-ure analysis, new-con-cept introduction, motivational talk	Problem Probable causes Comparative assessments Selected solution Implementation

then presenting the pros and cons of the various options and the rationale for selecting the proposed facility; and finally giving the proposed
plan of action to implement the proposed solution. This problem-
solution arrangement is extremely common in business, particularly
when the purpose is to obtain approval for a specific course of action.

An orientation program describing the features of a new product
might best be organized by product system, component, or function:
"Today we will be looking at three main systems of our new model:
body, engine, and electronics."

A presentation to the investment community might have these
modules: sales, earnings, assets, liabilities, and net worth. Presentations given to a professional group often are expected to follow certain
standards associated with that group. A presentation often uses different organizational patterns for the separate sections. As an example:

Main message: The Gizmo Program is generally on course.

Key point: 1. Financial picture is good.
                    a. Sales projections look good.
                    b. Earnings are expected to track well.
                 2. System design is well along.
                    a. Structure meeting key milestones.
                    b. Engine system earlier problems resolved

The first subpoint set follows a professional standard pattern; the
second is subject nature pattern.

Looking for Common Bonds

You might transform an unwieldy list of nine items into a clear, manageable list of three, such as:

radishes	*animals*
chickens	chickens
iron	horses
plastic	sheep
sheep	*vegetables*
horses	radishes
diamonds	wheat
cauliflower	cauliflower

wheat   *minerals*
                           iron
                           diamonds
                           plastic

The list on the left looks shorter; the list on the right is clearer.

Testing Outline Structure

Test the outline structure so it's clear, cohesive, convincing. Here are three tests, adapted from Samovar and Mills, to assure sound structure.[14]

1. *Relevance.* Do the main points truly support your main theme? Review this set:

Main message: The Model M computer is economical
                (persuasive)
Key points: 1. Initial cost is low
                2. Maintenance
                3. It's a pretty blue color

What does the third point have to do with the theme of economy? Eliminate it (and fix point 2 as well, since it's not clear). As a simple check of relevance, for presentations whose purpose is to persuade, place the word "because" between the main message and each of the main points. Try that for the first example above—the Model M is economical—and you can immediately see the lack of sense of the irrelevant idea contained in point 3.

Consider this one:

Main message: Vitamins and minerals are needed by the body
                (informational)
Key points: 1. Protein does this.
                2. Vitamins do that.
                3. Minerals do something else.

And the astute reader exclaims, "Huh? Where'd that first point come from?" It may be valid, but it is not part of what the speaker says is the message. For a presentation whose purpose is to inform, place the words "for example" between the main message and each of the main points and observe whether it makes sense. Items 2 and 3 track.

2. *Independence.* Are the main points truly independent? Often ideas put forth as key points are relevant to the main message but seem to overlap. For example:

Main message: Buy the Model M computer
   (because)
Key points: 1. Overall costs are low
   2. Maintenance cost is low
   3. Performance is better

All points meet the 'because" test. However, since overall costs include maintenance costs, point 2 is a subpoint of key point 1. It fails the independence test.

3. *Clarity.* Are the main points clearly stated or are clinkers in the set? Are parallel points consistent with one another?

Main message: Procurement is spread throughout the country
Key Points 1. Engines come from Texas
   2. Tires come from Ohio
   3. A Denver Company provides structure

Point 3 is worded differently from the first two. When a pattern is set, make sure all items follow the pattern.

Organizational Clueing Devices

Remember the value of road maps. Since the body is the bulk of the presentation and may involve complex material, it is often helpful to the audience to receive frequent direction signals. Here are some ways you can do this:

◆ *Moving Agendas.* Repeat the original agenda chart, with the up-coming topic highlighted.

◆ *Transitions.* These provide direction and regain attention. They're useful at major break points, as you move from one topic to the next, and as lead-ins to visuals or demonstrations: "With that background let's now look at my first major topic . . . Which brings us to my second topic . . . And in conclusion . . ."

◆ *Mini-Summaries.* These are capsule versions of the most recent key points, such as: "We've examined the new manufacturing plan with its three features: computer-controlled milling, an advanced production control system, and a modularized assembly technique. Now let's look at how this affects our personnel requirements."

◆ *Orientation Devices.* Visual aids can be designed with their own directional clues. Reduce an overview flowchart, copy it onto successive charts, and highlight the block being discussed. Use colors to code a series of block diagrams, sketches, or word charts.

Logical Progression

Development of material may proceed *from* the main proposition ("X is true for these reasons: A, B, and C") or *toward* it ("Our studies show A, B, and C, leading us to conclude that X is true"). The first is called deductive reasoning, the second, inductive reasoning.

If your audience is likely to take issue with your conclusion, it may be wise to move toward it rather than from it. For example, arguing in favor of gun control to gun enthusiasts and starting with the statement (your proposition) "Handguns are a menace and should be banned" would probably make for a short but stimulating presentation. Building toward it might give you a better hearing and enable you to establish agreement on some points, if not on the whole proposition. The latter approach would be inductive.

In inductive reasoning you attempt to gain agreement or acceptance on several pieces of evidence or argument, and keep building the case until you have shown that enough evidence exists (you hope) to gain acceptance for the proposition. For example:

"We are having quality problems in the shop." [prove it]

"Maintenance on our equipment is costly." [show the data]

"Production rates have been declining." [show the trends]

All this shows that:

Proposition: "We need to replace our machinery."

Deductive reasoning starts with an accepted generalization:

"We need to replace our machinery with a better-quality, lower-cost, and faster machine."
"The Brand X Mod-95 is such a machine."
"We should replace our machinery with the Mod-95."

The Summary: Tell 'em What You Told 'em and Ask for the Action

The summary gives you one more opportunity to hammer home the key parts of your message and to make sure the basic ideas are conveyed. Make this a must-have for your presentations as it is so important and often absent. I have seen vague and rambling presentations come into focus by the simple expedient of asking the presenters to write out summaries. This forces presenters to identify the true essence of what they want to get across, and it applies a fundamental principle of learning: that restatement is often essential.

A concise summary also provides flexibility when presentation time is shortened or some points take longer than planned. The presenter can cut material and still make sure the audience hears all the key points by going to the summary. Do what you must with the body—omit detail, cut charts, skip material—but do not shortchange your summary.

Here are the key elements (see Figure 5-6):

1. *Reiterate main points.* This is the final leg of the "tell 'em" triad, often presented on a visual aid as the summary chart. Restate only what you covered during the talk; no new material should surface here. Figure 5-7 shows an example of an actual summary (restatement) chart.

2. *Give conclusions and recommendations, as appropriate.* Ask for specific action, the objective you identified in your planning. What do you want the audience to do? This is also called "Ask for

Figure 5-6. The summary ties it all together. Select specific parts to fit the presentation best.

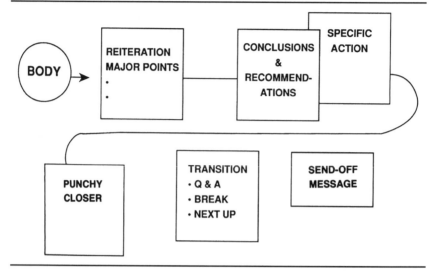

the order." Presenters often are timid about doing this ("My God, that would be selling!") or are not clear about what they want. "So, Madame Director, the next step is to enter negotiations with subcontractor X. Do we have your approval to do that?"

3. Close with punch. The wrap-up leaves the audience with a memorable impression about the topic or its importance. A good one also reinforces the impression of assurance and professionalism. A variety of methods work, just as for your opening grabber. For example:

   ◆ *Illustration.* A good way to show closure is to refer again to the illustration with which you began the talk. Recall how the speaker held up a printed circuit board, with the promise of having a far better product? Having shown that in the body, he might now hold up the board and say, "Remember this board? It's costing you $500 a copy. We've shown our approach will cut that to $3 each. How many do you want?"

   ◆ *Demonstration or Action.* The investment counselor might choose at this point to do his tearing up the $5,000 bill. One team closed a major proposal presentation with the CEO say-

Figure 5-7. The most important chart is the summary, which reiterates the main theme and primary points.

BIOTEK — PRIMED FOR GROWTH

- Market niche established

- Solid management team in place

- Key contracts secured

- Financing plan is sound

---

ing, "And to once more reinforce the point we've made that we absolutely are committed to being part of your team in Buffalo . . ." and at that point all eight team members put on their Buffalo Bills ball caps. The audience howled and the team won the contract.

♦ *Quotation, Poem, Cartoon, etc.* A favorite for many formal speeches is a closing of this sort (see end of chapter).

♦ *Entertaining Action.* The speaker had explained and demonstrated how to prepare a delicious margarita. To close, he then passed out glasses of the finished product, including one to the class instructor, yours truly (good audience analysis). He got a 10 for that talk.

♦ *Inspiration or Challenge.* The wrap-up can be a simple sentence: "At this point, winning the proposal is entirely up to us—let's get at it." Vivid demonstrations of this technique were applied by orators Bill Murray and John Belushi in the classic movies *Stripes* and *Animal House*.

♦ *Tie to Current Hot Topic.* During one of the September 11, 2001 terrorist attacks, passengers rushed the hijackers and prevented them from crashing the plane into an important target. The last words from one of the leaders on a cell phone to his wife were "Let's roll." Following the attacks, George W. Bush dramatically closed a major speech with the same words: "Let's roll." It was extremely effective (though after he used it several times more, it was getting trite).

4. *What about a final thank you?* Sometimes this is appropriate, for example, when the speaker has requested time to make an appeal for funds from the audience. Generally a thank you is superfluous and detracts from the final punch achieved by the wrap-up statement

5. *Make the transition to the next phase.* Now what? Don't leave the audience sitting there bewildered. Do you want to take questions? Introduce the next speaker? Pass out materials? Take a break? Let them know. To transfer to questions, use wording that will ease your audience into a new mode. "Any questions?"—the most common expression—is too abrupt and frequently means, "Don't ask questions." Try this: "We've covered the main points about my proposal. I'm sure you have more questions, and I'll be pleased to answer them now."

6. *After Q&A, end the meeting with a final send-off message.* The Q&A period may have been rough, and you may want to restore the right flavor to your message, or you sense a key player is about to leave and you'd like to get her ear one more time. Be assertive and close out the session with the message you'd like to have her carry out of the room: "Once again, the key point I'd like to leave you with is that our proposed new system will greatly add to our productivity."

Other Organization Formulas

The basic formula just presented is the one most commonly used in business presentations. Several other formulas have useful applications as well.

The Motivated Sequence

Alan Monroe and Douglas Ehninger are associated with this formula, which may be effective for certain persuasive presentations.[15] It may fit well for neutral to negative audiences, where revealing the true purpose and message early may bring the presentation to an abrupt halt. This formula does not "tell 'em" in advance. The main message is not stated until late in the talk, after an important need has been established and developed. It is roughly how Mark Antony in Shakespeare's *Julius Caesar* turned around an audience that initially was opposed to his proposition.

Here's an example of how the formula might be applied in a presentation.

ATTENTION:	"Losing the Program K contract was a major blow."
NEED:	"To remain competitive, we must fix our main problem, namely high costs."
SATISFACTION:	"The Model H50 computer will reduce our costs."
VISUALIZATION:	"With the H50, we can win the upcoming Program Y contract."
ACTION:	"I ask your O.K. to buy the Model H50."

AIDA

AIDA does not refer to the Verdi opera; it is a mnemonic frequently used by toastmasters, similar to the motivated sequence.[16]

(CATCH) **A**TTENTION:	"With your present setup, two dump trucks a day go to the scrap yards."
(AROUSE) **I**NTEREST:	"Suppose you could cut that down to one per week."
(STIMULATE) **D**ESIRE:	"Our Framzis Fixit can do that. The proof is in the dozen units we've sold your competitors, which have averaged 90 percent scrap reduction."
(MOVE TO) **A**CTION:	"Sign on the dotted line, and we'll deliver tomorrow."

Borden's "Ho-Hum" Formula

Richard Borden's formula covers the four stages of audience reaction to a speaker.[17]

HO HUM	"Twenty-five billion dollars of prime real estate was sold last year to a new group of buyers—foreign oil millionaires."
WHY BRING THAT UP?	"They got to be rich because of the huge outlay we pay for oil imports."
FOR INSTANCE	"Look at this graph showing how our gasoline use is escalating, with 85 percent from foreign oil."
SO WHAT?	"We can keep pouring out dollars for foreign oil or cut down consumption. Let's choose the latter."

Example-Point-Reason

Dale Carnegie called this the "Magic Formula" for short talks to get action.[18] Here is an example:

EXAMPLE:	"I recently spent time with an enthusiastic bunch of business-people. They're making flotzinjammers and selling them like hot cakes. These are teenagers, getting business experience through Junior Achievement."
POINT:	"To get these kids started in business takes money. I'm here to ask you to donate $100 to get another group started."
REASON:	"What will you get out of it? The satisfaction of helping kids understand our economic system."

PREP

Communications consultant June Guncheon discussed the PREP formula in an article in *Nation's Business* and noted it was particularly useful for impromptu or short-notice situations.[19] Many of my students have commented favorably on the value of this formula. It can help quickly organize your thoughts prior to speaking or going into a meeting, or even before making a telephone call. It can help prevent that sinking feeling that often hits one minute after you've finished speaking: "Oh, why didn't I say that?" or "I forgot the main point!"

POINT: "Boss, I deserve a raise."
            "Oh really, what makes you think so?"

REASON: "Because I've been doing good work this year."
            "Oh? Such as?"

EXAMPLE: "The study you put me in charge of. We finished that under budget; the customer said it was great and gave us an add-on."
            "Hmmm."

POINT: "I think that shows that I deserve a raise."
            "Hmmm."

Straw Man, or Point/Counterpoint.

This is my own formula, which quickly lays out an easily understood framework for argument. Setting a straw man (the opposing position) against your own view provides a dramatic confrontation, shows you have given some attention to opposing views, and allows flexibility of attack.

POINT: "Many people feel that nuclear energy is not safe because of the waste disposal problem."

COUNTERPOINT: "Others feel the disposal methods are adequate and that we should proceed."

ARGUMENT: "A study conducted by the Department of Energy shows. . . ."

CONCLUSION: "I believe these analyses have shown . . . and that we should. . . ."

Organization Tools

Sifting through ideas and material and arranging them in a logical and effective order is by no means simple. The process can be greatly aided with the help of several manual and computer tools.

Brainstorming and Sorting

Once the main theme is set, a useful step early in the organizing phase is to list all the topics that the presentation might cover. Brainstorming, which can be done alone or with a group, lists all ideas as they come, with no attempt to evaluate or categorize. The fullest range of potential topics is the goal. After the flow of ideas slackens, sorting and evaluation begins. The objective is to identify and establish priorities for the half-dozen or fewer major topics to be covered and to eliminate those of lesser value.

Visual Outlining/Mind Mapping

Many people are more spatially oriented than word oriented. For designers, computer programmers, and schedulers, diagrams are an integral part of the thinking process. GANTT charts, decision trees, flowcharts, and exploded drawings are examples of spatial thinking. The same concepts can be used to map out the design for a presentation, which is why one variation is called mind mapping. This process can provide insight and structure as it helps generate ideas and reveal relationships. Diagrams often develop ideas better than verbal outlines (Figure 5-8).

Notes and Folder

A common method is writing key ideas down on 3 × 5 cards, then arranging them into common groups on a table top A handy variation of this is to use Post-It Notes with a manila folder to brainstorm and develop a quick layout of key points. I've used this method for years to organize speeches, lesson plans, articles, and meetings quickly. Many who've tried it have become ardent advocates.

Outlining: Beneficial and Underemployed

One seasoned presenter, frustrated after spending "two weeks wrestling with this presentation," said, "I've been going round and round trying to tie all these graphics together and to get this thing to flow. Then I decided to go back to square one and write an outline. I spent one day working on it, and was absolutely amazed at what it did for my presentation. For the first time I could see what I was really trying

Figure 5-8. Mind mapping can stimulate idea flow.

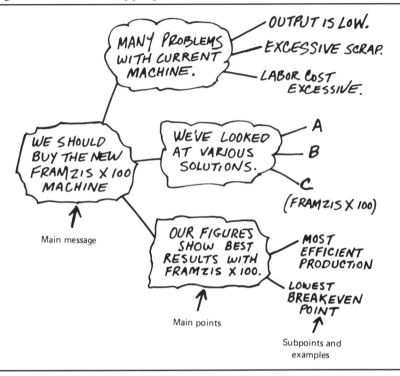

to say. The outline sorted out a whole jumble of ideas that had been racing around in my head. The obvious question is, why didn't I do the outline first and save all that time and energy? Next time I'll know better.''

The outline is a planning tool. It is a way of forcing or disciplining the selection and ordering of ideas. Presenters sometimes say that they don't outline because it will constrain their thought process and take away their natural flow. Yet a presentation must be constrained. It must be tightly packaged, with all the extraneous ideas and material excluded. An audience deserves and will insist upon a concisely organized message that achieves its goals in the least possible time.

Writing an outline is a much better use of time than writing out a presentation. If there is one thing that constrains speakers, it is a written speech. The basic ideas are often poorly organized and are hard to assess and improve because they may be buried and rambling. Writing style is different from speaking style, and written speeches often sound dreary and lifeless.

   Outlines come in different forms. Simple key words can be helpful. My recommendation is to develop a complete-sentence outline, where main points and subpoints are written out in complete sentences (Figure 5-9). This removes the vagueness associated with briefer outlines and permits the tests discussed above to be readily applied.

Figure 5-9. Outlining, manually or by computer, is an important step in clarifying thinking.

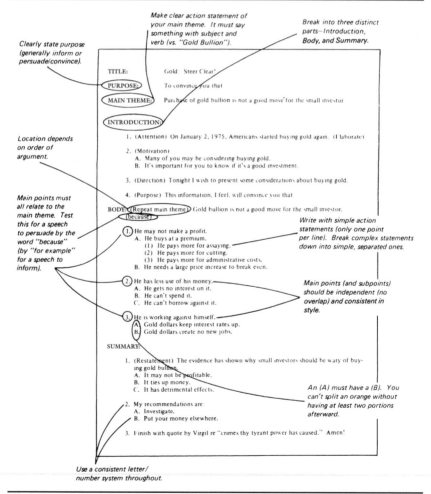

Storyboards: Visual Outlines

Storyboards—a most important and useful tool in the planning of visual aid presentations—have proven valuable in many applications for developing materials and meeting cost targets. Advertisers match the visual and spoken elements of commercials. Filmmakers lay out their action sequences via a series of wall sketches to create and refine each step of an activity before they go into the studio or on location to shoot the scene. Musical videos rely heavily on storyboards, as evidenced on a CBS-TV news program about hugely successful Irish pop singer, Enya.

Because storyboards are part of the design process, they can be created, reviewed, and redone quickly and cheaply. Their visual nature is easier to follow for some than written outlines or narratives, and the rough visual ideas give reviewers an actual picture of what the audience will be seeing during the presentation. Presentation length can also be quickly estimated from the storyboards. Business presentations typically take thirty seconds to two minutes per visual.

A storyboard (also called a thumbnail sketch) is a visual aid outline. It is a layout or flowchart of the presentation in a series of sketches (Figure 5-10), with each sketch representing one visual. Each should make one point only, and that statement should be written out. These intended messages suggest the visual—not the other way around. A storyboard developed further will add the spoken points that would go with the visual.

Figure 5-10. The storyboard is an excellent tool for getting outlines tied to visuals.

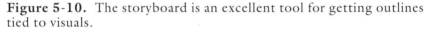

Storyboards come in various forms: 3×5 cards laid out on a table; a set of forms or 4×6 cards that show both the visual and likely spoken notes; $8^1/_2 \times 11$ sheets of paper mounted on a wall, cork board, or magnetic wall.

Let's look at a quick example: Assuming that the point is "We should expand our vacation time from three to six weeks," what visual aid might convey that? Brainstorming quickly surfaces these graphic candidates:

A graph showing how productivity is improved with six versus three weeks.

Clip art of three employees barely lively after three weeks, perky after six weeks.

A table showing employee retention figures for three versus six weeks.

And even more. From these the presenter selects and develops the most promising storyboard.

Computers as Organizing Tools

Computers can greatly expedite the organizing process. Presenters can use software programs to develop outlines, shift each key point into a storyboard of visual aid concepts, and develop each into a finished visual. Most programs have back-and-forth linkages, so changing the outline can automatically change the visual content, and vice versa.

A word of caution: Computers can streamline the process, but they don't ensure a sound presentation. That immediate bridge from outline to visual, for example, can quickly create slides, but, without further development, they may be mostly words. Presenters may be inclined to stop at this point, yet further development may lead to significantly better visuals.

Outlines

When you use the outlining tool in the graphics program (e.g. Power-Point), it immediately transfers into visuals. Doing the outline in word processing software requires the added step of copying into the graphics program. Why not start there?

Storyboards

The software (the slide sorter option in PowerPoint) can display as many graphics as you choose, for you to peruse and progressively develop. This makes it easy to move slides around, to insert slides from other presentations, to delete or temporarily store ones you won't be using. You can also print this out for you or others to review (instead of using the wall storyboard).

Slide Development

With the graphics software, you can instantly copy over from your outline the points and subpoints, which become titles and bullets, then add visual enhancements to work up each visual aid.

Delivery Scripts and Speaker Notes

This is the bridge between outline, graphics, and delivery. Use this option to add notes to be spoken for each visual (Figure 5-11). This is an underused, yet valuable option to match spoken word with on-screen graphics. Use this to focus key points, cut material, smooth out

Figure 5-11. Delivery or talking scripts help tighten spoken messages and meet time targets.

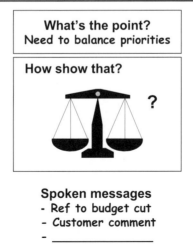

transitions, and track better to time requirements. Some audiences have required that paper copies of the notes pages be provided along with the visuals.

An important point is that speaker notes are good tools for *preparing* presentations, not for delivering them. Some speakers cling to the notes and become dependent on them, taking away much of their delivery credibility and personal style. Use them if needed during early rehearsals, then wean yourself from them so that most of your thought triggers come from the on-screen graphics and your mind.

Titles: A Full House May Depend on Them

Two papers on a similar subject given at a national speech conference had different titles. Which is likely to draw the bigger crowds?

> "Structural Coherence Production in the Conversations of Pre-school Children"
>
> OR
>
> "I'll Give You a Knuckle Sandwich!': Preschoolers' Resolution of Conflict."[20]

For most everyday business presentations, titles are not particularly significant. In-house management and customers generally know what the subject will cover, and the title's main function is for reference and to go on the front page of the visual aid brochure. In this category I would put "Proposal for NASA Electric Propulsion System" and "Production Readiness Review."

Titles take on more significance when the presentation is given to outside groups, particularly those whose members can be selective about whether they even show up. At a professional society's annual convention, attendees may be able to choose from a half-dozen presentations, all occurring simultaneously. The title may be the determining factor in the choice of which talk to attend.

If the title is to be used in advance publicity or the talk is to be printed in seminar proceedings or some other publication, a punchy title can help promote attendance and ensure that the talk will be read. A political club's newsletter announced that the speaker at the next club meeting would talk about prison reform and rehabilitation. The talk was titled, "Penal Reform and Rehabilitation." A real crowd puller. I suggest that an equally informative and much punchier title might have been "Ex-Cons—Recyclable or Lost Causes?"

A catchy and effective title has several key characteristics:

◆ It is appropriate to the occasion.

◆ It provides enough information about the subject so that potential attendees can tell whether this is likely to be of interest to them.

◆ It is succinct and to the point.

◆ It piques the interest of the reader or listener.

Here are some ideas, with examples from actual speeches:

◆ *Play on Words:* "The Yen to Make a Mark with the Dollar: A Franc Look at Our International Economic Policy" (from former Senator Frank Church); "Let's Put Some Esprit in de Corporation" (from a *Harvard Business Review* article).

◆ *Satire:* "Can't Nobody Here Use This Language?" (to professional communicators).

◆ *Variation of a Common Axiom:* "Guilty Until Proven Innocent—Advertising and the Consumer" (to an advertising club).

◆ *Tie to Current Topics (Movies, Slogans, Songs, Books):* "Organizational Encounters of the Third Kind: With the Ombudsman" (your author).

◆ *Figures of Speech:* "Resources, Results, and the Seven Deadly Sins."

In Summary: Take Time to Organize— It Carries a Lot of Power

Great orators realize the power of good openings, clear and persuasive story lines, and inspiring closings. Here is an especially effective closing.

In 1951, at the height of the Korean War, General Douglas Mac-

Arthur was relieved of duty in a controversial move by President Harry S. Truman. Because MacArthur had many supporters, he was invited to deliver a speech to the U. S. Congress. This is how he closed: "I am closing my fifty-two years of military service. When I joined the army even before the turn of the century, it was the fulfillment of all my boyish hopes and dreams. The world has turned over many times since I took the oath on the plain at West Point, and the hopes and dreams have long since vanished. But I still remember the refrain of one of the most popular barrack ballads of that day which proclaimed most proudly that "old soldiers never die; they just fade away." And like the old soldier of that ballad, I now close my military career and just fade away—an old soldier who tried to do his duty as God gave me the light to see that duty. Goodbye.[21]

MacArthur's closing, delivered with his dramatic vocal style, received enormous applause, and led to a top musical hit "Old Soldiers Never Die." (He still got fired.)

CHAPTER 6

Support

Make Your Case

Many presenters focus a lot of energy on getting just the right graphics, trying to illustrate their ideas and prove their propositions are sound. Another means of support, and often far more riveting and powerful, is not visible on screen but related via the spoken word. Recall how many communicators have somehow won over their audiences without PowerPoint. Remember Homer's tales, Jesus' parables, Disraeli's pithy metaphors, Emily Dickinson's poems, Abe Lincoln's humorous stories, and on up to current speakers. Used often to make a point, much of this clever support material is still well known centuries later.

From the Organize phase came the presentation skeleton: the layout of themes, topics, and ideas. Now comes the time to flesh it out, adding the supporting material to illustrate and back up the main points. "Where's the beef?" is the cry from the audience, a slogan that Wendy's hamburgers coined to suggest that other products lacked substance (Figure 6-1).

Contracts and budgets are rarely won by enthusiasm alone, but by also making a solid case. Good support adds spark to presentations, much as the color analyst does in a sports broadcast. It offers one of

Figure 6-1. For good support, anticipate the audience key question "Where's the beef?"

the best ways to get an audience actively involved, and it helps a presenter add personality and experience to message and style.

Today's master communicators, such as Paul Harvey, Tom Peters, and Oprah Winfrey, are among the most proficient users of supporting material to inform and inspire. Humorists such as Bill Cosby and Garrison Keillor are masters at using stories to entertain audiences. *Consumer Reports* relies on hard data, garnered from research, testing, and investigations, for their assessments of products. These are all forms of support.

One of the staples of major presidential speeches is the example to bring in at the appropriate point. The President will make an argument about the success or importance of doing topic X (getting off welfare, helping others, or helping foil an attack) and then, dramatically, point to the balcony (the usual position, often next to the President's spouse), and ask the person who exemplifies the theme to rise and be acknowledged. Guaranteed applause.

The Reinforcement Role

Presenters use support for four primary reasons:

♦ To increase understanding, such as for topics that are complex or outside the audience's knowledge level

◆ To convince, backing up claims with solid support

◆ To inspire or move, relating something so vivid, moving, or catchy that it leads to action

◆ To entertain, as for a roast or an after-dinner speech

Consider the following presentation by a representative from an electronics company to a potential customer:

> Our innovative new Mod 75 is the perfect solution to your problem. It has worked fine for many other companies. Maintenance costs are almost nothing. It is a significant technological advance over the brand X unit, but it's a bit complicated to explain and much of it is proprietary, so I can't say much about it. Suffice it to say it will do the job you need. Now, how many do you want?

It is possible for a presenter to make such a series of statements to a potential customer. It is also possible the customer will throw the presenter out on his ear. The presenter has made a series of claims, all of which the customer is supposed to accept on faith.

That same presenter could have also given this presentation

> We believe our innovative new Mod 75 is the perfect solution to your problem. The people at Magnacom had a problem similar to yours and the Mod 75 worked beautifully for them.
>
> You asked about maintenance costs. Here's what Frank Gonzales, Magnacom's chief of maintenance, said about the 75: "Our experience has been phenomenal. We've reduced down time from three days per month to two hours. We love it."
>
> What makes the Mod 75 so much more effective than the competition? It's the difference between a car alternator—always charging—and a generator—often not. Unlike other products, our 75 is a form of alternator—it never drains off energy from the system it works with. . . . And how many do you want?

Both presentations contain the same ideas and make the same claims. In the first version, however, none of the claims are substantiated; in the second, they are. The reinforcement not only adds support to the claims; it helps the listener understand the concepts presented. If the support material is effective, the listener may become convinced that the Mod 75 is indeed just what his or her company needs. If it is weak, no sale.

The principle here is, "assertion needs reinforcement to be successful" (Figure 6-2). Winning over the audience to the proposition depends largely on how well the presenter uses supporting material to clarify, substantiate, and inspire. The reinforcement repertoire is sparked by the words "for example," as discussed in the second Mod 75 presentation (which you'll recognize is itself an application of support).

The following nine basic ideas apply to the use of any form of supporting material (summarized in Figure 6-3).

1. *The material must fit the needs and style of the receivers.* In planning support material it's essential to know how the principal listeners want material presented to them. Are they big on numbers? Are they no-nonsense, get-to-it-now types, or are they likely to allow a more leisurely pace? Do they enjoy a good story? This is where many presenters fall flat. In my organization, the engineering vice president was a stickler for details, so people learned to be ready with lots of those. His successor was vastly different; his eyes would glaze over and his interest would visibly shift after the second data chart. Would you have prepared for and presented the same way to President George W. Bush as to President Bill Clinton? (One company makes it easy to tell the difference. On

Figure 6-2. Assertion needs reinforcement, with the key words "for example."

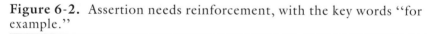

Figure 6-3. Apply these tips to use support material well.

◆ Use support to illustrate, validate, inspire, and entertain by applying the term "for example."

◆ Select material to help the presenter's delivery as well as the message.

◆ Make sure the material is relevant to the topic and in appropriate taste.

◆ Use a variety of support types to account for differing audience backgrounds.

◆ Provide enough support to illustrate and prove your case, but don't overkill or bore people.

◆ Be sure of your facts, and use them ethically.

◆ Use examples from your own experience where possible.

◆ Capitalize on the power of analogies, but don't overdo their use.

◆ Be sparing in your use of statistics and convey them in terms the audience can understand.

◆ Use sources the audience will respect and in the context the author intended.

◆ Keep your material nitpick-free by pronouncing names correctly, making sure numbers and totals match, and being ready for challenges.

◆ Practice so you can deliver material well.

◆ Don't rush your delivery. Make sure key points are clearly spoken and even repeated. Allow sink-in time.

---

each person's desk is a color-coded card identifying the dominant style of that person. The objective is to expedite dialogue.)

A related factor is that receivers process information in different ways, and it helps to know the primary ways used by your principal audience members. It is well researched that three basic styles are common (Figure 6-4).

Years ago, without knowing anything about this research, I worked with a manager who wanted everything put into visual format. So we used lots of graphs and illustrations in developing information. Attorneys know this approach well; through jury selection they ask questions to establish the primary mode for each jury member and then tailor their spoken words to match each jury member's style. Being aware helps you prepare your material and approach. For example:

◆ People who process information visually, the most common mode, are big on pictures, relationships, illustrations, and graphs. Use plenty of these, plus visual language: "Picture the smashed window, with broken glass on the carpet. . . ."

Figure 6-4. Different styles mean different approaches.

- ◆ Auditory people rely more on hearing information. "Can you hear that glass breaking as the burglar smashes it with his club?"

- ◆ Feeling people internalize information. "Imagine the terror in the victim's mind on hearing that intruder approaching. . . ."

2. *The material must be relevant to the subject being discussed.* One of the problems with stories selected from published collections is that the speaker may not tie them well into the ideas he or she is presenting. In business presentations listeners are there to hear ideas put forth, not a series of jokes and one-liners. Unless your purpose is to entertain, make sure the balance is proper. Have something to say first, and then present the examples to back that up.

3. *The material must be meaningful to the audience.* A speaker from the eastern United States might find a western audience puzzled by references to Kroger's or to Mogen David wine. A speaker to a youth group might be better off speaking about Tiger Woods than Jesse Owens. (This is a common problem with international audiences, as will be noted in Chapter 17.)

4. *The material must be accurate and fairly presented.* This avoids the biggest and most legitimate criticism: Support material often is biased, phony, taken out of the original context, inaccurate, or selectively presented to show only the good and not the bad. Ethical speakers use material fairly; pragmatic ones do also, realizing that phony material can come back to bite them.

   Frequently sad or inspiring tales come across the Internet, some legit, but many falling into the never-happened urban legend category. The "Protocols of Zion" have been used by dictators and demagogues for decades (maybe centuries) to justify anti-Jewish attitudes and actions, and have been thoroughly discredited as fabrications for just as long

   In early 2003, in a major policy speech justifying going to war against Iraq, George W. Bush claimed that the Iraqis were acquiring uranium from Nigeria (to verify that they might have been developing nuclear weapons they could use against the United States). Later it was determined that this was not a true statement, and that the Central Intelligence Agency and perhaps some White House officials had known this to be incorrect but had neglected to remove this item from the speech. This became a contentious issue in Congress and for opponents of that war.[1]

5. *If it's satire, make sure they know that.* Jonathan Swift's *Gulliver's Travels* is a classic for its memorable ways of criticizing society through the use of Lilliputians and Yahoos. Humor columnist Dave Barry uses many fictitious examples to titillate his readers; some readers even take them seriously, sometimes questioning the accuracy of the examples cited.

   In an article about a golf tourney, the sports editor of a New Mexico newspaper included some quotes from a course employee named Carl Spangler. He neglected to note that he took the dialogue directly from the movie *Caddyshack*, and that Spangler was the character played by Bill Murray. The editor was trying to liven up the somewhat uneventful event with writing that he said was intended to be tongue-in-cheek. He got fired anyway.[2]

6. *The material must be workable.* Will the presentation or activity fit within the time allowed? Can it be completed as intended? When a participative activity at a conference took far longer than the speaker expected, it became a total flop.

7. *The material must prudently balance quantity and variety.* Because listeners bring different backgrounds and interests to a presentation (recall also Maslow's needs differences discussed in Chapter 4), several types of material are generally desirable. What registers with one may not resonate with another. It is also possible to saturate listeners with so much material that they lose interest. The "rule of three" has proven sound; citing more than three examples or statistics is overkill and sleep inducing.

8. *The material must be presented smoothly.* A great story falls flat if the speaker forgets the punch line. If the speaker stumbles when reading a testimonial or gets numbers confused, credibility and impact suffer. Prepare material well, and practice so it goes smoothly. When delivering, read as little as possible, and pause long enough to let the punch line sink in. (If they don't laugh, tell it again. That's a joke.)

9. *The material must be absolutely appropriate and nonoffensive.* It's surprisingly easy to shoot yourself in the foot by using off-color humor, ethnic jokes, and sexist references. I was amazed at a recent conference when the keynote speaker told several clearly-sexist jokes to an audience of which at least half were women professionals. In the 1990s a woman faculty member resigned from a major university because of a prevailing sexist environment, including professors showing slides of *Playboy* centerfolds. (We saw that a lot in meetings during the 1960s, supposedly used for humor and to wake us up. I thought speakers had wised up long ago about that no-no.)

    Here are two communicators who found out the hard way, when a front-page outcry followed their pronouncements:

    ◆ Prior to a U.S.-Soviet summit conference, White House Chief of Staff Donald Regan said that women would find the activities of the two president's wives more interesting "as they'd have trouble understanding the weightier issues."[3]

    ◆ The Italian minister of tourism, apparently forgetting his job title, came up with a description of Germans—Italy's largest tourism customers—as beer-swilling, chauvinistic boors, "those stereotyped blondes with a hyper-nationalistic pride who have always been indoctrinated to be first in class at any cost." He resigned shortly thereafter.[4]

Choosing the Right Support Material

Presenters have a variety of methods at their disposal for supporting their message.

Specific Cases

The following examples are references to specific instances, not detailed stories, that provide support for the point being made. In his books and speeches about managing, Tom Peters makes extensive use of such examples.

Captain James Woolway, commanding officer of the U.S. Naval Air Depot North Island, described a low-key presentation given one-on-one across the desk. "Their product was overhauled bearings. They clearly stated the objective of the presentation and made their point quickly, briefing from paper copies of their slides. What was especially effective were examples of equipment from which they'd taken the bearings, overhauled them, and brought them back for installation. And they had a shrink-wrapped sample of a reworked bearing. Very believable. I gave them some contacts to talk with and they concluded in twenty minutes. All well done and highly successful."[5]

Here are some other examples of how specific cases might be applied:

◆ "Drugs are bad news. You don't believe it? Neither did John Belushi, half of the Blues Brothers and a superb comic talent. Nor did rock singer Janis Joplin. And apparently not baseball's Darryl Strawberry, whose drug arrests have severely curtailed his career."

◆ "You've raised an important question—what makes us think this new scheduling system will work here? The answer is that we know it will work here. This system is identical to one that has been working at Standard Oil for six months. IBM installed one a month ago, and they're ecstatic about it. The problem they solved is the same one that you have here."

Stories and Illustrations

More than likely you have been part of a group in conversation and found yourself shifting your attention to an adjoining conversation.

Why? Probably because someone started to tell a story. Or you may have been listening to a sermon or presentation and your interest had drifted when the speaker said something that brought you right back to full attention. Again, the most likely draw was a story.

The interest capability of a well-told story has been demonstrated throughout history. If the Greeks, Romans, Vikings, and American Indians have had one thing in common, it is that their cultures have been heavily flowered with myths and stories. The great religious leaders made parables and stories a major force for getting their ideas across. Abe Lincoln and Mark Twain were noted for their storytelling as well as for their political skills or writing accomplishments. Ken Blanchard, author of *The One-Minute Manager*, in his speaking programs is a master story teller (and holder of audiences).

How does someone convince her own management or a source selection board that she is the best one for the new project? Listing college degrees and job titles is only marginally effective and does little to distinguish this person from other candidates. One of the most effective ways is by telling about her experience on one or two similar assignments, with enough specifics to demonstrate she's been there, met tough challenges, and played a significant role in getting the job done. This is the place for one or two war stories, with enough detail to establish credibility and instill confidence. (Revisit the PREP organizational formula in Chapter 5.)

We applied this approach on a major proposal. The program manager was well qualified but was having little success at imparting his qualifications to the coaching team. Part of the reason was his reluctance to brag, a quality he shared with many people. After some probing about what successful and relevant past experience he'd had, he finally mentioned one:

His role?	"Program Manager."
Requirement?	"Design and build a bridge."
Results?	"We saved the customer $1 million."
Relevance?	"We'll use many of those methods on this proposed contract."

Bingo! This example was a real grabber. These four Rs can trigger more valuable support, leading to the "Been there, done that . . . well" statement and high comfort to customers.

Sometimes hypothetical examples are just as effective as real ones, often starting with the words "suppose" or "picture." For example:

> Ladies and gentlemen of the council, let's follow first-grader Johnny as he leaves his home on Cowen Street. A block away he meets his classmate, Maria. They walk to Second Avenue. Here they have to cross over because that's where the school is located. As they get almost to the center, they're startled to hear a squealing of tires. It's two high-school kids drag-racing. The children run, but the drivers don't see them until it's too late. Johnny and Maria don't make it across the street, and they'll never make it to school. This story hasn't happened . . . yet. But it is inevitable, and the names won't be Johnny and Maria, but the names of some of our kids, unless you approve the new stoplight we've requested for that corner.

Assertiveness is a term often used and often confused. Alberti and Emmons define the terms by noting behaviors in a restaurant where Mr. A. has ordered a rare steak and gets one that was well done:

Nonassertive	Mr. A. grumbles to his wife but says nothing directly to the waiter. He leaves a tiny tip and later says he won't eat there again.
Aggressive	Angrily summons the waiter, berates him loudly, and demands another steak. Mrs. A. is embarrassed, but Mr. A doesn't care.
Assertive	Motions the waiter to the table. Notes he had ordered a rare steak but got a well-done piece of meat. Asks politely but firmly that it be replaced.[6]

These definitions could be made vivid and memorable by role-playing the various behaviors, creating punchy visuals, and drawing similar experiences from the audience.

Analogies

Disraeli was once asked to define the difference between a misfortune and a calamity. "Well," he said, "if Gladstone [his political opponent] were to fall into the river, it would be a misfortune. But if anybody dragged him out, it would be a calamity."[7]

A business executive gave a talk about the U.S. economic system to an elementary school class, not a group especially tuned into stocks and corporate takeovers. He introduced his topic by suggesting they form a company to make a product this group knew well: skateboards. He led them through the process of selecting the type of boards, getting a facility to build them, buying the raw materials, making the product, and getting it sold. Where would the money come from to do this? With a few more of the right questions, the children got the sense of how the system works. How well can be seen from the newspaper headline about the story: WHEN THIS EXECUTIVE SPEAKS, 6TH-GRADERS LISTEN.

Analogies help listeners understand and more fully appreciate the significance of complex concepts by relating topics unfamiliar to the audience with those they know. They show an interesting and possibly unusual way of looking at something.

Figurative analogies compare things that differ considerably in their appearance or function. They are a close cousin to similes, such as "Your eyes are like diamonds." Figurative analogies are frequently used by experts in a field when talking to persons not well versed in that field or to people from other disciplines.

A presenter applied an analogy in explaining the concept of trade studies to a general audience: "You're familiar with the magazine *Consumer Reports*. In every issue they compare how different models of refrigerators or lawn mowers stack up against various set criteria. Those are trade studies." The formal definition would have taken longer and still left misconceptions.

A speaker discussing the problems with government regulation presented it this way: "In my own company, for every dollar spent in our chemical division for the development of new agricultural products—such as those chemicals that increase crop yields around the world—we spend an equal amount to prepare regulatory paperwork. A one-to-one ratio of productive to nonproductive. I've read that a leading drug company spends more man-hours filling out government forms than it devotes to cancer and heart research combined."

Literal analogies compare items with similar characteristics. They are comparisons of green apples to red apples, to use a figurative analogy, as distinct from comparisons of green apples to elephants.

Statistics

"Somewhere on this globe, every ten seconds, there is a woman giving birth to a child," observed humorist Sam Levenson. "She must be found and stopped!"

While any of the forms of supporting material can be used in a confusing and questionable manner, statistics are perhaps subject to more chicanery and selective use than any of the others. It was Disraeli who observed, "There are three kinds of lies—lies, damned lies, and statistics." Yet statistics that are demonstrably valid can add powerful support to an idea. For many presentations they are essential.

Suppose you're finding that your departmental meetings are taking up way too much of your time. You need a presentation to convince management that something has got to be done. But you're weak on hard evidence. Some research turns up a relevant survey. Now with some solid ammunition, you include this tidbit in your presentation: "The amount of time wasted in meetings is probably more than any of us realize. None of us have time—remember, we spend a lot in meetings—to get quantifiable data, but someone else has done it for us. In a survey of 100 companies, Robert Half Company asked the question 'How much time do executives spend in meetings, and how useful were they?' What they found is that the average is 16.5 hours per week, and of that 4.8 hours is a waste of time. Carry that through to a year and wasted time is over six weeks per year. Imagine what we could do with an extra SIX WEEKS PER YEAR?"[8]

References

Statements by other people are the final form of supporting material. As in a courtroom, the testimony of recognized authorities can provide important support to a presentation. People may not be swayed by statistical analyses or specific cases, no matter how powerful they seem, but they may listen to and believe the comments of someone else they respect. This is widely recognized in running for office, selling new cars, or plugging a new movie.

A department director may have difficulty convincing her colleagues that affirmative action is important by showing the ethnic and racial makeup of the workforce relative to the local community, but she may be successful by quoting the company president's statement in favor of the program: "Affirmative action is a fundamental part of our operation. I expect all supervisors to comply fully with both the spirit and the intent of our program. Each supervisor will be evaluated on how well he or she contributes toward achieving our goals." (O.K. I got it—will do.)

A salesperson may find it invaluable to have on hand a few testimonials from previous buyers on the virtues of the salesperson's gadget.

Of course, your sources may have superb credentials and lousy insights. For example, in 1945, Admiral William Leahy, President Truman's chief-of-staff, pronounced: "This is the biggest fool thing we have ever done. The atomic bomb will never go off. And I speak as an expert in explosives."[9]

Quotations, Poems, Sayings

Mountaineer Jim Whittaker gave a slide-illustrated presentation about his four decades of climbing. Observed a reporter, "But what left the crowd nodding in agreement was his quoting John Muir on the rewards to be found only at altitude: 'Climb the mountains and get their good tidings. Nature's peace will flow into you as sunshine flows into trees. . . .'"[10]

This form of support is often used to add flavoring, entertainment, or a dramatic touch to the message. Quotations from the Bible or Confucius, old saws from the *Farmer's Almanac*, and selections from *Bartlett's Quotations* are used for these purposes rather than as true evidence.

Here is an opening from a talk by Walter Beran, a partner in Ernst & Young: "It certainly was an act of reckless courage on someone's part to have selected an auditor as your speaker today. For some of you will recall Elbert Hubbard's damning description of the typical auditor as 'a man past middle age, spare, wrinkled, intelligent, cold, passive, noncommittal, with eyes like codfish, polite in contact, but at the same time unresponsive, calm, and damnably composed as a concrete post or a plaster of paris cast. A human petrification with heart of feldspar and without the charm of the friendly germ, minus bowels, passion, or sense of humor. 'Happily,' he said, 'they never reproduce, and all of them finally go to hell.'"[11]

John Kennedy often wove poems, such as those by fellow New Englander Robert Frost, into his speeches. Maya Angelou, an honored poet, in her conference programs weaves her own poetry into her messages.

In my own talks, seminars, and writing (as you've seen), I've found Shakespeare's relevant quotes useful as novel reminders about important communication concepts. Commentator David Gergen drew on the Bard of Avon with this observation, following the speech to the nation by President George W. Bush shortly after the 9/11 attacks: "This was the night that Prince Hal became Henry V."[12] Those lacking knowledge of Shakespeare's plays would have missed the comparison, but Bard fans noted the changed perception of the president from party guy to statesman.

Popular News Items, Cartoons, Columns, and TV Programs

Among the richest sources for materials are the daily newspaper, magazines and the Internet, with moving and juicy items arriving in e-mail often (and some of them are even legit). The local happenings (especially from the Police Blotter), *National Inquirer*, the "Dear Abby" column, *Dilbert* cartoons, news clips from the various sections, the popular column "Weird News," and even the sports pages—all provide gist for rich support. In his conference programs, *Dilbert* creator Scott Adams discusses the relationships and frequent miscommunication among various parts of the business world, while displaying his cartoons on the big screen from an overhead projector.

Personal Experience

Look for examples from the world around you. You won't have to scratch very hard to come up with your own good examples, and they'll probably be more germane than borrowed material. Your own experiences at work, play, home, or daily encounters may be the richest and funniest sources available. You'll be more comfortable relating them, and they'll probably come across with more vitality to the audience. In particular, humorous stories told at your own expense almost always go over well.

Using Support Material Well

"Start with a joke" is common advice, and yet many people can't tell jokes well. "Dazzle 'em with statistics" is another old saw, which often quickly leads instead to the MEGO ("My Eyes Glaze Over") syndrome. And if support is proven faulty, it can come back to erode the speaker's credibility.

Having dandy support is good; using it well is even better, as the following examples show.

◆ *Avoid lengthy formal definitions, especially if shown as a lengthy paragraph on a visual aid.* This is one of the easiest ways to add lead to your presentation, as pure dictionary descriptions are deadly dull. Generally better are brief paraphrased definitions with specific examples used to create clearer understanding faster. "There's a difference between involvement and commitment," said one speaker. "Take a plate of ham and eggs. The chicken was involved, but the pig was committed."

◆ *Use discretion in presenting ground rules.* I have seen many presentations quickly bog down because the speaker was so meticulous in presenting every assumption. Immediately some listeners started to argue about the appropriateness of certain minor assumptions. They took on an importance far beyond what they actually had and would have been much better left for the question period or as an exercise for the reader as he reviewed a written report giving all the details.

◆ *Be sure of your facts and know the specifics.* Astute or critical audiences may cause problems either during or after the presentation if the information is erroneous. An example that is vague and lacks key information is often better not told. The presenter who doesn't know the details is open to attack and embarrassment.

◆ *Start with the story itself.* Don't say "That reminds me of a story."

◆ *Speak clearly, deliberately, and project well.* Make sure that all can hear your story, especially names, places, and numbers. Not "Five [mumble, mumble] . . . What do you think about that?" Huh?

◆ *Let your natural body language operate.* If it's funny, enjoy it. An amusing story may be hampered if the teller's jaws are clenched. A story about terrorism and the 9/11 attacks will probably not be well received if the presenter is grinning from ear to ear.

◆ *Above all, tell it right.* Here are three who didn't:

  • Vice President Dan Quayle became infamous for his frequent gaffes in speaking. An oft-cited one is his speech to the United Negro College Fund. His attempt to quote the fund's motto, "A mind is a terrible thing to waste," came out instead as, "What a waste it is to lose one's mind or not to have a mind. How true that is."[13]

  • Xerox Corporation speechwriter Tony Francis prepared a talk for a company executive, smooth at manufacturing but rough at speaking. He wove in a quotation, which the executive delivered thusly: "To quote the famous British author, W. Somerset Muggam . . ."[14]

  • Even the great communicators can blow it occasionally, usually to the amusement of the audiences. President Ronald Reagan closed out a speech to the United Nations with a reflection from "Mahatga Magandi": he meant Mahatma Gandhi.[15]

Analogies

◆ Make sure the analogy has a direct correlation to the idea it is intended to reinforce. "Olympian Charley Smith eats Smackos every morning for breakfast. Eat Smackos and you too can become an Olympic champion." As listeners, we are highly susceptible to analogies and far too frequently accept them as valid without questioning their logic. Common examples are found in political advertising, where a candidate is shown jogging to indicate he is vigorous and thus will make a good president. Or a candidate's success as a business executive is used to shows that she will be successful at running the government.

During Senate confirmation hearings, the nominee for secretary of defense, John Tower, was under heavy attack. In an appearance before the National Press Club, he defiantly vowed to fight on. Quoting from the last letter written by Lieutenant Colonel Travis, leader of the Alamo defenders in 1836, he said "I shall never surrender or retreat." Applause ringing in his ears, he stepped away from the lectern. Moments later, he retook the lectern to say: "I'm a little sorry I brought up the Alamo analogy because it just occurred to me what happened at the Alamo." Tower's nomination had the same fate.[16]

◆ Make sure the conditions of both parts of the analogy are close enough to render the comparison legitimate. This is especially important for literal analogies. "We turned the tide in the Korean War with a surprise amphibious landing at Inchon. We can do it again in the _____ War by making a similar surprise attack on _____." While the first statement may be correct, the situations may be so different that the speaker's argument will be shot down immediately.

Statistics

◆ *State the truly significant point about the statistics.* Is the value for 2004 significant, or is it that it's down 30 percent from 2003? Often the trend is more useful than absolute values. If you present a visual array of numbers, listeners are likely to have a hard time ferreting out the hot stuff unless you do it for them. You may be better off showing the data in graphic rather than tabular form.

◆ *Round the data off:* $505 million is probably close enough, $500 million is often just as good; and $532,505,279 is probably deadly—especially if it follows $276,597,873.52. See, you can hardly read it without having your eyes glaze over.

◆ *Be prepared to provide the assumptions behind the numbers and the procedures followed to develop them.* Once I was presenting data generated by someone else and was not clear about all the ground rules used. Sure enough, the key member of the audience queried me on those, and when I was not able to answer adequately, there went the presentation.

◆ *Make sure the numbers add up.* Don't give your listeners golden opportunities for nitpicking by having columns that don't add up or figures that aren't consistent. *The Chicago Sun-Times* gleefully pointed out an error in an ad run in *Forbes* and *Fortune*. A sample tax return shown in the ad contained a subtraction error of $1 million. Adding to the embarrassment of the advertiser was the fact that it was a major accounting firm, and the ad was touting the value of its services in preparing tax forms.[17]

References

◆ *Use legitimate authorities with valid and current credentials.* During the 1980 Presidential campaign debate, Jimmy Carter lost points by citing his daughter, Amy, as a source on the subject of nuclear proliferation.

◆ *Select sources the audience will respect.* A speaker advocating expanded use of solar energy quoted the head of the solar manufacturing lobby. If his audience had been pro-solar, this would have been no problem. Since he was trying to convince neutral-to-negative listeners, they rejected his source as biased in favor of the speaker's position.

◆ *Give sources where appropriate.* It may be helpful to identify the authority or document from which the information came. If a business audience knows your information came from the *Wall Street Journal* of August 5, 2003, it might add credibility.

What About Humor?

"Now that reminds me of a story." This statement can bring on a pleasant interlude or cause the audience to groan, "Oh, not again!" Do jokes or humorous stories have a place in business presentations? Maybe. Almost any audience appreciates a bit of levity, and I have seen many business presenters incorporate humor into their talks with good effect. The "maybe" is to put up a caution that humor can fall flat if it is out of place, is not pertinent to the subject, or is atrociously told. We're not all great joke tellers, and obvious attempts to add levity at any cost generally backfire.

Why use humor at all? Says Dr. Jerry Tarver of the University of

Richmond: "Mainly because it can help hold attention and interest. Also, humor helps establish a friendly atmosphere. It can relieve tension and allow an audience to appreciate the human qualities of a speaker. I recall watching John F. Kennedy on television as he won over an audience by explaining his reaction to a political setback. 'I feel like the old pioneer lying on the ground after being shot full of arrows,' he said. 'It only hurts when I laugh.' "[18]

Using humor does not automatically mean success. In a study testing results from speeches delivered with and without humor, (a) there was no significant difference in content retention for a speech on totalitarianism, and (b) significantly less learning occurred with the humorous approach in a technical speech.[19]

From speech writer Jean Pope comes this advice: "The rule of thumb concerning a joke is threefold: The speaker can deliver it effectively; it flows out of the experience of the speaker; and it is appropriate to the subject."[20]

"The single most common mistake in the delivery of humor is announcing you're going to tell a joke," said humor consultant Malcolm Kushner. Rather than, "That reminds me of a joke," he suggests substituting, "It's like . . ." and then the humor arrives as a surprise.[21]

"But I can't tell jokes!" you may protest. So don't. Professional speaker Gary Beals says humor isn't just telling jokes: "Everybody has a sense of humor. To sharpen it, find out whose humor you like by watching other speakers or comedians on TV. Write down what you like and you'll start to find your own humor. This is better than reading a book of jokes."[22]

Here are some ways to use humor to help get your message across.

◆ Practice privately before using publicly.

◆ Test your material in advance with knowledgeable listeners; humor can backfire if it is inappropriate or offensive. Many public figures have discovered this message, too late.

◆ Have fun with your audience. Professional speaker Susan Clarke interacts heavily with her audiences, salting her messages with entertaining and relevant examples the audience responds well to. As she wanders through the groups she sprinkles bubbles from a wand, putting listeners into a playful mood for her topic, the "fun"-damentals of relationship.

◆ Stretch your creativity as you develop material. Consider visuals, props, demonstrations, activities, and concepts adapted from late-night shows. One manager livened up the dreary annual lecture on time cards by using a cartoon character on each chart. "First time I ever paid any attention," said one grizzled supervisor.

◆ Try humor to help grab or revive audience attention. In a manufacturing organization, funding for a new idea had to be approved by a review board notorious for its negative attitude. A designer opened his presentation to the board with a viewgraph cartoon. In it a medieval general was surrounded by enemies, armed to the teeth with bows and arrows. A salesman attempts to sell him a new product, but the general rebuffs him: "Don't bother me. I have a battle to fight." The salesman's product? A Gatling gun. The board members recognized his point in good humor and heard him out, something they'd never done before.

◆ Add punch to your purpose. As mentioned in Chapter 5, in a competition for a contract to be performed in Buffalo, the source selection board required presentations from eight proposed project team members who would all move to Buffalo should they win the contract. To close the four-hour presentation, the team leader reaffirmed their commitment to the project by publicly declaring loyalty to their new team. At that point all eight team members stood up and placed new Buffalo Bills hats on their heads. The audience roared with laughter. Was it effective? They won the contract, and in later meetings several board members chuckled about the ploy.

◆ Look for opportunities to do something unique—perhaps even outrageous—to make your message more memorable. Mike Hale, Tootsie Rolls' human resources director, told of an executive who started a meeting in a gorilla outfit. "We laughed and relaxed. Then we listened and remembered. Fourteen months later, I can still tell you several points he made."[23]

◆ Even puns have a place. David Goodstein, chairman of the faculty at California Institute of Technology, likes to end his lectures with puns because, he said, they bring forth a loud and exquisitely predictable groan, waking up everyone for lunch. Here is one of his examples: "Heroes in the history of science may come and go, but Ampere's name will always be current."[24] You may now groan.

Using Support Material for Increased Audience Participation

According to Elbert Bowen and colleagues: "The attention span of even an interested cooperative listener is startlingly short. . . . Experimentation indicated that listening spans are a matter of only seconds or fractions of a second . . . The speaker is faced not with holding attention but with constantly regaining it, performing in such a way as to bring the listeners back alive as often as possible." [25]

A proven way of increasing audience interest and degree of learning is to get members of the audience to participate, physically and mentally, in the presentation (Figure 6-5).[26]

Professional speaker and master humorist Joe Griffith advises: "By

Figure 6-5. Involve your audience to keep them tuned in.

I HEAR and I forget

I SEE and I retain

I DO and I understand

sprinkling illustrations throughout your presentation, you will grab the imagination of listeners in a way that films or television are hard pressed to duplicate. Never forget that as a communicator you are appealing to the most powerful image-producing mechanism on earth . . . the human mind. It thrives on images. Good stories are triggers that release an explosive, powerful, positive form of communication energy.[27]

Support material is a powerful means of getting audiences involved in your presentation. Here are some specific ways to do that:

◆ *Make their activity an essential part of the communication process.* Role playing exercises and application activities are methods commonly used in presentations.

- Nutritionist Candy Cumming spoke to an elementary school class about the importance of eating better foods. To spice up the talk, she had the students work through a puzzle similar to a children's game. She was a hit on a subject the children normally paid little attention to.

- A lecturer on intercultural communication divided the audience into two artificially created nations. Each group quickly learned the rules of its new culture and then interacted with the other culture. By making the audience experience the intercultural difficulties, the key concepts were driven home far more effectively than would have been possible with a straight lecture.

- My associate Leslie Johnson applied her theatrical directing background to helping a corporation pay tribute to (and roast) their CEO with a tailored and humorous version of "A Christmas Carol." The actors were the company's employees, with the targeted CEO portrayed as Scrooge. Lots of fun for the employees and the CEO.

◆ *Let them handle the gadgetry.* Let the designer try out the new interaction graphic computer terminal, or take the customer's production experts out to the factory floor and let them operate the proposed assembly tool. If you don't have real objects, have models, hardware samples, cutaways—anything people can touch, handle, or operate. In a presentation about the effects of employee drinking on job safety and quality, bring in a recent *Wall Street*

Journal article about the subject, a box of liquor bottles confiscated from employees in the plant, and a damaged part produced by an intoxicated employee.

◆ *Ask them to supply material for illustrations.* The most effective professor I ever had was a master at keeping his students active. One of his methods was to ask them to provide material he needed to illustrate propositions. In a discussion of statistical probabilities, he needed three choices of different degrees of value. He could have said A, B, and C or provided his own examples of real choices. What he did was have us generate them—specifically, three restaurants, in categories of deluxe, not bad, and everyday. He not only kept us awake and involved, he came up with choices that were more significant to us because they were ours.

◆ *Have them assist with demonstrations.* Kit Goldman, president of Live Action Edutainment, speaks to many audiences about such workplace issues as harassment and violence. Bringing her theatrical background into training sessions, she develops customized scenarios and then has professional actors performing. Audience members become part of scenes and engage in dialogue at various pause points. Results are increased level of engagement and high retention.

◆ *Integrate audience responses into your presentation.* Take a tip from the stirring speakers who love repeated themes (e.g., "I have a dream . . ."). Once the pattern is seen, the audience gets on board and joins in each time the theme is repeated. In a training session, leave some blanks on the slide or lecture notes for participants to fill in with responses. Ask questions. Get the left side of the room into competition with the right side ("Tastes great!" "Less filling!").

Developing Support Material

Support material doesn't materialize out of thin air. Business presenters and public speakers develop such material from three basic sources.

1. *Studies and Analyses.* Statistical data in particular are developed during efforts undertaken prior to the presentation, and those

studies, analyses, and investigations may be key parts of the presentation.

2. *Specific Research.* A presenter may need to conduct a literature search to locate material to support a topic. A wealth of written and oral communication about any subject can be readily accessed using computer search methods or searching manually through the many reference systems found in public, educational, and corporate libraries. Identifying journals or digests pertinent to the presenter's general area of interest can be of value when the need arises to conduct a literature search.

3. *Ongoing Accumulation.* Here are some suggestions for accumulating and organizing material so that it will be of best use to you when needed.

    ◆ Identify topics of relevance. If you start accumulating material on all topics, you'll soon be driven out of the house by paper.

    ◆ Transcribe key material into a database or onto cards. Even if noting only a single anecdote, quotation, statistic, idea, or personal reaction, this will record and make retrievable at least a part of many articles, which typically will soon find their way into a stack of unread or hard-to-find articles. By noting the source, you can easily go back to the full document if needed.

    ◆ Create separate files for the various topics.

    ◆ Carry a small notebook of 3×5 cards. You will find a rich source of material in the experiences, observations, and thoughts that are part of your everyday business or personal life.

    ◆ If you intend to use it for publication, document the source information completely. You may not be able to use it if the source is not specified adequately, or you may find yourself spending valuable time searching for the missing information.

In Summary: Good Supporting Material Is Powerful

A presentation without supporting material is hard to conceive. Well done and executed, supporting materials add color to a presentation, in addition to providing their main service: clarifying points and backing up claims.

In August 1963, probably the most memorable speech of the decade was the "I have a dream" speech given by Reverend Martin Luther King in Washington, D.C. Just over two weeks later a terrible bombing of a church in Birmingham, Alabama, resulted in the deaths of four young black girls. In his eulogy, King vividly demonstrated the power of support material with these words to close: "Shakespeare had Horatio utter some beautiful words over the dead body of Hamlet. I paraphrase these words today as I stand over the last remains of these lovely girls. Good night, sweet princesses. May the flight of angels take thee to thy eternal rest."[28]

CHAPTER 7

Visual Aids/Graphics

A Picture Is Worth 1000 Words, Maybe

n many organizations, the word presentation automatically implies "visuals" or the more current term "graphics." Visual aids have been valuable to communication from Day One. Religion provides some well-known examples. The apple was a prop to impart an important lesson to Adam and Eve. Moses' Ten Commandments (or were there fifteen, Mel Brooks fans?) were carved on stone plaques. In the Sermon on the Mount, Jesus said "Behold the lilies of the field . . ."

To be truly proficient in today's presentations world, one needs to know how to create good visuals and how to use them well. The term oral communications, used to describe the content of many books on public speaking, is inadequate to describe business presentations. Because visuals are so integrally woven into presentations, the term *oral and visual communications* would be more appropriate.

"A picture is worth a thousand words" is a widely cited axiom that touts the value of visual aids. Add, "unless it is a thousand words." (See Figure 7-1. Perhaps you're familiar with charts like that.)

Figure 7-1. Nothing like a good old visual aid to clarify your communication.

SOURCE: Courtesy Rick McKee/*The Augusta (GA) Chronicle*. Reprinted with permission.

Visuals Can Add Greatly to a Presentation.

Research shows that adding visuals to the spoken word increases communication effectiveness by 40 percent to 50 percent.[1] Another statistic should also be kept in mind: If the visuals are poor, the result may lower communication success (Figure 7-2). I've been in many meetings where the best event would be for the bulb to burn out.

According to *AV Communication Review*, "The battle for supremacy between seeing and hearing has been waged presumably ever since man was endowed with eyes and ears. . . . Because of between-channel interference, it is not by any means a rule that the audiovisual is always better than the audio or visual only."[2]

When well done, visuals add to:

◆ *Audience Interest.* People are attracted to what catches the eye as well as the ear. Adding punchy visuals to a talk can pique and revive interest.

Figure 7-2. Visuals can help or hinder.

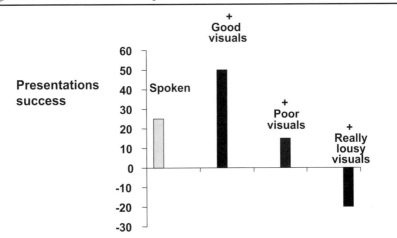

◆ *Understanding and Retention.* The complex nature of business and technology demands that information be presented visually as well as verbally. Trying to understand the propulsion system of the space shuttle or a complex business plan is well-nigh impossible without visuals. Even simpler information, such as three main points, can be grasped and understood better if seen as well as heard.

◆ *Clarity and Insight.* Many times in meetings, a disputed point is resolved by someone using a board or a flipchart to clarify the issue. (Research in the field of neurolinguistics shows that people process information gain from one sensory channel better than from others. An auditory person picks up material readily by hearing it; a visual person needs to see it. For the latter, visuals are particularly important.)

◆ *Results.* Maybe. In one well-known study at the Wharton School of Business, audiences significantly favored the presenter's proposition more with visuals (65 percent) than without (35 percent). This conclusion shouldn't be applied across the board because it depends on many factors, among them the quality of the visuals.[3]

◆ *Professional Image.* The medium is the message, as Marshal McLuhan said. A presenter who comes to a meeting with well-prepared visuals and uses them effectively conveys an image of competence.

◆ *Efficiency.* Empirical data strongly indicate that the same message can be communicated faster, and often better, by using visuals. A U.S. Department of Education study found that instructors could cut fifteen minutes off one-hour lectures by using an overhead projector. At the University of Wisconsin a fifty-minute lecture was boiled down to twenty minutes by using audiovisuals. The Wharton study previously noted found that using visuals reduced meeting time by 28 percent.

Poor Visuals Hurt Presentations' Success

"We don't make visual *aids* in our company," said one director. "We specialize in visual *hindrances*."

◆ At a professional society meeting, the articulate presenter used a series of computer-based graphics, many of which were barely readable due to poor color choices and overloaded content.

◆ At an annual convention, a highly paid and internationally known speaker showed visuals on a screen placed in a far corner of the room so that only half the audience could see them. The lettering was so small that those who could see could barely read the visuals.

◆ At a major conference sponsored by a prestigious university, roughly half the presenters showed visuals that were completely unreadable beyond the first few rows and were so cluttered as to make them impossible to follow.

Each of these examples is a case of poor visuals seriously damaging the presentation and the speaker's credibility, plus wasting the time of many people.

Technology Is Integral to Today's Presentations

The rules have dramatically changed for preparing presentation visual aids. Getting good-quality visuals in the past meant using the services of in-house or outside professional graphics designers. Those services were generally available only for major presentations and were costly. Visuals for most everyday presentations were usually created by the presenter: typed, cut-and-paste versions of whatever art existed, shrinking illustrations on the copy machine to fit viewgraphs, and even hand printed.

"Technology has been a tremendous boon to presentations," said Nick Vlahakis, Alliant Tech Systems' chief operating officer.[4] Computer technology provides presenters with an entire graphics department right in their offices. Low-priced scanners enable photos, illustrations, and other content to be quickly copied. The Internet means that photos and other content can be readily located or transferred. With digital cameras, pictures can be immediately copied over to the software or printer. Graphics software enables presenters to create bold titles, lay out flowcharts, instantly transform tables into graphic layouts, and incorporate clip art. Most software comes with professionally designed templates to steer amateurs along the right paths.

With better graphics come many output and display options that formerly were only in the domain of expensive presentations. The quality of presentations has significantly increased for everyday presentations as well as for the major ones.

With increased use, the term PowerPoint Ranger has been coined, referring to briefers who are heavy practitioners of this form of presentation. That's not always a complimentary term.

Computers Mean Better Visuals, Don't They?

Nevertheless, poor visuals are still being used in presentations. Many can't be read, or they obscure more than illuminate. Those handy software templates may be useful somewhere, but for many business presentations they are not appropriate and are best deleted to avert negative responses from audience members. Some presenters can't resist trying out the many options, leading to presentations that are more exercises in technology than communication.

An article in the *Wall Street Journal* was a wake-up call to many briefers and business development directors around the country. Titled "What's your point, Lieutenant? Please, just cut to the pie charts," it quoted high-level military leaders' dissatisfaction with many high-tech presentations. An order issued by the Chairman of the Joint Chiefs of Staff said, in essence, "Enough with the bells and whistles—just get to the point. . . . We don't need Venetian-blind effects or fancy backdrops. All we need is the information." The Secretary of the Navy had a similar lament: "The idea behind most of these briefings is for us to sit through a hundred slides with our eyes glazed over, and then to do what all military organizations hope for . . . to surrender to an overwhelming mass." Another problem noted was that all the fancy gimmicks of "booming tanks and spinning pie-charts" were gobbling up way too much Internet bandwidth.[5]

Having nifty tools is one thing; knowing how to use them is another. Graphic design is a specialty in its own right, and having managerial or technical talent doesn't ensure graphics capability. Computer specialists have long used the term GIGO: "Garbage In, Garbage Out." If visual knowledge and presentation wisdom are weak, the computer will give only prettier garbage. And when you do use the graphics pros, you need to supply the strategy, organization, and content. By adding basic knowledge of visual aids, you can come up with more creative ways to get that knowledge across, whether making visuals yourself or working with experts.

Why Not Better Visuals? Check the Right Brain

Almost anyone can make visuals. We started doing that as tots the first time we got crayons and walls together. Then we spent our early years drawing houses, trees, and doggies. We soon stopped doing that, because crayons were for kids. Over the next decade or two we learned stuff. Our heads got filled with information, and we solved problems, wrote a lot of essays, and answered lots of multiple-choice questions. We did a lot of communicating—written and oral. Only rarely were we asked to do anything "visual," except to go to the blackboard occasionally and work through some formulas.

Then we went to work and got steeped in detail and specialization. We learned to turn out seventy-five-page reports and make illustrations of minute details of design and scheduling and cost analysis. And then the boss said, "Jones, I want a half-hour presentation on what you're doing." And since we already had a lot of that information, we went to the almighty reproduction machine and copied our illustrations and got instant transparencies showing all those minute details. Since we now had computer graphics, we added ten more charts. True, they were all words and a little busy, but they looked clean. (Truth is, we never had mastered those better options in the software.)

So we gave the boss the presentation and she said, "Yeechhh!" And we were stunned because we thought she wanted a thorough report, and here we had all these visual aids to help her get that. She said the visuals stunk.

Why, in this television and computer world, are many visuals still mediocre? One explanation—that society is afflicted with massive visual atrophy—is suggested by Robert McKim in *Experiences in Visual Thinking*. It is the result of an almost exclusive stress in school on the three Rs: reading, (w)riting, and (a)rithmetic. "Opportunity for visual expression usually ceases early in the primary grades," he said, adding that "any mental ability that is not exercised decays, and visual ability is no exception."[6]

Research into learning suggests that the two sides of the brain handle different types of information and activities For the typical business and technical person, the left side is continually exercised and well developed while the right side often gets little workout and thus may be only slightly developed. The result is stifled visualization and imaginative ability. Deliberate stretching of imagination exercises the right side and helps the visual ideas flow (Figure 7-3).

Selecting the Right Audiovisual Form

Hardware, Models, and Props

Hardware, models, and props are among the highest interest media when used well. For the audience, they can add a change of pace from sitting through an hour of viewgraphs, bring in a dramatic or humorous touch, and add credibility. They also have high recall quotient. (For example, from TV ads what products come to mind when you see a falling needle, or two hands gripped together in an inviting manner? Perhaps a phone company and an insurance company?)

As an Air Force colonel said, "A picture is worth 1,000 words and

Figure 7-3. Right-brain atrophy stymies visual creativity.

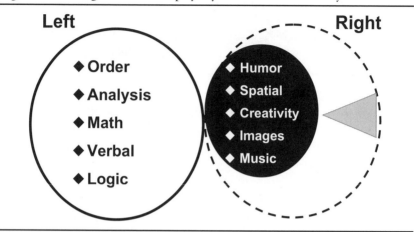

a piece of hardware is worth 1,000 pictures." People love to handle gadgetry, see real stuff, and watch things work, a bit like kicking the tires and test-driving an automobile before buying it. Here are some examples that worked well:

◆ A Miami priest whipped out a handgun during his Palm Sunday sermon and then asked his flock to turn theirs in and stop shooting each other. Said one parishioner, "It was the most dramatic thing I've ever seen in a church in my life." (Only one gun got turned in; nevertheless, the presentation was dramatic.)[7]

◆ A speaker used puppets, among them Sergeant Sammy Sperm and his regiment, in sex education lectures to junior and senior classes. A reviewer described this as "the most comfortable, clearly-presented class I have ever attended on the subject."[8]

◆ A large crowd had gathered for community plan review meeting, with several diverse viewpoints represented. The plan administrator opened the meeting by juggling, first a tennis ball (the recreational interest), then a monkey wrench (the off-road contingent) and finally an acorn (the environmental faction). As he kept adding items (and never dropping any!) he spoke about the need for the plan to integrate the competing needs. All were engrossed, and his opening set a positive tone for the meeting that otherwise might have been contentious.

Demonstrations

Demonstrations can be powerful forms of support and add high credibility as they vividly illustrate some activity relevant to the purpose of the presentations. Consider the hold that demonstrations by magicians or product hawkers at county fairs have on their audiences.

As mentioned in Chapter 5, a thoroughly engrossing presentation was given by a student demonstrating how to make margaritas from scratch. The choice of subject and promise at the end was a good starter for keeping our interest. In addition, he brought several listeners into the demonstration by having them squeeze the limes, measure out some of the ingredients, operate the blender and ice crusher, and, most importantly, by having the instructor (your author) sample the finished product.

As another example, in a marketing presentation the bidding team was made up of several large firms with complementary specialties. Anticipating a customer concern about how this multi-hued team would actually be able to work well together, they set up a demonstration as part of the proposal presentation. Several subteams were positioned across from the customers. The project manager directed a potential delivery order by showing viewgraphs of each step in the process. The overhead projector was then turned off, and a subteam of three people arose and, placing hats for that team on their heads, described how they would function. The project manager went on to the next task, and the next team arose and described how they would work. The whole sequence was well staged and executed and showed clearly the competence, teamwork, and spirit of the bidder.

Many governmental proposal requests specify that a scenario or sample problem demonstration will be required as part of each bidder's presentation. These may be specified in advance or during the meeting, with the analysis, solution, and communication to be done in a specific time, such as two hours. Typically the program head leads the team through a series of activities, all developed on the spot, which provides a challenging but important demonstration of how this team works under fire.

Visual Support, Nonelectronic

In a high-tech world, the nonprojected formats still have many applications and often are necessary because the setting precludes electric outlets, screens, or darkened rooms

Paper copies are especially useful for one-on-one discussions across the conference table. Their informality and easy use stimulate interchange, which could be inhibited when higher-tech formats are used. Paper copies can also serve as a backup in case the computer or projector conks out. For example, a team had prepared and rehearsed several times with their computer-based presentation. When setting up their own equipment in the meeting, they discovered a snag in the software. They immediately shifted to the paper copies, had a productive session, and won the contract. Without those paper copies, it's highly doubtful they'd have won.

Chalkboards, flipcharts, and posters are widely used. In his much-noted Gulf War briefing, General Norman Schwarzkopf chose poster boards to convey troop locations and movements. Architects rely heavily on paper drawings and pictures on poster boards. Quality presentations or safety talks on the shop floor are often done from flipcharts. In workshop sessions, participants often develop and shape their ideas with hand-written posters and stick them on the walls. Sales people use paper copies or small flipcharts for one-on-one meetings.

Projected and Electronic Media

Electronic chalkboards offer a useful capability for primarily dialogue sessions, as these provide instant transfer to a computer or to printouts, plus they allow the speaker to bring in previously-prepared graphics.

Overhead projectors and viewgraphs (also called transparencies or foils) are still widely used, especially in situations lacking computer-based capabilities. They can be quickly prepared and changed, they allow high flexibility and interchange during meetings, and paper copies can be quickly made. The art is generally done with computer graphics programs, but their operational use is much the same as in the 1970s. Color viewgraphs are common, obtained quickly and cheaply from ink-jet printers. Hand-drawn transparencies still have a place for interactive programs. In a recent major procurement presentation, only hand-drawn transparencies were permitted to support the different scenarios being presented.

Full-color slide presentations remain common, especially for industries that use lots of pictures, such as designers and builders. Slides are easy to create from any camera and are a high-quality medium, with versatile capability through multiple projectors and special effects.

Opaque projectors display objects or printed materials on a screen without using photographic material or reproductions. One advantage is enabling large audiences to view objects without passing the objects around; another is the ability to project examples of color advertisements without having to make slides.

Computer graphics is the term often used to mean presentations linking computers with projectors or monitors. This brings a vast array of presentation possibilities—including animation, movement, 3D effects, reality simulations from different viewpoints, and video segments—that can't be done with simpler devices. With small laptops and projectors these are also easily transported. Computers offer a high degree of flexibility, such as presentations being tuned up on airplanes en route to a meeting. Changes can be made right up to the time of the meeting or even while it is going on. In response to a question, the speaker can immediately call up the program and display the changed data with a new graph. A trainee can engage in an interactive dialogue to acquire knowledge or skills.

Video provides another dimension to presentations, bringing realism, actual events, processes, and people into the conference room and generally enlivening the program. Applications are many:

◆ For dynamic activities—rocket liftoffs, safety procedures, and of course, freeway pursuits—video clips are more valuable than static formats.

◆ Personal commentaries or stories can be powerful. In a short public service announcement, a woman used a throat mechanism to talk because she'd had throat cancer. It was made unforgettable when she then drew on a cigarette through that same throat opening.

◆ For training purposes or team building, short films or movie clips can be used to make a point.

◆ Proposals often include video summaries or team commentaries.

◆ For proposals, interviews, and hearings, presentations are often recorded for later review or for the record.

◆ Presentation rehearsals can be enhanced with video recording and playback.

Video/Internet Teleconferences

Satellite TV, cable, and the Internet can incorporate all of the above during meetings and presentations linking different locations. These allow convenient and timely communication to occur while cutting out travel time, preventing aggravation, and reducing expenses. With air travel complications and traffic congestion, the use of these formats continues to increase.

Multimedia

Historically the term multimedia has referred to presentations using two or more audiovisual forms, such as slides and video. The term also refers to computer-generated presentations incorporating slides, video, animation, sound, 3-D effects, and beyond. These bring added dynamic effects, adding power and interest to presentations.

Factors in Selecting the Right Medium

Captain James Woolway, commanding officer of the U.S. Naval Air Depot North Island, experiences many briefings running the gamut from low to high tech.

> Technology can be useful or of no value. Recently a guy gave us a briefing using hand-marked transparencies. It was very effective as he made very good points and it added a personal touch. Very believable. Another briefing integrated video clips into a PowerPoint presentation, showing cross hairs on a target and then the weapon coming in. Sure made the point. On the other hand, I've seen others with video segments thrown in that aren't worth much as they don't make the point. . . . We also rely a lot on videoteleconfer-

ences. They're very useful, saving time and money as we don't have to travel.[9]

For many presentations, selecting the right medium is an easy decision. It's whatever is standard and easy. Perhaps the organization always uses viewgraphs, or for serious presentations, color slides or computer graphics. But the easy decision may not be the best one. The "we've always done it this way" syndrome may stifle alternatives that achieve a better result, or may not adequately consider related factors, which can lead to serious aggravation and rework later.

- ◆ Do preset specifications apply? In a request for proposal contract, a customer may ask for viewgraphs, paper copies, and a thirty-minute video summary. (They may also say, "Don't spend much money on fancy presentations," thus driving marketing directors crazy trying to figure out how to do that and not get aced out by competitors.)

- ◆ What's our capability for producing and using visuals? Can we farm it out or use local facilities (such as a video-teleconference)?

- ◆ What's best for this situation, environment, audience, and purpose?

- ◆ What's the budget and due date? With today's computer graphics capability and low cost, this is less of a decision than during the time when "Class A slides" were only reserved for major occasions due to the cost.

- ◆ How else might these visuals be used? It is increasingly common that visuals get used in several modes, each of which has different requirements. Viewgraphs designed for conference room use may not work well for a video-conference.

- ◆ What about production? Will they need to be printed as well as shown? If we select color, how will that affect making paper copies?

Principles of Good Visual Aids

From a customer review board: "We said we wanted a presentation, not a written proposal projected onto a screen." With that scathing comment as a major yellow flag (or was that red?) waving in the air, here are some guidelines on creating visual aids that achieve their purpose (summarized in Figure 7-4).

◆ *Remember, they are aids.* The most important element in the presentation is you, the presenter. The aids may be your most important tool, but your words and the way you conduct yourself are primary. If the entire message is on the visuals, why do we need you? Just send a clerk, who costs a third as much, to flip the charts. If the aid does not help you convey your message, it's a poor visual.

◆ *Visuals or graphics must be an integral part of the larger picture, the story.* Thus the topics dealt with in the previous chapters—sound strategy, theme, clear organization, and good support—all are essentials. Without them, stunning graphics mean nothing, except to note that a lot of energy was wasted producing them. To have visuals track the story line, use the process dis-

Figure 7-4. Apply these guidelines for creating punchy visual aids.

◆ Choose the best audiovisual medium to suit audience, purpose, situation, environment, and budget. High tech is not always better.

◆ Good visual aids help communication go better and faster; poor visuals are seen too often.

◆ Computer graphics programs can increase graphics quality and productivity, but they're only as good as the thinking that goes into them.

◆ Hands-on visuals, such as props, displays and models, are strong audience attention-getters.

◆ Visual power can be increased by better application of right-brain thinking.

◆ Excessive reliance on bullet charts leads to boredom. Look for better ways.

◆ Design visuals that help audiences get it better and faster.

◆ Ensure that each visual conveys only one main idea. Use the title as a headline vs just a topic.

◆ Make visuals readable. Choose fonts and colors wisely.

◆ KISS—Keep It Simple, S____.

◆ Present no more than seven items—lines, labels, blocks.

◆ Present material in bite-size pieces to keep the audience's attention focused.

◆ Apply the wisdom that a picture may indeed be worth a thousand words.

◆ Select the right graph form for best communication.

◆ Be sure to proof visuals before heading to the conference room.

cussed in Chapter 5, specifically moving from outline to story-board rather than just popping in charts.

◆ *First ask, "What's the point?"* A visual serves one main purpose: to help make a point. This concept often gets forgotten, and charts are tossed into the presentation because they're there. It's better to figure out the message and then determine the best way to show that. Many visuals have been wisely eliminated or extensively modified by that question (Figure 7-5).

◆ *White space is O.K.* One manager, who has sat through many presentations, said "Our philosophy seems to be that if there's an inch of white space, fill it!" I've worked with many presenters whose idea of graphics is to keep adding on info ("So I won't forget to say it."), leading to the kitchen sink chart, which includes everything but the kitchen sink, is overloaded, and is way too complex.

◆ *KISS—Keep It Simple, Selene!* This is a well-known adage, often ignored. For the audience, following a presentation is much like driving down a freeway. The passengers (listeners) have only a few moments to pick up the messages from the billboards, but they do, because the messages on the billboards are so simple. How

Figure 7-5. Each visual must answer one primary question.

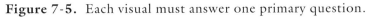

many messages would they pick up if billboards looked like a page from the phone book? Not many. In the presentation, we want the audience to grasp our visual message quickly and listen to our words without moving on to other agendas in their heads or giving up because of information overload. Complex charts make that hard to achieve. "This may be the most common failing," says the Electro/Wescon Midcom *Speaker's Handbook*, "trying to reproduce a novel on the 35mm slide."[10]

◆ *Making them readable is paramount.* It shouldn't be too much to expect that your projected graphics, with presumably useful information, be readable. From a long-time high-level governmental official: "With anybody I've ever talked to in the government, the first thing they'll bitch about is the visual they can't read. This is so fundamental yet so commonly violated."

Mistake #1 is to display a chart that can't be read. Mistake #2 is to say, "I know you can't read this . . ." Guess what, we knew that the instant it hit the screen.

A common response from audience members is, "Looks like another eye chart," referring to the optometrist's wall chart with several lines unreadable to the average eyeball. Keep in mind that many upper-level management audiences include older people. On numerous occasions, I've heard those executives remind presenters in this fashion: "This may surprise you, but my vision is not nearly as sharp as it was twenty years before. In other words, don't make these old eyes work so hard. Print larger."

◆ *Ensure logical flow from chart to chart.* Consider how easy it is to follow a cartoon strip. Each visual logically leads to the next until the story is complete. It is much easier for the audience to follow your presentation if each visual ties in with the one before it. The storyboard and delivery script helps this to occur. If the visuals are disconnected, it comes across as jerky, and the audience has to reorient itself for each visual.

◆ *Interpret, don't just report.* As the presenter, you are the expert on the subject being discussed. "The data speaks for itself" is a common expression. The trouble is, it may say different things to different people. Your job is to apply your expertise and insights to help those not as expert as you to understand the information.

◆ *Present more messages and less information.* Information overload is universally hated and, unfortunately, extremely common. It's the main contributor to the MEGO Syndrome: "My Eyes Glaze Over." The value of a presentation is to help listeners understand the essence of the subject, to be alerted to vital conditions.

◆ *Focus on and highlight key information.* Out of three factors, which is the most crucial at this moment? When explaining a ten-step process, is one step potentially the most likely to go wrong? If you've had five related assignments, did one in particular provide the best lessons learned for your proposed position? Design the visual so that these key items will be obvious and so they almost jump out at the audience.

◆ *Technology can add much to presentations, but watch that it doesn't backfire.* Recall the comments from the Pentagon's top audience member about too many bells and whistles interfering with presentations. "It is nice to see the tools used in creative ways. They help, without a doubt," said Mike Cogburn, Anteon Corporation's COO. "They're especially valuable in creating proposals and presentations." And he cautions against getting carried away with gimmicks. "People are looking for content and message. For a while, presentations got too flamboyant; some went crazy as the technology had all these capabilities. It was irritating to be on the receiving end. Now they're not so jerky and jump around less."[11]

◆ *Change happens, so be ready for it.* In many meetings, the presentation does not proceed on the planned course. Audience questions and directions may omit certain charts, delete entire segments, revisit previous charts. In planning your visuals, consider how you will be able to respond to such diversions. Learn about the options available in your computer systems so you can adjust, meet the need and impress the audience by your management under fire. This topic is addressed in the discussion on "staging" in Chapter 8.

Ten Tips for Getting Visuals to Come Through Loud and Clear

1. Understand and Make Clear "What's the Point?"

Make sure each chart communicates one primary point, and one only. More than one confuses the audience and often shows that the presenter hasn't thoroughly sorted out the ideas. Two messages on one chart also divide the attention of the audience. While you are explaining point 1 (say, the graphical data), the audience is thinking about point 2 (the conclusions about it) that you put on the same chart.

Write the title so that the point is clearly understood. Titles tend to be expressed as "topics," but it's not easy to grasp the point from just a topic. To more clearly make the point, write titles that convey a message, the point, as if it were a newspaper article. The most powerful message in a newspaper article is the headline. Most people never read beyond that. In a visual aid, the most powerful position is the title. Yet few presenters take advantage of the potential power in the title. How many charts have you seen whose titles read something like "Cost versus Years" or "System Improvements"? As one observer said, that's like showing a picture of a horse and titling it "Horse." Of course it's a horse. Titles like that add little to the chart.

A headline title states in catchy terms the main message of the chart or interprets the chart. Even if readers don't get to or follow the body or detail of the chart, they will understand what the chart is intended to show. Like newspaper readers, they get the message from the headline and can then digest the rest of the material as they choose. For general audiences or those with mixed levels or disciplines, action or interpretive titles are particularly useful aids to understanding. (The term varies for different organizations: message titles, action captions, or take-away messages.)

My experience shows that many presenters have difficulty grasping the value of headline titles compared to topic or "horse" titles. For reference, consider these research findings. As cited in *Communication and Persuasion*, following a persuasive presentation, significantly more people (over 50 percent) changed toward the speaker's proposition when the speaker explicitly stated conclusions than when he didn't (30 percent).[12] That's what a headline title does: It states the point (or conclusion) of the chart.

Here are some examples of headline titles, with the proviso that the body of the chart must back tip what the title says (see also Figure 7-6):

Subject/Topic Title	*Headline Title*
Horse	Polka-Dot Horses Run Faster
Cost vs. Years	Initial Cost Outlay Quickly Recovered
System Improvements	System Changes Expand Performance

Figure 7-6. Use title to make the point clear.

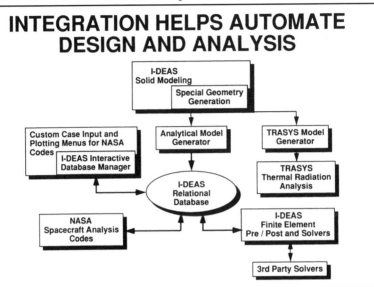

INTEGRATION HELPS AUTOMATE
DESIGN AND ANALYSIS

SOURCE: Courtesy of Structural Dynamics Research Corporation.

A headline title may not be appropriate for every chart, and the flavor of the message should match the situation and audience. A heavy sales flavor may turn off some listeners, particularly with an informational audience. The boss may prefer to draw his own conclusions. Generally, however, interpretive titles add to understanding.

Writing full titles can prove extremely beneficial for the presenter, as well as for the listener. This process can help focus and clarify the message the presenter wishes to convey, which often is clouded in a mass of data.

The location of the interpretive title varies. Many companies place it at the top of the chart. Others use a simple title or no title at the top and place the interpretive statement at the bottom, often adding in the title after the chart is explained.

2. Make Visuals Viewer-Friendly

You can make audiences work hard to grasp the essence and content of your visuals, or you can put more effort into helping them get it quickly. This means providing information and layouts that are intuitive, easily followed and absorbed.

◆ *Put page numbers on slides.* This makes it much easier for the viewers to take notes and refer to the slides when asking questions.

◆ *Limit items to seven.* Show them more than seven, and you will lose control of their attention, and their comprehension will probably be less than you expect.[13] If more than seven items are needed, disclose them progressively.

◆ *Tighten wording.* Many visuals are overloaded with verbiage. It's amazing how application of the delete button and some word-tightening can reduce words in titles, bullets, or boxes. Work toward the fewest and shortest word possible. Cut qualifiers, connectives, and articles. Active tense has more zip than passive. Compare the wordier version on the left to the trimmed on the right:

The selected component is acquired.	Buy part.
Rigorous testing procedures will be employed.	Test it.
The production decision is ascertained, pending application of the various assessment factors.	Evaluate and decide.

◆ *Start with the general; move to the specific.* Frequently a presenter shows a complicated visual and proceeds to describe the detailed design or operation of some gadget or process. After five minutes listening to a description of all the intimate workings, a bewildered audience member may hesitatingly ask: "Uh, what does this thing look like?" or "Just where does this gadget fit on the vehicle?" Then the presenter comes, belatedly, to the realization that these people haven't the foggiest idea of what he or she has been talking about for the past five minutes.

It's almost always worth an extra thirty seconds to give people the big picture before getting into the details. If it's an engine valve under discussion, shoot a photo of the entire engine. If you're explaining a computer software module to users, first show how that fits into the overall system and what it looks like (Figure 7-7).

◆ *Don't expect your viewers to have ostrich necks.* It's O.K. in a written report to have the y axis written vertically on the page; the

Figure 7-7. Provide a brief orientation before diving into details.

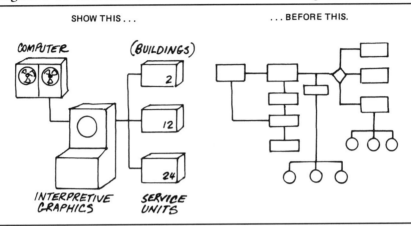

reader just rotates the page. This is not so easy in a presentation, where that y axis (usually in tiny print) is impossible to read, especially in the short time available while the speaker is discussing the details on the graph. The rule for presentations is that all printing must be easily readable. Thus replace any vertical printing with horizontal. Viewers should not have to cock their heads sideways to read vertically aligned graph labels, column headings, or labels on bar or pie charts (Figure 7-8).

◆ *Use labels not legends.* So often you're trying to figure out which line is what on a line graph by reading the legend in the lower right corner, trying to figure out which line that applies to, while the speaker is blithely chatting away. Once you finally get it,

Figure 7-8. Make charts easily readable.

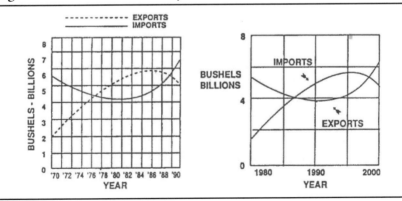

if you do, the speaker has already moved on to the next chart. Legends are fine for written reports, not for presentations. Put labels right on the lines (Figure 7-8).

◆ *Keep the visuals moving.* Audience members will read your visual material much faster than you can talk it. They won't be listening to you if you give them too much material to look at. Simplify the visuals to aim for no more than one to two minutes per visual for talks of some substance. If a chart needs a longer time on screen, find a way to show it as a buildup of several charts.

3. Use Visual Power

On a plane to Washington, D.C., my seat mate was a U.S. Navy captain. Upon hearing that I train and coach presenters, he said: "I sit through a lot of presentations, as our organization lets a lot of contracts. I am constantly amazed at how many presenters lack visual creativity. They seem to only think of bullet charts. Do you know how boring it is to sit through presentation after presentation seeing mostly bullet charts? Tell your clients to put some more thinking into their graphic layouts."

Low-key or highly apprehensive presenters can benefit greatly by using high-interest visuals—those with lots of pictures and few words. Perky visuals promote a more zestful delivery; dull visuals compound the dullness problem the speaker already has.

◆ *Look for obvious visual opportunities.* In this highly left-brain world, we often overlook the obvious. If a picture is worth a thousand words, why do we see so many words-only charts, especially ones describing things that can be pictured? A useful ground rule is this: if it's real, show it; if it flows, flow it (Figure 7-9).

◆ *Think relationships.* Objects, processes, operations, sequences, time lines, and A versus B data lend themselves to visual displays (right brain) rather than wordy descriptions (left brain). Transforming a dull bullet chart to a matrix often makes the data easier to grasp (Figure 7-10).

◆ *Present concepts, not just data.* Which is more important, showing all the details of your topic or showing trends, changes, impacts, and insights? Present the data so that the desired concepts

Figure 7-9. Look for better ways to show data than bullets.

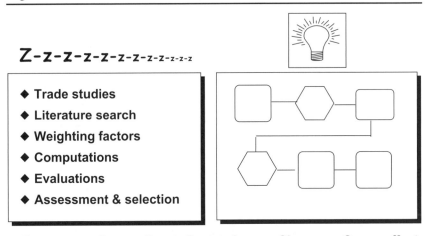

Z-z-z-z-z-z-z-z-z-z-z-z-z

- ◆ **Trade studies**
- ◆ **Literature search**
- ◆ **Weighting factors**
- ◆ **Computations**
- ◆ **Evaluations**
- ◆ **Assessment & selection**

Processes - Connections - Comparisons - Changes - Cause-effect

can be readily understood. This is an area of particularly rich potential for a presenter, where communication can be vastly enhanced by creative visual thinking.

◆ *Apply the "picture equal 1000 words" principle.* After a dozen word-only charts, up pops a photograph. The audience stirs, looks intently at the screen, and wakes back up. Pictures, sketches, abstractions, and cartoons are high-interest items that enable people to grasp ideas quickly—to "see the picture"—better than with words alone, spoken or written. Pictures or animation often can effectively complement the necessary words or phrases. Some examples are shown in Figure 7-11.

Figure 7-10. Transform bullets into matrix for clearer communication.

- ● **Option A has 30% lower cost, 40% faster output, 90 days delivery**
- ● **Option B, 40% lower cost, 30% faster, 120 days delivery**
- ● **C has no savings, 25% faster, off-shelf**

Factors	Options		
	A	B	C
Cost	-30%	-40%	0
Output	+40%	+50%	+25%
Delivery (days)	90	120	now

Figure 7-11. Pictures can add much to presentations.

Quality Circles Need Timely Response to Suggestions

Innovative Technologies Have Saved Time and Money

◆ **In situ remediation**

- Zero valent iron injection to remediate chlorinated solvents

- Enhanced aerobic and anaerobic biodegradation

◆ **Screening technologies**

- Immunoassay

- XRF

- Geophysics

Data displays—graphs, pie charts, column charts, and bar charts—are staples for presentations. Suggestions for using them effectively will be discussed later in the chapter.

4. Use Color Power—Wisely

With advances in computer graphics and output capabilities, color visuals are much more commonly used. The value of color has been demonstrated in numerous studies. A Xerox Corporation study showed significant benefits in learning and retention from use of color materials over black and white.[14] According to *Audio-Visual Instruction: Technology, Media and Methods*, color can add to visual effect in three ways:

1. To attract attention (e.g., using the Red Cross logo to stress safety).
2. To emphasize or contrast (e.g., highlighting the super sales trend of one product line relative to several others).
3. To create moods (e.g., a sunny logo for a solar energy company or blue for a Caribbean cruise company advertisement).

Poor use of color can damage visuals in three primary ways:

1. Poor readability due to improper color combinations—the most common flaw.
2. Misuse of color associations. In a presentation to demonstrate how much better team A was than brand X, a bar chart compared financial performance. The team A bar was in red; brand X's was in black. Who had the apparent red ink, a standard measure of financial loss?
3. Culture traps. What plays well in Peoria may backfire in Hong Kong.

5. Make Visuals Readable

Several factors go into achieving visuals that meet the test for readability: font type and size, color, and interference.

Computer graphics programs have fonts that can assure good

readability when slides are projected. They also have fonts that are too small or unsuited for presentation graphics, leading to way too many unreadable items on screen.

The wording might be readable, if it weren't that red-against-black combination. Hopeless and also very common. Poor use of color is regularly seen even in presentations that have received extensive preparation. It also appears on the computer screen with e-mail that uses color combinations that defy legibility.

Graphics software also has many templates and effects that presenters can use to theoretically add pizzazz to the visuals. Some will do that well; others, such as fadeouts from top to bottom, mean that parts of the words are obscured. Another dandy is the background that is so busy it resembles the kids' game *Where's Waldo*, only in the game the intention is to hide Waldo. This is visual interference. Avoid it (see Figure 7-12).

Other color choices fail to consider that people who are color-blind will not be able to read what's on the screen. About 10 percent of the population fits this category, with the most common bad color combination being green and red. (It should not be comforting to know that many templates use this combination.) A director found out the hard way that his corporate boss was color blind, when he showed up for his first meeting with a well-honed graphics set, all based on red bullets and green background. Ouch, that smarts!

Specifics of how to ensure that your visuals meet the readable standards are discussed on pages 155 to 160.

Figure 7-12. Make sure that cute backgrounds don't wipe out readability.

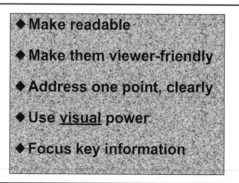

- ◆ Make readable
- ◆ Make them viewer-friendly
- ◆ Address one point, clearly
- ◆ Use _visual_ power
- ◆ Focus key information

6. Focus on Key Information

A major purpose of presentation is to quickly help others get the information they need. Visuals provide an excellent mechanism to give them relevant information and then focus their attention on what is especially pertinent.

◆ *First, present only information you plan to discuss.* This deletes potentially troublesome baggage. Whatever you leave on is fair game for viewers to raise questions about. Exercise that red pencil, correction fluid, or delete command liberally.

◆ *Don't overload them with unnecessary detail.* Will anyone remember the last six digits in "The program cost will be $946,275,172"? Does anyone care? Try $946 million or maybe even $950.

◆ *Highlight the most pertinent items.* On a flow chart, put the most critical box in a different color. On a bullet chart emphasize the key line or word with an arrow, highlighted color, or by underlining. On a table highlight the column or line that is the important one. Show a Gantt chart, schedule, or detailed list for context, then blow up the most pertinent information (Figure 7-13).

◆ *Use progressive disclosure or overlays to build to complexity and for dramatic effect.* Since the eye is quicker than the mouth, showing lots of information is a sure way to lose your audience. Yet when considerable material has to be displayed, a way to do that and still hold the audience is to use progressive disclosure, also called "revelation." Show one part of the chart, then bring in another, and perhaps one more (Figure 7-14). This can work well with flow charts, bullets, tables with add-ons, agendas, or a series of pictures. Use this technique with care. Be sensitive to the situation and audience; for example, advancing bullets one at a time can irritate some audiences. It can also cause speakers to stumble and cause excessive mechanical manipulation.

◆ *Show a reference (comparison, example, or analogy) for heightened insight and impact.* The significance of the accuracy achieved during a series of missile firings was barely grasped by an

Figure 7-13. Don't just present information. Focus and interpret.

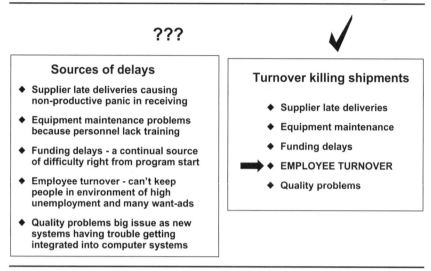

audience shown a visual aid giving the test results in the form of miss distances. An astute presenter changed the visual aid to a dartboard showing the actual miss distances all clustered tightly around the bulls-eye. Instant recognition of a sensational performance was achieved (Figure 7-15).

Figure 7-14. Progressive disclosure shows segments in sequence.

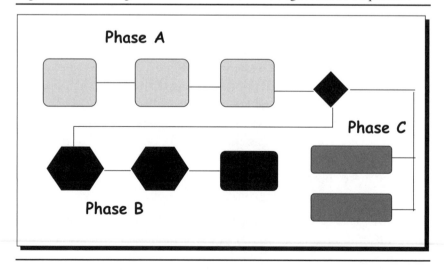

Figure 7-15. Giving a frame of reference increases comprehension.

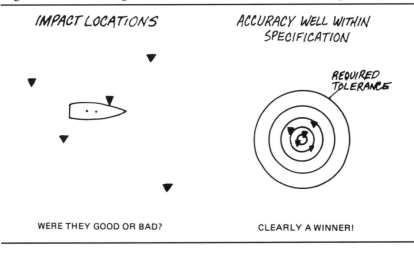

Often audiences have trouble catching key information (re-flected by comments such as "That's interesting, but was it good or bad?") because the presenter has failed to give them a frame of reference.

Complex concepts are more quickly grasped if a familiar anal-ogy is made. An instructor was able to get across the idea more quickly of how to steer a sailboat by relating it to the steering of a car. Another presenter drove home his point that a relatively sim-ple structure was costing the government too much money by showing it next to four brand-new Cadillacs. Other examples are a pencil next to a circuit board, a woman holding a new cruise missile engine in her hands to show its compact size, and a changed procedure next to the old one.

7. Proof Your Visuals

Particularly embarrassing to a presenter is when a slide appears on screen and the audience immediately picks up a misspelled word. Or they scan that column of numbers and find that they don't add up to 100 percent. Or key information is obscured due to poor use of color? Or the picture shown is not of the product being discussed but of another one. "Oops, that slide is out of order." Perhaps you've seen a few of these (see Figure 7-16).

Figure 7-16. People love to nitpick. Check your visuals carefully before you show them so that you are not guilty of making avoidable errors.

Although computer graphics programs have spell checkers to pick up spelling errors, it often appears that the presenter has failed to use them. Of course, some words survive the spell checker: they are spelled correctly but they're the wrong word. Other mistakes may not be caught by the speaker because it's hard to see your own goofs. Someone else might spot them immediately, which is why it's important to have others proof your materials or to rehearse with others before going public.

For example, here is a set of bullets, each containing one or two typical errors. What are they?

◆ Color chosen compliments design

◆ Green is favorable too it's reception

◆ Totals are 48 percent green, 30 percent blue and 25 percent red

Here are some tips to avert that sinking feeling that comes when you see several audience members giggling and pointing at the screen.

◆ *Make sure the quality fits the occasion and audience.* Having mediocre quality graphics for a significant audience sends a bad message: "You're not important enough for us to do a good job."

◆ *Spell words correctly.* This is the most common flaw. Gremlins often creep into visuals, detracting from the message and the speaker's credibility. Pay attention to these little details, for their impact is way out of proportion to their actual importance. Use a computer spell-checker, have someone else review your visuals, and have a dry run with an astute audience.

◆ *Use a consistent style.* If you underline titles, underline all titles, so people don't start guessing about something that isn't there. If you establish a format, stick to it. Use consistent terminology, not:

Achieves goals

Lowers costs

Schedule is met

◆ *Present material that will advance your idea, not sabotage it.* Often presenters overlook words or pictures in their visuals that cause trouble as soon as the audience sees them. Special-interest groups or minorities can easily become offended when the wrong visual symbol is flashed before their eyes, such as a new design being proposed to the U.S. Navy and shown with an Army logo, a presentation to Saudi Arabia that features a map identifying the Persian, not the Arabian, Gulf, or visuals that show women only as secretaries.

◆ *Check for inconsistencies within a presentation.* Inconsistencies, such as logos in different locations, fonts changing for titles or bullets, or different styles for graphs often occur when graphics are pulled in from different presentations. Set a template that all graphics will adhere to.

◆ *Check for inconsistencies across segments.* Many presentations involve several speakers, each having prepared their own graphics, which are often different from those of their colleagues. It gives a poor team impression when obvious differences in style appear from one presenter to the next.

8. Verify That the Visuals "Talk" Well

It's important that as the presenter you must truly believe what you're going to say. A term we often use is that the presenters have to own their own charts. If you delegate chart preparation to someone else, and are not fully involved in development, it will be difficult for you to deliver the presentation with the right degree of conviction and knowledge. So if you're the speaker, be involved with the graphics preparation.

In many presentations the graphics may not have been prepared by the one who gets to discuss them. For example, people from several disciplines may have prepared charts for the program manager, who delivers the actual talk; or the designated manager for a competitive contract might not be available during the graphics preparation, and so a colleague prepares them. As often happens, the actual presenter may not be thrilled with the graphics that someone else has prepared.

A related situation occurred during a coaching session for a major bid. The program manager was a detail person, and very concerned with getting the perfect visual aid. He pored over the wording of each bullet and over the exact layout of each illustration. We kept nudging him to practice these with us to see how they flowed and talked. No, they weren't quite right yet. Finally, the day before the major review he agreed to a practice session. It was a mess. The charts that had looked reasonable good on the wall or on the computer monitor didn't talk well. The messages were obscured, and the manager got hung up on fine points, such as finding what was on the left would work better on the right, etc. This led to a lengthy rework session well past midnight, and still a mediocre walk-through the next day.

This experience also showed the value of working up the delivery script in linkage with the actual visuals, a useful concept the manager had also refused to apply. The delivery script has another value, even if worked up by someone else. For example, the very busy VP has had little time to be involved with the graphics, but tomorrow morning she has to jump on the plane for LA for the important meeting. With a well-honed script, she can now use her laptop during the five-hour flight to go over the presentation slide by slide. She can consider what wording she would prefer and change it as needed.

9. Be Ready with Back-up Visuals

This tip addresses two primary needs:

1. *When the projector fails what do you do?* When the viewgraphs you put into the luggage (mistake) got lost, what's your alternative approach? When Plan A fails, the astute presenter is ready with Plan B. This is a surprisingly frequent need.

2. *How do you handle questions that are not covered in your charts?* Here's where having Just-In-Case (JIC) or backup charts comes in. Anticipating potential questions, and where workable, preparing backup charts is an important part of being ready with your visuals.

10. Finally, Make the Visuals Sell You and Your Story

If you've applied the many concepts discussed in tips 1 to 9, you will have achieved this major value of good graphics—to enhance the presentation objectives for both presenter and receiver. These include:

◆ Quality that shows you care

◆ Headline titles

◆ Information that is interpreted and focused

◆ Designs that help the audience get it quicker and better

◆ Technology use that adds value, not distraction

◆ Speakers who clearly own their charts, not vice versa

Getting Better Visual Aids: The Mechanics

When you use the services of graphics professionals, heed their advice about how to lay out visuals properly. Get them on board early and have a schedule that allows time to consult with them. Avoid showing up on Friday with thirty rough visual ideas and expecting them back in finished form for a Monday morning presentation. If you're preparing graphics yourself, you need to know certain mechanics about getting workable visuals prepared.

Making Sure Hands-On Support Works

Props, gadgetry or demos can add much to a presentation, if they are used well. Used badly they can backfire with lasting detrimental effects. For example:

- ◆ A famous prop was used in a high-profile trial. In the O.J. Simpson trial, the prosecutor brought out the glove that had been found at the murder scene and asked the defendant to try it on for the jury? He tried but it wouldn't fit. Was that due to shrinkage or was it not his glove. No matter. That was the turning point of the trial, and the defense attorney's summation repeated the central theme "If it doesn't fit, you must acquit." And they did.

- ◆ During the 1988 Presidential race, an ad for candidate Michael Dukakis showed him wearing a helmet while riding in a tank. The photo backfired as it made Dukakis look like a misfit.

- ◆ At a large conference, the CEO of a software firm stirred the audience by showing a series of vignettes prepared with his software. Many were ready to buy, and credit cards were coming out of wallets. Continuing on, the CEO showed the details of his software, except it snagged a few minutes into it. He tried again, no good. Now cronies were checking connections, rebooting, etc. And then the CEO looked at the program diskette and said, with much chagrin, it was a faulty disk. He'd dashed to the airport and grabbed the wrong one. Back into the wallets went the credit cards.

Care needs to be given to using these forms of support. Interest fades fast when people can't see items, and having people handle gadgets can create distractions when the speaker has moved on to a different topic. If demonstrations are part of your presentation, advance try-outs are a must.

Choose Fonts Well

Figure 7-17 shows recommended font types, sizes, and layouts for good readability. These were developed long before computer graph-

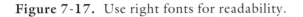
Figure 7-17. Use right fonts for readability.

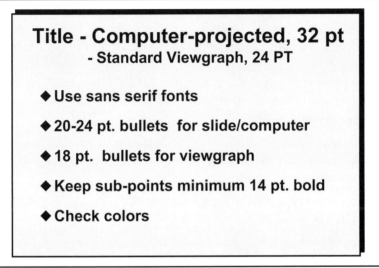

ics arrived. Many presentations display slides that violate these guidelines, and their audiences reach for the binoculars. Follow these suggestions:

◆ *Use easily readable fonts.* Use sans serif styles, such as Arial, Helvetica, or Comic Sans Serif rather than serif, such as Times Roman or Courier. Serif fonts are fine for written documents, not presentations. Look at most road signs—those are sans serif.

◆ *Select readable type sizes.* For reference, font size for a newspaper article is about 10 to12 points, and the front-page headlines are perhaps 50 to 60 points. Assuming an adequate screen size for the room, for typical computer-based projected presentations a safe title size is 28 to 32. Bullets might be 20 to 24 points, with a minimum of 14 point bold for boxes, legends, etc. These sizes work well for most videoconference applications (unless a small monitor is used). For viewgraphs in a small meeting room, these can be reduced, though stick with the 14-point bold minimum.

◆ *Choose lettering case with care.* Tests have shown that for presentations, lower or mixed case, with only the first letter capitalized, are better than all capitals for two main reasons: We're used to seeing this form in print, and changes in lettering elevation with mixed case are easier to pick up than all-capitals with all the same height.[15] Still, if you want a specific phrase or line to stand out strongly, all-capital lettering can focus attention (which is why many people prefer it for chart titles). For titles, the standard is to capitalize each main word. For bullets, I discourage this style: (a) it de-emphasizes words that should be capitalized, and (b) errors keep creeping in.

◆ *Make it strong enough for good legibility.* Use filled letters, not open ones. Avoid italics. Be careful about using shadows because they may hamper legibility.

◆ *Focus on key words.* Change font color, style, or size; underline or change the look.

◆ *Stick with one family for a matched group.* For example, always use bullets, call-outs, or boxes. Using another font can add punch, but more may be distracting. Within one family, use no more than three variations per chart.[16] Some people have to try out all the computer options, so the first bullet is Old English Script, the second Broadway Bound Italics, and so forth, which makes for mass confusion.

◆ *Space for readability.* A simple rule is to keep a two-line statement tight and separate it distinctly from other parallel statements. Then make the space between statements a minimum of one-and-a-half times the line height.[17] Increase this space as needed to fit the vertical page space well.

◆ *Keep all lettering horizontal.* Keep lettering horizontal even for y graph axes, unless your audiences have ostrich necks.

Select Colors Smartly

The best way to make sure your color choices won't backfire is to follow the wisdom of the experts. If you're using an in-house graphics department or outside service, ask for advice and listen to it. If you're using computer software, a generally sound approach is to stick with the choices the software designers used to create preset background lettering combination or templates. They've developed these following good color principles (you hope).

◆ *Watch out for the WYSIWYG trap.* This means "What You See (on the computer monitor) Is What You Get [in the finished product]." Except you often don't get what you see. Many people have made color choices because they looked fine on the monitor and then were dismayed to see on-screen slides that could barely be read.

For better understanding of color combinations, review the color wheel (Figure 7-18).

◆ *Warm-side colors are yellow, orange, red, and their cousins.* They have associations of fire, sun, intensity, and movement. These are also called advancing colors, because they seem to move toward the audience. They are good choices for focusing areas or items; poor choices for large sections or backgrounds.

◆ *Cool colors are violet, blue, and green.* Associations are meadows, oceans, peace, and harmony. Because these seem to recede from the audience, they make better background colors than focusing colors.

◆ *For best contrast or visibility, choose colors opposite from each other on the color wheel (called "complementary").*

Figure 7-18. The color wheel is the key to wise use of color.

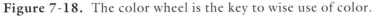
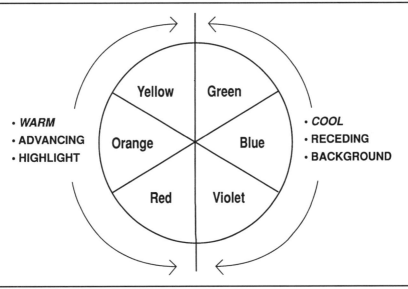

Thus, with a blue background, good visibility is likely with its opposites—orange or yellow.

◆ *For subtle effects, choose colors adjacent to each other ("harmonious").* For example, with a blue background, a green or violet logo would show subtly. Another choice is to use the same basic color in a lighter or darker shade (e.g., a dark blue background with a pale blue logo).

◆ *Avoid gray as a background.* No colors seem to contrast well with it.

◆ *Help color-blind people, roughly 10 percent of the population, get your visual message.* Do not place red and green (the most common problem colors) next to each other. Don't place red letters on green background, and don't put red pie slices next to green ones, unless you place a line between them. (Note that many prepared templates violate these guidelines.)

Some safe color combinations are shown in Figure 7-19. Remember that these are guidelines; test your color production system from computer to screen.

Be moderate and consistent in color use. People often pull presentations together from previous ones or from other sources. Often the various sources have different color combinations; using them as is would lead to confusion and a slapdash look. Some graphics programs can apply the same design to all visuals, which leads to a more uniform appearance.

Figure 7-19. Typical backgrounds and suitable emphasis colors. Choose color combinations carefully.

Background Color	Best Legibility	Lower Legibility
Dark (black, blue, green)	White, yellow, orange	Red, green, gray
Light (blue, green, brown)	Black, red, other dark (test)	
White, clear	Black, other dark	Yellow, pink, gray
Gray	Almost nothing	Blue, black, green, yellow
Red (for spot areas)	White, yellow (test)	Black, blue, violet
Brown, rust, wine (not red)	White, yellow, blue (test)	Black, red

Selecting the Right Data Display Form

For data presentation, select the visual format that best portrays your message. A major function of visual aids is to display statistical data—the figures. Of the many visual forms that exist to do this, the most frequently used are tables, line graphs, bar charts, and pie charts (Figure 7-20).

If you've followed a suggestion made earlier in this section, you've identified the specific point you want the visual to help get across,

Figure 7-20. Select graph type to best display data: Four common graph styles.

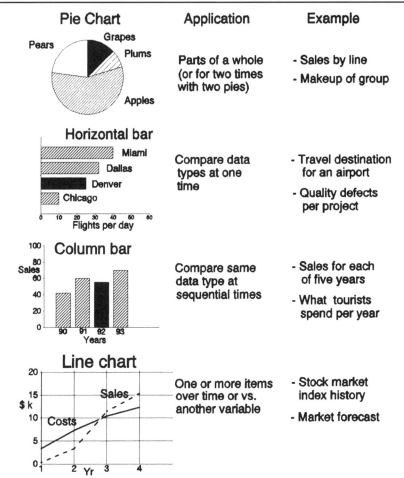

Pie Chart	Application	Example
Pears, Grapes, Plums, Apples	Parts of a whole (or for two times with two pies)	- Sales by line - Makeup of group
Horizontal bar Miami, Dallas, Denver, Chicago Flights per day	Compare data types at one time	- Travel destination for an airport - Quality defects per project
Column bar Sales / Years (90 91 92 93)	Compare same data type at sequential times	- Sales for each of five years - What tourists spend per year
Line chart $ k / Yr Sales, Costs	One or more items over time or vs. another variable	- Stock market index history - Market forecast

rather than generated a bunch of data that probably ought to be shown. Knowing the purpose of the visual is a good starting point for choosing the best display method. For example:

Message	*Display choice*
"We're losing market share."	Three side-by-side pie charts for three years.
"The recession has barely affected sales, but it has hurt profits."	Column chart with two segments—sales and profits—for the past five years, (or) a line graph showing these changes over time.
"The best alloy for required conditions is number 310."	Line graph showing the strength of three candidate alloys over the temperature range.

Design the graph so that the message will stand out. For the three examples above, highlight the most pertinent pie segment, column, or line by using shading, boldface, or color to focus the audience's attention. If you are using tables, use block, arrow, larger type, or color to focus attention on the vital entries.

In general, if your purpose requires that specific numbers be seen by a knowledgeable audience, the best method is probably a table. If you wish to show general trends, relationships, or changes, especially to a general audience, one of the more pictorial forms is probably better. Recall this headline from a Tektronix Company ad: "The difference between a page of numbers and a graph is ten minutes of explanation."

Don't just present data. You're the expert; display information so that nonexperts can better grasp the significant aspects. Headline titles are a big help. Showing information in different perspectives can add to comprehension and help get your point across (Figure 7-21).

What works well for one audience may work poorly for another. A detailed financial table appropriate for internal top management reviews may baffle newly hired employees at an orientation program. A graph, bar chart, or pie chart may be a better choice.

Figure 7-21. Showing data in several ways may give a truer picture and help make your case better (another example of progressive disclosure).

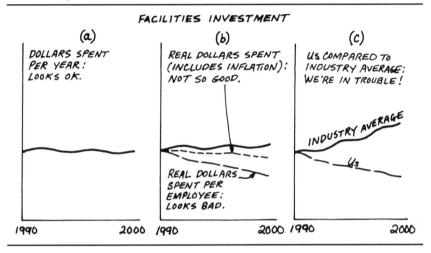

Here are suggestions for wise use of standard graph forms. For good examples read *U.S.A. Today.*

Graphs

◆ Position the graph on the page so that there is enough room to print the ordinate label (vertical axis) horizontally. Print words in full. Make sure that symbols will be understood.

◆ Use broadly spaced grids rather than finely spaced ones to improve chart visibility and reduce nitpicking. A few grid lines help viewers grasp numbers better than no grid lines. (The more general the audience, the fewer the grid lines.)

◆ Space grid markers at regular, fairly large, and easily handled magnitudes—for example, not 5, 10, 15 . . . or 35, 70, 105 . . . but 0, 25, 50, 100.

◆ Start the vertical axis at zero. If using a section (such as 700–800) to show detail, insert a break or separate chart with zero value.

◆ With a series of graphs of the same type of data (like sales histories for products X, Y, and Z), keep the same scales for the axes.

◆ Built-up graphs, where each line adds to the line below it, are often hard to figure out. Make it clear that it is a built-up graph and that the lines are not independent. If changes in each segment are to be understood to any degree, using separate charts for each segment or bar charts may be better.

◆ Use of more than three lines on a graph gets confusing. If more lines art needed, use progressive disclosure or color coding to help keep lines straight.

◆ Tie identifiers directly to the lines instead of showing them as a separate legend. If color coding is used and black-and-white copies are to be made, distinguish the lines by other means, such as dashed and solid lines.

Bar Charts

◆ Be careful when using three-dimensional effects, because they can make values, such as vertical bar quantities, hard to read. When making comparisons, change one dimension only (e.g., bar heights) rather than two (e.g., bar areas).

◆ Try using symbols instead of bars to establish a stronger relationship between numbers and the information. Be creative: For example, use stacked trucks, trains, planes, and ships to show different shipping quantities, or use figures of a man, woman, and child to report incidence of diabetes. But don't let symbols or graphics interfere with clarity.

◆ Use shading, spacing, colors, and arrows to increase clarity and punch. Distinguish key information by the richest shading, an arrow, or notation of activating events.

◆ Reduce the clutter by thinning out axes markers, making all labels horizontal, and designing layouts to cut redundant information. Place labels close to the bars rather than using a reference legend.

◆ Subsets of data within bars can be effective, but categories (other than the first one from zero) may be hard to compare. One category (e.g., profits as subset of sales) can be easily grasped, but dividing sales into four product categories can be difficult.

Pie Charts

◆ Start a pie at twelve o'clock, and place the most important element clockwise from there. Make it obvious by using strong shading or color or spill out a key segment to focus extra attention.

◆ Too many pieces ruin the pie. Stick with no more than six segments, and put any other little segments into an "all other" category.

◆ Make all labels horizontal for easy readability. Color code to match pie segments..

◆ Pie charts work well with other graphical forms or for coding. The pie can be placed in a corner, with the key element high-lighted, and then presented more fully in a table, bar chart, or word chart.

In Summary: Make Them Aids, Not Ailments

Visual aids are integral with presentations. Good visuals can add greatly to presentation success, and computer technology has brought high-quality graphics capability out of the realm of graphics designers only and onto office desktops.

As Shakespeare wrote 400 years ago, "To see sad sights moves more than hear them told." That's the basic premise of why we use visual aids. The caveat is that we will see those favorable results when we make sure our visual "sad [or happy] sights" are well prepared and used.

PART III

Stage

CHAPTER 8

Arrangements
The Devil's in the Details

President Bill Clinton arrived at the joint session of Congress ready to deliver a speech about a major issue—health care. It would be nationally televised as well. The president looked at the TelePrompter in front of him. There was an immediate problem: The speech he was seeing was not the health-care one but his earlier State-of-the-Union address. He signaled the Vice President about the problem and continued on, reading from his paper manuscript on the lectern. Several minutes later, the right speech appeared on the TelePrompter.

Another Bill—Gates—was also before a large audience for the momentous occasion of introducing "Windows 98." After the usual introductory meeting flourishes it was time to show the product . . . except it wouldn't show due to a technology snafu.

Speakers today have many technologies they can use for high quality presentations. They can walk into a conference room, set up their laptop computer and projector and be up and running in five minutes. If everything works. Winning presenters are on top of the operational aspects; they know that wise planning and attention to detail are vital to success. They also know that not paying attention to those operational details has caused countless presenters to be embarrassed and clobbered.

Proper attention to arrangements results in trouble-free operations, thus making a valuable contribution to presentations success and meeting productivity. Missed planes, lost visual aids, burned-out projector bulbs, and upside-down slides can sabotage a presentation beyond repair (Figure 8-1).

These irritants or disasters may be amusing to audience members, especially when it happens to the competition. But they are embarrassing to the presenter, who is now trying to recover from sloppy preparation (and occasionally fate). And they quickly become costly as the meeting is delayed while problems get fixed (maybe) or principal listeners get fed up and move on to something else When presentations go smoothly, audience members scarcely notice anything about the mechanics; when something goes wrong, that may become the most dominant and lasting impression: "I don't recall anything he said, but I'll never forget what he did."

Arrangements Fundamentals

Here are six axioms about arrangements that have been developed over years of hard lessons, learned from my own and others' painful experiences. They will serve you well if you apply them rigorously.

1. *Remember that the medium may be the message.* Marshall McLuhan's famous observation—slightly adapted—definitely applies to presentations. A smoothly run presentation not only helps get the message across—it also enhances the confidence listeners have in the speaker and the material. Conversely, speakers who have serious operational problems are doing serious damage to their cause. Observers may assume that such carelessness applies to the work being presented as well.

    "If a presenter fumbles with the audio-visual equipment, it's unprofessional and a waste of time," says Captain James Woolway, commanding officer of the U.S. Naval Air Depot North Island. "It's an embarrassment and reflects poorly on the speaker, a poor way to start."[1]

Figure 8-1. Staging goof-ups have caused grief for many a presenter.

WILL THEY BE COMFORTABLE ABOUT CHOOSING YOUR TEAM?

2. *Be prepared.* Give thorough attention to every detail necessary for putting on the presentation smoothly: the who, what, when, where, and why questions. Assurance comes from knowing all the incidentals have been taken care of and all the necessary equipment is in place and working. Few things can more quickly sap the confidence of an already apprehensive speaker than discovering at presentation time that some key incidental has been overlooked.

3. *Anticipate disasters and be ready when they hit.* The classic example is the projector bulb that burns out—generally at the most critical part of your talk. If you follow this axiom, you will assume the bulb is going to burn out and will have a spare with you. And you will know how to put it in.

4. *Test everything.* Despite extreme exhortations to inexperienced presenters, it usually takes one or two trials under fire before the critical importance of this axiom truly registers in the MANDA-TORY section of the brain. Show time is not the time for on-the-job training.

5. *Make arrangement your own responsibility.* The presenter, not the support people, will be embarrassed and set back when a

promised projector isn't there, or when your laptop won't work with the host's projector. Unless it comes from a trusted and experienced helper—a most valuable resource—be wary whenever you hear, "It'll work, trust me," or "Joe said it's all set."

6. *Never underestimate the power of Murphy's Law, which says that whatever can go wrong, will.* Various corollaries and axioms have been put forth over the years, many of which, I suspect, were derived during business presentations. My set, all reality-based, is shown in Figure 8-2.

Figure 8-2. Murphy's devious law applies to presentations, too.

♦ When you must have a dozen copies of your 30-slide presentation, the ink runs out in the copier, and that's the only cartridge.

♦ Graphics packed with luggage headed for Cleveland will end up in Detroit.

♦ Your plane will just be taking off as you realize you left your laptop back at airport security.

♦ On a major two-speaker road show, your colleague will get hit with the flu thirty minutes before show time.

♦ When you make a final run to the restroom, a prominent zipper will catch, in either the closed (before) or open (after) position.

♦ While racing to a meeting across town, you suddenly remember you left the directions in the office, right beside the client's phone number and the cell phone.

♦ A person can partake of coffee hundreds of times without incident until he is the next presenter—and then he spills coffee all over himself.

♦ The one time you neglected to check the projector bulb is the time just after the last person who used the projector burned out the bulb—and didn't replace it.

♦ When a bulb burns out half-way through the presentations, the person with the key to the bulb storage closet is in another building.

♦ The pointer that is always there, won't be.

♦ When the graphics expert advises, "You don't need to check it—it will work fine," it won't.

♦ If a presenter must have a specific type of equipment, such as a TV player for his VHS cassette, the other type will be delivered, such as a digital player.

♦ An upside-down slide or viewgraph will not be projected correctly until all other erroneous positions are tried.

♦ Whenever a speaker says, "As you can all see . . . ," half the audience can't.

♦ If you bring the resident expert on a specific subject to the meeting, that subject will never come up.

Facilities and Equipment Planning

Presenters seem to be lightly consulted when planners design presentation rooms or buy audiovisual equipment. Presenters themselves seldom have raised their voices in advance about their needs, because they don't know such planning or buying is going on, and they have other priorities—until the time comes when they have to present. Then the cries of despair bellow forth: "What idiot designed this room!!?"

To those with responsibility for planning and acquiring facilities and equipment that presenters will have to use, here's a suggestion: Get input from the users of that facility and equipment and pay attention to it. That might help prevent some of the problems that presenters are continually faced with, such as:

◆ Lecterns that won't hold notes or can't be moved

◆ Ceiling lights that shine directly onto the screen

◆ Overhead projector tables with no room for transparencies

◆ Projectors with no obvious on/off switches

◆ Equipment cords that are always about five feet too short

◆ Nonchangeable temperature controls leading to either melting or frozen audiences

◆ Sound systems that blast here and squeal there

◆ Restrooms totally inadequate for the size of the groups that will meet there

◆ Add your own

Key items for consideration of arrangements are shown in Figure 8-3.

Facilities

The following discussion is directed not just at presenters themselves but also at those who are involved with the planning for and acquisition of facilities and equipment that presenters will have to use.

Figure 8-3. Key how-to's of arrangements.

◆ Make your concerns and needs known to planners and buyers of facilities and equipment.

◆ Assume responsibility for specifying facility, equipment, personnel, material, transportation, and other requirements.

◆ Make a detailed checklist well in advance. Have checkpoints to ensure that arrangements are being met as planned.

◆ Give deliberate consideration to how the presentation will be affected by timing, location, and attendees.

◆ Know the facility and equipment and have access to needed controls.

◆ Make sure all equipment is in place and tested well enough in advance that fixes can be made.

◆ Public address systems are notoriously poor quality and cantankerous. Check in advance or bring your own.

◆ When traveling, allow enough time to get there and inside. Do not entrust your visuals to the baggage department.

The Meeting Room

The location for meetings varies widely, with the most common being the organization's conference room. Safety meetings might be held out in the workplace, all-hands meetings in the dining room or auditorium.

External meetings run the gamut from hotel conference rooms, convention centers, to cruise ships. Jesus delivered his Sermon on the Mount from the mount. Shakespeare had Mark Antony deliver his famous opening line "Friends, Romans, Countrymen . . ." from the Roman Forum, and Henry V rallied his troops right on the battlefield with his "Once more into the breach!" appeal.

The room itself can add to or detract from meeting productivity. As an example, a change in setting for a weekly production meeting had dramatic effects. The meeting had always been held in the factory area in a poorly maintained and crowded room. Speakers and other audience members were continually interrupted, foul language was prevalent, and shouting was the normal level of discourse. When the meeting was shifted to a first-class conference room, with carpeting, a controlled environment, and comfortable seating, one regular attendee said: "I couldn't believe the change. People stopped interrupting each other, cleaned up their language (a little bit), and started giving the presenters a chance. Things got done a whole lot faster."

Some meeting room tips:

◆ An off-site location may be more desirable than an on-site one, with increased attentiveness, self-image, and productivity often offsetting the cost of the facility.

◆ Check soundproofing carefully. Find out who will be using adjacent facilities and what effects this will have on your meeting.

◆ Room walls should be plain—no photos, charts, or drawings. And especially remove distractions in the section where the presenter operates. These are powerful attention getters, and they compete with the presenter.

◆ Have a clock to help presenters keep to schedules, and put it at the back of the room, not the front.

◆ Entrance and exit should be at the opposite end from the speaker. That way, latecomers and early departers create less of a disturbance than when the door is near the speaker. Also, message bearers or refreshment servers can do their tasks more discreetly.

◆ The fewer barriers between speaker and audience, the better. Elevation, distance, podiums, microphones, and other obstacles between speaker and audience serve to impede communication.

Room Lighting and Darkening

With the excellent quality of today's low-cost projectors, presenters can generally keep room light up (unlike with early models, which were so dim that the room had to be kept nearly totally dark for people to be able to read the slides on the screen). To check lighting needs, visit the facility well in advance to locate light switches and window blind adjustments.

If room lighting has to be dimmed, the light should be kept on the presenter. Most rooms have rheostat controls to adjust lighting or switches to control sections of ceiling lights. Unfortunately, the on-off sections are often unrelated to the darkening need and don't kill the lights in the right place. Also many rooms are set up with a light that shines directly onto the screen. If the screen is portable, the problem can be overcome by moving it. In some situations the best solution is to remove the bulbs near the screen.

Lecterns

Since most people aren't clear about the difference between a lectern and a podium, here's some help. What doctor type do you go see when you have a foot-related problem? Most likely a pod-iatrist, thus the pod-ium is what you stand on; the lectern is what you put your notes on (and if typical, lean on or grip mightily).

For presentations, a lectern, placed so not to interfere with audience ability to see the screen, may be helpful as a place to keep notes, copies of visual aids, a laptop, and other materials in the storage areas. A moveable lectern provides more flexibility for use than a fixed one (usually set up for hard-wiring of controls for audiovisual systems.

Lectern designers seem not to have asked speakers what they'll use the lectern for. The 1/4-inch back edges of lecterns are sure bets to have materials sliding to the floor at inappropriate times. Lights shine directly into the speaker's face, preventing him or her from seeing materials and creating a Dracula-like glow.

Power Capabilities

If you want that equipment to work, it generally needs electrical power. Are the outlets in the room adequate and located where you need them? Do you need power extensions? Who provides them? How will you keep people from tripping over the wires and killing the power at a crucial moment? (Tip: Wide duct tape is most helpful for disaster prevention.)

Environmental Control

Nothing kills meeting productivity faster than an overly warm room, after lunch, with a slide presentation in the dark. Keep the room too cool rather than too hot. If you as the presenter do not have the capability to control the room temperature—which is often the case—at least try to specify the desired temperature, with 72°F a generally acceptable target.

In most U.S. facilities, smoking is banned in conference rooms. That may not be true in non-U.S. facilities. The meeting coordinator should communicate the rules in advance, and all should respect them.

Seating and Tables

Adequate and comfortable seating for all attendees is essential. Each member of the audience should be able to see the key elements of the presentation—speaker, screen, displays—without strain. Higher participation can be facilitated by arranging tables so that audience members can see one another as well as the speaker (see Figure 8-4). In contrast, theater seating, common in most classrooms and auditoriums, defeats audience interaction. For small groups (ten to fifteen people), a large conference table with attendees seated on three sides works well. By opening up the center and making a U-shaped table arrangement, the speaker can operate with the group better. For larger audiences, groupings of five to six people at tables are still preferable to theater seating.

Projection Screens

A large audience was assembled to hear a high-level military briefing by an admiral and several senior officers. Each gave a twenty-minute

Figure 8-4. Common conference room presentation setup.

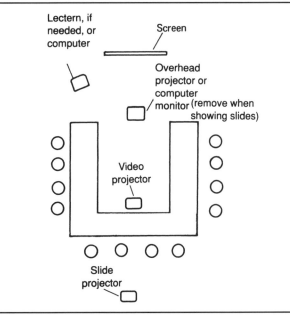

presentation, profusely illustrated with excellent full-color slides. There was one problem: At least half the audience was unable to see the slides from where they were seated because the screen was too small for the room. Scratch another well-intended and expensive presentation. Here are some guidelines:

- *Size.* Make sure the screen is large enough. The standard guideline is to use a screen width at least one-sixth the distance from the screen to the last viewer.[2]

- *Visibility.* Place the screen so all viewers can see it. Consider both side angle and elevation. Depending on the screen type, anyone seated more than 20 degrees to 30 degrees to either side of the screen center won't be able to see the image. (For a beaded screen, the angle is about 20 degrees; for matte or lenticular screens, the angle is up to 30 degrees and perhaps more.[3]

- *Projection.* The screen image should be projected high enough that viewers won't be trying to look through the heads of those in front of them. The screen bottom should be at least four feet above the floor if everybody is seated at the same level. For some conference or hotel rooms, however, the room height may preclude the four-foot minimum, resulting in people jumping up and down to read content on lower part of screen.

- *Interference.* Columns, hanging fixtures, other lights, and inadequate darkening capability can all cause interference.

- *Brightness.* Type and age of screen, projector powers, lens type, room darkness, and extraneous lights all affect brightness. The type of visual material is also a factor. Full-color slides require brighter projection or a darker room than black-and-white slides or viewgraphs. Highly reflective screens, such as beaded or lenticular, can be used in a dim light; a matte screen will require a darker room or brighter projection. In general, keep the room dim rather than completely dark. Make sure lights from the lectern, exit signs, or outside source don't interfere with the image. Check that window coverings block the sun or nighttime outside lights.

- *Quality.* Yellowed, damaged, or patched screens may reduce image sharpness or add distracting marks (most commonly caused by presenters who used a marking pen as a screen pointer or scraped the pointer across the screen, another audience irritant).

◆ *Distortion.* Angled projection makes a distorted image. With overhead projectors, this "keystoning" is often severe. Slanting the screen forward from the top will help keep the top and bottom image widths constant.

Sound Systems

Standing at the side of the conference room, the upcoming presenter listened as the current presenter spoke into the microphone to the large audience. Knowing he had several minutes before he was due up, he stepped out into the hallway and into the men's room for some final personal arrangements. He proceeded to comb his hair, straighten his tie, and, being a bit nervous, go to the bathroom. Unfortunately, he was wearing a wireless microphone, switched to "on." The current speaker's words on the public address system were joined by the unmistakable sounds of a gentleman relieving himself. The audience roared with delight, and as the new speaker took the podium cheered mightily. In the movie *Naked Gun*, the same thing occurred to the cool but hapless police detective, Frank Drebin.

In fiction or reality, sound systems can be tricky. In large meetings, if anything is likely to go wrong, it is the sound system.

Presenters in small meetings generally don't use a sound system. They will do so, however, when presenting at a large conference, speaking to a civic group or at a management club dinner, conducting a walk-around tour through the factory, serving as a panelist or emcee, and testifying in court or to a Congressional committee. In those cases, it pays to be able to use sound systems properly.

For starters, work with the professional sound specialist, who is usually on the scene. If none is there, you're on your own. Even with the pros, sound problems are widespread. For example, at a national conference, neither the emcee nor the keynote speaker could be heard by half the audience.

Here are some useful tips.

◆ If you're speaking away from your office, you will be taking your chances about the adequacy of the sound system. Either you or a trusted aide should visit the facility in advance and check out the system or take along your own equipment. Try out the system with a helper located where the audience will sit (all locations). Remember that the noise level will go up with a real audience as compared to an empty room.

◆ Have each presenter become comfortable with the microphone. A rule of thumb is to hold the mike at a 45-degree angle six to ten inches from the mouth or vertically near the chin. Holding it too close can create a popping effect.

◆ Know where the system controls are, how they work, and that they will be operating or accessible when needed. Note the desired settings, so the system can be instantly activated without experimenting before a live audience.

◆ Fixed or hand-held mikes often create problems. Practice with presenters so they can tell when the mike is not adequately picking up their voices. Clip-on, lavaliere, or wireless mikes may work better; they allow the presenters to move their heads or bodies freely. Practice till you can put the mike on smoothly. A mike windscreen can help reduce wind noise if outside or popping from presenters who talk too closely into the mike.

◆ What about the painful squeal caused by sound system feedback? Often the cause is having the mike located in front of the audio speakers.

◆ Small, portable systems are good for multistop talks, such as plant tours. Make sure the quality is good and the batteries are fresh. Take along a spare set, just in case.

Audiovisual Equipment

Today's presenters have a vast array of tools at their disposal. Here we'll examine the options, proceeding from high to low tech.

Computer-Based Presentations

Computers, tied to projectors and displayed on screen, are today's standard format for business presentations. Computers include those that are part of the in-room setup, portable laptops, or those tied into the organization's network. Projectors come in a variety of types, from small table-top LCD devices to large floor or ceiling three-gun systems. Today's small, light-weight projectors provide easy-to-read screen images with little need to darken rooms. Older ones will require dark rooms. Here are some specific cautions, roughly in order of importance and sequence:

1. Verify compatibility between projector and computer. When making offsite presentations, this can be a problem. Check as soon as you arrive at the facility.

2. Make sure connectors are long enough for good placement of the laptop. The standard connector is often too short; for insurance spend ten dollars and buy your own extension cord.

3. Make sure you have enough power for the likely meeting duration. This is easy to overlook when you do your setup on battery power, and then forget to plug into an outlet. It's no fun about ten minutes into the presentation to hear the low battery warning, then realize the nearest 110V outlet is fifteen feet away (and your power cord is ten feet long). More insurance: Carry your own extension cord.

4. Place gear for ease of use without blocking or distracting the audience. With laptops this problem has mostly faded as the speaker can easily operate the computers from a lectern or a convenient table. Try not to sit behind the computer (often done with early systems) as this greatly impedes audience contact. Placing the laptop right next to the projector on the conference table may have the speaker constantly going back and forth from screen to computer. Better to place it off to the side, on a separate table or lectern, or have a colleague operate it. Practice timing in advance. Better than the irritating "next slide" are clear verbal and non-verbal cues from the presenter.

5. Test in advance the entire system—computer plus projector—to verify readability and wise color selections. People are often surprised at the colors that appear on the screen, as they can be different from what the computer screen shows.

6. Use a wireless controller or mouse to maneuver slides, for more freedom of movement and so as not be tied to the computer loca-

tion. Make sure that what you buy has all the options you would like to use (transition effects, darken screen, reverse image, laser pointer, etc.). A wireless keyboard can be helpful for interactive meetings.

Video

Video can be operated from camcorders, playback devices (VCRs), and often can be inserted directly into the computer graphics presentation. It can add a vivid element to the presentation, but it offers some traps for the unwary.

◆ For a serious video recording, bring in the experts. Preparing a video summary of a major proposal, for example, is too important for amateurs. Experts can ensure proper lighting, backgrounds, and clothing; eliminate distractions; and make good use of TelePrompters.

◆ Specify video equipment needs in detail. Check for compatibility so you won't be surprised later, when you find out the recorder and separate playback won't work together. Are all the connecting and power cables there? Is the zoom adequate for where the key players will stand or sit? Special lighting may be required to get the desired quality. Is tripod there and adequate for camera?

◆ Check audio system. Will the camcorder's built-in mic be acceptable. Or do you need separate mic, perhaps clip-on?

◆ Who is going to operate the equipment? That needs to be arranged, and the operator needs to be instructed and clued.

◆ Above all, do a test run with the equipment in the actual conditions you'll be using, and test the entire system.

◆ Make sure your playback monitors are adequate. The most common problem is having a monitor that is too small, yet many people persist in using one 19-inch video monitor for a large meeting of thirty to forty people. Even several monitors may not be enough. I watched a presentation die in a large auditorium with 500 people: the dozen video monitors placed around the room were not enough. Here are some guidelines from General Telephone Company of California, a major corporate video producer.[4]

Monitor Size	Number of People
19 inches	5 to 6
25 inches	12 to 18 (up to 30 if dark, quiet room)
4 to 6 feet	50 to 75 (check for side visibility)

Playback can also be done via LCD projectors, the same ones used for computer-based presentations. Projecting on a large screen eliminates most of the visibility problems with monitors.

Video/Internet Conferencing

Video/Internet conferencing links two or more locations by Internet, video, and audio, allowing live interactive presentations among people who may be thousands of miles apart. This can greatly reduce travel time, expense, and aggravation. They are common for a variety of applications, such as meetings, presentation reviews or development, major conferences (product introductions, expert speeches, all-hands meetings), and on-line Web seminars.

If you are called upon to participate in a videoconference, don't assume it is business as usual. Lack of awareness and preparation have humbled many seasoned presenters. The first rule is to seek out the experts and follow their advice.

Video/Internet-conferencing setups vary widely. In a typical corporate facility participants are likely to be seated facing a camera and facing a monitor that shows the people on the other end. A separate camera may be focused on visual aids or other materials. For an Internet conference both ends may not have video but will share the same information (e.g., a PowerPoint presentation) on their computer monitors or projection screens.

Be aware of these key elements:

◆ Time is money. Agreed-upon objectives, an agenda with timed targets for each segment, and speaker preparation are more important in video/Internet conferences than in regular presentations. All participants need to cooperate by sticking with the agenda so that all topics get suitable attention and people interested in upcoming topics don't get fidgety or short-changed.

◆ Visual aids, props, or hardware are especially valuable but need to be checked for suitability and possibly adapted to meet video's stringent requirements. Visuals passable in conference rooms may be inadequate for video/Internet conferences. If you follow the earlier guidelines for minimum visual aid type sizes and colors, your graphics will generally be O.K. for this application. Anything less than a 14-point, sans serif font will likely be unreadable.

◆ Timing is definitely trickier than for standard presentations. Since visuals may not be under your control, you will have to give strong clues to the operator so that your words match the visual on the screen.

Electronic Boards

Electronic boards see a lot of use for discussion or problem-solving sessions with words or illustrations drawn on the board, then instantly printed out or tied to a computer for later use. You can also call in prepared graphics from a computer hookup, facilitating the discussion.

35mm Slide Projectors

Only a decade ago, these were the standard for high-importance presentations. They are still used in some industries, such as by architects who display many pictures of projects, but they've been mostly supplanted by computer-based media.

◆ *When requesting equipment, be explicit about your needs.* You don't want to show up with a Kodak Carousel tray full of slides and be greeted with a noncompatible projector (rarely a problem in the United States, but often one elsewhere). The automatic focus option is handy.

◆ *Ensure that you have the right lens.* Many people overlook this consideration and end up with mediocre results. The typical culprit is a fixed lens that is not suited to the room conditions and leads to tiny screen images or having to move the projector way to the rear of the room. For flexibility, use a zoom lens, which adjusts the image to fit the screen without moving the projector.

◆ *Determine whether the bulb is strong enough.* If you can't see much on the screen, maybe the bulb is too weak for the room conditions or the images you're trying to project. First try to make the room darker, especially around the screen. Then consider a higher-powered lens, such as a xenon.

◆ *Make sure the tray or slide holder is compatible with the projector and slides.* If you are using a Kodak Carousel type, use only the 80-capacity tray (the 140 size is more prone to jamming).

◆ *Put the slides in properly.* Who hasn't seen an upside-down slide, or several of them? This is so common that it's almost expected— and it's always embarrassing to the presenter. For front-screen projection, hold the slide so you can read it. Turn it top to bottom, and place it in the tray. Once you know a position is correct, mark or number it in order in the upper right corner (as in the tray). For rear-screen projection, follow the same procedure but reverse front to back. One presenter only found this out, to his dismay, after all the slides had appeared backward.

◆ *Lock the slides into the tray.* Failing to do this is extending an invitation to disaster. Right before a meeting, I watched a team on hands and knees picking up and sorting fifty slides spilled onto the floor.

◆ *Know how to control the projector, and from where.* Most projectors come with a control device and a wire that is never long enough. Two solutions are to use a wire extension cord for the controller or a wireless remote (an excellent investment). With either one, get focusing control plus forward/reverse. Another handy option is a projector on-off control.

◆ *Get a workable projector table.* The projector has to sit on something, and mostly it's a last-minute jury-rig (projector box, TV set in the back of the room, or stray carton). It may work from the conference table or from a high table at the rear of the room. For more flexibility, carry along a 1-inch-high portable shim for more upward tilt.

◆ *Make sure the images appear properly on the screen.* Often a slide image is crooked or tiny or overlaps onto the wall behind. Check it out. If you're using mix of horizontal and vertical slides (not advised), be sure to check both.

◆ *Know in advance whether you'll need a power extension cord.* Carry one with you anyway.

Overhead Projectors

Even with the widespread use of computer-based systems, the low-tech overhead projector is still widely used. (Even for $100 million proposal presentations, the specified medium is still often transparencies.) Nearly every conference room has one, and presenters can easily tote small portable ones with them. Here are some tips:

◆ *Check your equipment in advance.* I've seen dozens of presentations get off to poor starts because the projector wasn't there, it was the wrong projector, or the speaker didn't know how to operate it or even turn it on. That's a terrible first impression and a disservice to the audience, which may now have to wait several minutes while the presenter does what should have been done in advance. Don't forget to check that the power cord is long enough to reach the outlet.

◆ *Make sure the images are large enough.* In advance, position the projector (and the screen, if you have that option) so the image fills the screen. Many projectors stationed in conference rooms don't match the rooms; finding that out at show time can be painful. Get one with a wide-angle lens (e.g., 11-inch or $12^1/_2$-inch focal length creates an image 15 to 20 percent wider than the 14-inch standard). Some projectors offer a dual capability for either standard or wide angle by flipping a switch.

◆ *Test it with the visual materials you intend to use.* Place the actual transparencies and framer (such as Instaframe, a wise forty dollar investment) on the projector and check the image quality. If the image is fuzzy, the projector optics may require that transparencies lie flat on the glass surface, precluding use of a framer.

◆ *Choose a projector with a built-in spare bulb.* This is a high confidence builder, if you've remembered to check both main and backup bulbs and know how to change them. If the projector doesn't have a built-in bulb, keep the correct spare handy and know how to insert it.

◆ *Place the projector on a waist-high table.* Don't use a chest-high table because it will block audience ability to see the screen.

◆ *Make sure the table has space for your viewgraphs.* Allow for two stacks—for upcoming and past—with both on the same side. This is so obvious yet frequently overlooked.

◆ *Decide on your pointing method.* Avoid pointing at the projector—you're bound to block some viewers. It can be effective to place a pointer on the transparency, then move back so all can see.

◆ *Arrange for a chart flipper if beneficial to get visuals on and off.* This is especially helpful with lengthy or particularly important presentations. The operator sits unobtrusively next to the projector, and the speaker stands on the opposite side of the projector, not behind the operator.

◆ *Take extra care with multiple projectors.* It's not unusual for presentations to use two or three projectors. Used well, they can help. Used poorly, they provide twice as much opportunity to confuse the audience. Will you use one or two screens? Are the projectors compatible? Are the images still readable? Don't let images overlap. With two overheads, decide where you'll place transparencies, and who will operate them? Where will the speaker be positioned—seated or standing? How will pointing to screen items be done?

Flip charts, displays, and posters

If using an easel, make sure you have the right type. Do your charts hang from or rest on the easel? Displays of illustrations, photos, and diagrams—common for many public hearings, short list interviews, and team meetings—play an important role, with the primary key being visibility. For example, in a public meeting for an environmental report, the presentation included many large diagrams hung from the wall. Disaster hit in the first minute when all the wall hangings collapsed to the floor. Even had they stayed up, few in the public audience would have been able to see them.

Props, displays, and models

These three-dimensional, hands-on objects can add much to a presentation, or they can subtract if not used properly. The first key is planning, knowing what objects you will use, when you will display them, and how you will use them. For tips watch the real experts at the county fair, as they hawk the latest gadget, typically applying good principles suitable for business presentations:

- ◆ Have the object in position, and generally out of audience view.
- ◆ Show it only when you are ready to talk about it.
- ◆ Hold it up so viewers can see it.
- ◆ Put it away when moving on to the next phase. Do not pass it around yet as this creates a series of distractions.

Backups

This is a final alert that applies to any of the media mentioned. When engaged in Plan A, problems may occur, and the presenters who are prepared with Plan B, a backup, can save the day. This happens often and many have found that extra attention absolutely worthwhile. Here's just one example. The team heading in for a major competitive presentation had to bring their own equipment and set it up rapidly at the customer's facility. It was in a field office, so resources were limited. They rehearsed two times with the setup—a laptop and projector—to make sure they could set it up quickly. At the 8 A.M. meeting with the customer, they went through the same setup operation, and it would not work. Immediately they shifted to their backup—paper copies of the presentation—and communicated from those. They won, which would not have happened without their low-tech backup.

Incidentals

This category covers the whole raft of things that must often be taken care of to make the presentation go well, Because overlooked factors can have repercussions far greater than one would think possible, attention to detail is the byword. Even in the era of e-mail and instant communications, overlooked incidentals can still sneak in and upset the plan. I arrived at a firm and checked in to conduct a seminar. Several others weren't so lucky, as they were unable to get in because their clearances had not been taken care of. They were not pleased, and they were the *customer*. Not a good way to begin your important program review. Some of the areas to consider are:

- ◆ Shipping of equipment and written materials
- ◆ Travel for speaker team and other participants, including mode, travel time at destination, directions, parking, and entry
- ◆ Human needs, such as refreshments and meals
- ◆ Arrival needs, security clearances, greetings, and movement
- ◆ Rank and ritual needs, such as protocol and special appearances
- ◆ Operational details, such as who does what and when, name tags, ID badges, and message processing

Reducing the Unknowns: An Arrangements Checklist

The best way to ward off the insidious sneak attacks of Murphy's Law is by using a rigorous checklist of all arrangements requirements, as shown in Figure 8-5. If only a few areas are regularly of concern, use a simpler list. Remember—Murphy awaits you.

Figure 8-5. An arrangements checklist is key to heading off trouble.

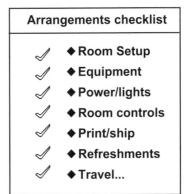

ATTENTION TO DETAIL PAYS

Arrangements checklist

- ✓ ◆ Room Setup
- ✓ ◆ Equipment
- ✓ ◆ Power/lights
- ✓ ◆ Room controls
- ✓ ◆ Print/ship
- ✓ ◆ Refreshments
- ✓ ◆ Travel...

In Summary

Ensuring that operations go smoothly is critical to presentations success. Attention to detail is key to success in arrangement planning; slipshod attention is disaster waiting to happen. However, in spite of careful attention, snafus will occur. When Murphy makes an appearance to create mischief, the smart presenters are able to shift into Plan B and continue on toward success.

I was part of the preparation team for a major conference with 500 franchisees. The theme was based on the movie *Back to the Future*. The meeting opened with a dazzling six-projector slide show, with images flashing and the movie theme pounding away. The company president was to appear from the curtains on the side of the stage in a chauffeur-driven Delorean automobile, the same model as used in the movie. The moment came and no car came out. The music kept pounding, and then the Delorean slowly appeared with simulated clouds of smoke behind it. It rolled a short distance in, the chauffeur got out and opened the door and out came the president, to the cheers of the throng. It came off fine. Later we found out the reason for the delay—the Delorean wouldn't start.

CHAPTER 9

Working the Charts, Successfully

A t a major financial conference the CEO was speaking at the lectern, forty feet from the screen, where a series of graphics were shown. We heard him, glanced over at the screen, became baffled as the spoken words seemed to have little correlation to what was on the screen. A dilemma: Which do we try to follow: the speaker's words or the visuals? Well there is that interesting *Wall Street Journal* article I wanted to read. . . .

How well visuals are used can have a major influence on how effective they truly are. Poor use of good visuals can make a very bad presentation. Here are suggestions for the effective use of visuals (summarized in Figure 9-1).

◆ *Before you start, verify that you are ready to work your gear.*

◆ *Decide where you and your colleagues will sit and stand.* The general rule is to stand to the left of the screen as you face it. Why? (1) To have the discussion go from you to the visual, and as we are used to reading from left to right, that's the logical way (unless you're in Saudi Arabia). (2) The bullets are on the left side, making that side a more logical place to use a pointer. Some speakers

Figure 9-1. Apply these tips for using audiovisual equipment and visual aids.

- Pre-set procedures for yourself *and* your colleagues.
- Have a colleague manage graphics if doing it yourself is awkward.
- Get away from the lectern; position yourself for good audience interaction and smooth use of gear.
- Don't block the screen; do talk with audience, not screen.
- Use gadgetry in an efficient and nondistracting manner.
- You run the graphics, don't let them run the show.
- For complex visuals, orient listeners before delving into details.
- Make sure your spoken message tracks the visual message.
- Avoid verbatim reading of bullet charts: Overview, paraphrase, and focus.
- Direct audience attention to key items with hand, pointer, and vocal inflection.
- Use pointers in a helpful, not distracting manner.
- Keep the visuals moving to prevent glazed eyes.
- Selectively use animation or builds to display a section at a time.
- When no longer using a visual, remove it so you don't sidetrack audience attention.
- Bring out and use props or materials smoothly; pass around when they won't be distracting.
- Keep your eye on the clock and trim material to stay on schedule.

---

argue that they are right handed, thus pointing with their left is difficult. That's not only irrelevant, as the primary factor is good audience connection, but it's also not a hugely difficult skill to learn to point with your left hand. The overriding concern is which side lets you better communicate with the principal audience members. If they are all seated on the left side of the room (facing the screen) it's hard to maintain eye contact. Move to the right side of the screen so you can use the charts and talk with the audience.

- *Display images only when ready to use them.* Too often, before they even say anything, presenters turn on the projector. Then for the next five minutes, listeners look at a lighted screen containing no image, or at an image that adds nothing to the opening comments. It's better to make sure visuals are ready and focused before you start, then darken the screen until the right moment to show the first visual.

- *Computer-based systems.* Get the projector lined up and focused, and use software to blank the screen. (In PowerPoint the letter "B" is an on-off toggle.)
- *Overhead projector.* Place the first viewgraph on the projector and focus it. Then turn off the projector until you are ready for the first visual.
- 35-mm slide projectors. Use the remote on-off capability or make your first slide an opaque one. Turn the projector on before you start to speak, thus keeping a dark screen until you advance to the first visual (not needed with most current projectors).
- Chalkboard. Start with a clean board or a blank chart or simple title.

Use aids to complement, not compete with, the message.

◆ *Make sure your spoken words and visuals match.* Often the speaker's words don't readily relate to the visual displayed. The result is internal disorientation, quickly leading to a channel switch in the brains of the listeners.

◆ *Stay in charge of your charts.* Many presentations come off as jerky, with the graphics only loosely connected. The time between charts is dead time, as the speaker changes charts, then looks up at the screen to verify that it really is there—surprise, it is—and then starts to address the chart, which audience members have already thoroughly examined.

Solution? Better lead-ins to charts before they hit the screen. This is one of the most effective techniques in the use of visual aids. It provides an opportunity to recapture attention before each visual, because listeners respond to words that suggest change is about to occur.

Here is a way a visual might be introduced: "The data just shown suggest that a significant benefit can result from a new marketing approach. We've looked at several of these, and now I'd like to show you the one we regard as most promising." At that time, and not before, show the visual.

◆ *Scope a chart before diving into the details.* Too often the speaker is explaining the significance of point A on a graph while listeners are trying to discover what the x and y axes are. Astute presenters first orient the audience by explaining such things as graph axes or column/row headings for tables. Then, having brought all listeners up to the same level of awareness, they go on to the details.

◆ *Use builds or animation (also called progressive disclosure) to develop complex charts.* Rather than show a flow chart with ten boxes—or an illustration with twenty labels—and lose the audience immediately, show initially only part of the set. Explain those. Then introduce the next group, and finally display the complete graphic. With computer graphics, this is a simple process, done with software. With viewgraphs, you can drop the new info onto the existing visual (definitely use a framer) or show a series of viewgraphs. Either needs to be done smoothly and without blocking the screen (having an associate handle the viewgraphs eliminates that problem). Some speakers use a blocking sheet to uncover a line at a time. However, with important or sophisticated audiences, avoid it unless you want this typical response: "I feel as if I'm being given the idiot treatment."

◆ *Give an overview of all main points on a chart.* Then go back and cover each in detail. Suppose you show a visual with three lines:

1. Initial cost is 20 percent less.
2. Maintenance cost is competitive.
3. Total life-cycle cost savings total 25 percent.

One approach is to discuss each item in order. But the overview approach seems to condition the listeners better and could sound like this: "Our approach achieves three major cost savings: initial, maintenance, and life-cycle. Let's first look at the initial cost savings."

◆ *In general, address all elements of a chart.* In the previous example, failing to address the third point would raise questions in the minds of the listeners. A workable alternative is to list and address several items as a group for completeness, then focus attention on one as being the critical one.

◆ *Paraphrase rather than read lines verbatim.* Perhaps the most detested practice in the use of visuals is when the presenter reads aloud every word of a busy chart. This is palatable if the chart contains only a few key words but is considered offensive if the chart consists of ten lengthy sentences. In the eyes of the viewer, the chart itself is a misdemeanor offense; reading it verbatim elevates the crime to the felony level.

Communicate with Your Audience

The speaker was clearly credible and articulate. It was troubling, however, that he never talked with us, the audience. I never could figure out which bullet he was talking about. When he got into that complex graph, the one with the six legends on the lower right corner, I never did figure out what x and y were. Was there something suspect in his material when he only looked at the screen? What if we all got up and left—would he know it?

Some tips for keeping your audience in the loop.

◆ *Provide direction to viewers.* It's aggravating to not know which bullet the speaker is talking about, or what part of the screen you're supposed to be looking at. For small conference rooms, use your hand to direct the audience to a specific bullet or box, being careful to stay out of the light so as not to create hugely distracting shadows. For topics beyond hand reach, use a pointer. For large rooms, use a laser pointer. More about these later.

◆ *Talk to the audience, not the screen or equipment.* This is one of the most important and commonly violated points. For many speakers, once the visual appears, it's goodbye eye contact. Yes, you might need to look at the screen as you point to specific items or lead the audience through a complex diagram or flowchart. But remember to face the audience as much as workable as you discuss the information (see Figure 9-2). Here's a useful formula:

  • DIRECT the audience to a specific item on the screen
  • CONNECT with your listeners by looking at them
  • PROJECT your spoken comments to them

Figure 9-2. Talk to people, not the screen. Direct, connect, project.

◆ *Don't block the screen.* Don't get in the way of projected images unless you intend to create hand shadows of giraffes or fish on screen (Figure 9-3). The worst culprit is the presenter who stands right beside an overhead projector and points to specific items right on the viewgraphs. Or writes on the viewgraph. This is a good way to irritate the audience members who lack Superman's ability to see through you. If you manage your own visuals, (a) place the viewgraph, then move away, usually to the side of the screen, or (b) place a pointer directly onto the transparency to highlight specific items, then move out of blocking range.

◆ *Cover visuals when they have served their purpose.* There is something fascinating about a visual aid; as long as it is there, it compels us to keep coming back to it, even if the speaker has moved onto another subject. If you discuss material not related to the on-screen visual, remove the distraction: Erase the board, turn to a blank flipchart, advance to a blank slide, turn off or cover the overhead projector, or use software to blank the computer image.

Use Visuals and Gadgetry to Add, Not Distract

◆ *Correct a problem immediately without calling further attention to it.* Ignoring an upside-down viewgraph, a badly focused

Figure 9-3. Don't block the audience's view of the screen or create your own distraction.

projector, or improper lighting prolongs the poor conditions. Apologizing, joking, or insulting the equipment or operators adds to the negative impressions possibly already created. What your audience wants is to get on with it and see how you perform under adversity.

◆ *Avoid creating your own distractions.* One of the biggest and most common distractions is a presenter who lets his body or arms get into the projected image. I once watched a series of presenters who stood right in the center of the screen, with images on their foreheads while they addressed a group of reviewers. (It's also amazing to see ads for projection equipment showing the speaker standing right in front of the light.)

◆ *Use gadgetry only as intended—not to juggle, lead the band, or toy with.* One speaker held a ballpoint pen in his hand, and clicked it about every five seconds. The laser pointer has a useful function, until the presenter forgets it's on and light flashes on the screen and around the room (and listeners duck for cover when that fierce light comes their way). When that wandering mouse appears on screen, it entices viewers to follow it, to nowhere of course. It is absolutely riveting to watch a speaker toy with a pointer or wave it around like a swashbuckler (see Figure 9-4).

Figure 9-4. Use pointer to direct attention to information on visuals, not to skewer audience.

How much of the message do you suppose is being heard while the sideshow is going on?

◆ *Look at the screen only when you want the audience to do the same.* If you look at the screen, we will presume you want us to do that too. If you frequently look at the screen as a nervous mannerism, you create your own distraction. I've watched speakers glance four to five times at a blank screen; it's intriguing to imagine what they were pulling from there.

◆ *Pass objects or materials around only after you have completed your presentation.* Doing it in the middle, a common occurrence, creates a whole series of little distractions as objects are inspected, passed along, or dropped. Show it, discuss it, and invite them to examine it when you don't mind losing their attention.

Use Graphics to Further the Dialogue

◆ *Stay alert for how the presentation is going.* How is the audience reacting? Are you starting to run out of time?

◆ *When a question comes up, if it relates to a specific visual, go to it quickly.* With the overhead, locate that transparency and show it. (If you've been sloppy about where you put used transparencies, lots of luck.) With a computer, know your software. (Tip: In PowerPoint slide-show mode, tap the slide number and "Enter.")

◆ *If the audience discussion is indicating "move on," adjust.* Perhaps shut off the projector and engage in dialogue.

◆ *If time is running out, make your choices.* Do not make the common mistake of continuing to address each chart and all bullets, except now at auctioneer speed. Decide which visuals are in the "must" category, and which items are key. Skip over everything else. With overheads, perhaps pull out several transparencies. Do your best to meet your time commitment.

◆ *Do not short-change your summary.* If you're running out of time, go to the summary and give that a good treatment. Then open for dialogue. Often some of the topics you had to skip now are open for discussion.

In Summary: Use Your Visual Aids to Help, Not Hamper

The speaker was one of those pointer fiddlers. It was fascinating to watch as he toyed with the pointer, twirling it clockwise rabidly, then counter-clockwise. He flamboyantly flashed it at the screen and twirled it in the air as if an orchestra conductor. We got a bit nervous when he would wave it wildly in our direction, then go back to toying again. Then, as he waved it in our direction for about the tenth time, the little tip came flying off and went right over our heads and caromed off the back wall. We all flinched. Some ducked for cover, shouting "INCOMING!!!" None of us ever forgot it. What did he say? None of us have a clue.

CHAPTER 10

Practice

Skip It at Your Risk

Two years after John F. Kennedy's death, the Canadian government named a mountain after him, and invited his brother, Robert Kennedy, to plant a flag on the summit. As a friend and ace mountaineer, Jim Whittaker was asked to lead the hike. Calling from his home in Seattle, Whittaker asked Kennedy what he was doing to get in shape for the climb. "Running up and down the stairs and practicing hollering 'Help!'" the senator replied. Oh great, thought Whittaker. (They made it fine.)[1]

The final phase of staging is to test the product, identify the weak spots, and fix them before taking the presentation to the actual audience. Many people firmly agree with the wisdom of doing this, yet in practice this step often gets skipped. Testing can do much to head off trouble, polish delivery and operations, and greatly enhance your ultimate comfort.

Some presenters stoutly maintain they don't need to practice, get coaching, or attend training seminars. Isn't it interesting that the top practitioners in any specialty—e.g., Tiger Woods, Serena Williams, and presidential debaters—practice with coaches. And they even listen to them.

In preparing for a major presentation for a competitive contract, I was coaching the team of four. When I discussed the need for dry runs, the main presenter (the assigned program director for the contract) resisted: "I don't believe in rehearsals. You can get too programmed." We did the dry run anyway, and it was obvious the one presenter most in need of coaching was the director. Vigorous feedback and seeing himself on video convinced him of that need. With a new attitude, he made the needed changes and did an excellent job for the actual presentation. Later he stated that forcing him to do the dry runs was valuable and would be standard practice henceforth.

Others have observed, "There's always a dry run." My question is, Do you want to have that occur before your real audience or in the privacy of your own conference room and in front of a couple of friendly colleagues? Put practice high on your list.

Having helpful colleagues play the roles of audience and feedback provider is key. If, as the old adage says, "Practice makes perfect"—when it comes to presentations, this is only partly true. If you're doing something wrong and don't realize it, you can practice all day and improve some parts of the presentation and have no effect on others. This is why having knowledgeable people, such as a presentation coach, give helpful feedback is so important. A truer adage would be "smart practice makes perfect."

What a Dry Run Can Do for You

A dry run serves several important functions:

◆ *Prevents Embarrassment.* For example, you may find out during the presentation that the print on the visual aid is so small it can't be read beyond the first row or that several misspelled words weren't caught earlier.

◆ *Checks Scope, Balance, and Structure.* Presenters are notorious for miscalculating the amount of material they think they can cover in the allotted time. It's not unusual for a presenter to show up for a fifteen-minute presentation with seventy-five viewgraphs that would require two hours to present.

◆ *Surfaces Fundamental Miscalculations.* Often presenters are so close to the topic, they overlook basic points—such as that the vice president doesn't care about all the technical details they are planning to cover. The dry run can refocus you on the presentation's true purpose and the appropriate method for achieving it.

◆ *Uncovers Holes in the Material.* You may discover while speaking that what you thought was valid or complete, isn't. A detached observer can often spot these holes more quickly than the presenter, who may be too close to the issue.

◆ *Prepares for the Unknown.* Since most presentations are interactive, with listeners commenting and asking questions, you need to be ready for more than what you are planning to cover. The unthought-of question can sabotage an otherwise sound presentation. A good dry run can go far toward surfacing questions that are likely to come up.

◆ *Makes for a Smoother, More Professional-Appearing Presentation.*

◆ *Enhances the Speaker's Self-Confidence.*

Planning the Test Phase

Planning for a simple dry run may take little effort. For major presentations, careful planning is key. Here are some suggestions for both reviewers and presenters, also summarized in Figure 10-1.

◆ *Test early and often.* Helpful reactions can be given at several key steps of development. The further along in the presentation phase, the more difficult and expensive changes become. Making

Figure 10-1. Testing and evaluation can greatly improve presentations.

◆ Plan to test at several steps during the development process.

◆ Conduct dry runs far enough in advance that needed changes can be implemented.

◆ Prepare carefully for dry runs for productive sessions.

◆ Test all parts: presenter, spoken words, graphics, operations, and Q&A.

◆ (Reviewers) Make feedback constructive, to help the presentation, not damage the speaker.

◆ Use video to help coaching and for self-evaluation.

◆ Listen to the reviewers and make changes where feasible and desirable.

◆ Do it again.

---

changes at the storyboard or rough-visual-aid level is simple and cheap compared to finding out that the presentation is off base and needs major work after all material has been gathered and finished visuals have been prepared.

◆ *Determine the specific purpose of each part of the test phase.* For a major presentation, several test formats may be in order. The intent of each may be different. To review visual aids for sequence and story, wall storyboards can be useful. To test the presentation and presenter, full-blown dry runs are in order. To prepare for questions, reviewers need to fire likely ones at the presenter and evaluate responses.

◆ *Schedule the dry run early and make it happen.* Often the test phase is done as an afterthought or skipped entirely. Planning and scheduling the test program are key to more effective presentation development.

◆ *Conduct dry runs well enough in advance to leave time for needed revisions.* If the dry run is not held until the day before the presentation, it is difficult to incorporate the suggestions of the evaluators.

◆ *Simulate the setting and the facilities.* If possible, practice with the specific equipment and at facilities that will be used for the presentation. If that's not possible, match the conditions as closely as possible. One major presentation involved extensive last-minute rework because the preliminary dry run failed to simulate the exact screen size and audience location. When these were later tested, it was obvious that most of the visuals had to be redone.

◆ *Simulate the audience.* Often people in the presenter's organization have backgrounds like those of key people in the real audience. A marketing manager who is a former Air Force colonel may be a good person to have as an evaluator for a military presentation. Fellow professionals can listen much like the technical experts in the audience.

◆ *Determine other participants.* To get needed graphics changes made quickly, include graphics designers in practice sessions.

◆ *Prepare the reviewers.* Send reviewers important information needed for well-informed review and feedback, and strongly suggest they come prepared. I've been part of many Red Teams where reviewers had not read the presentation requirements.

◆ *Arrange for dry-run support gear.* This may include video or audio recording and playback equipment, copies of visuals, evaluation forms, timing signs, and a stopwatch.

Conducting Productive Rehearsals and Reviews

The following suggestions apply to both the presenter and the evaluators.

◆ *Agree on the ground rules.* Let all participants know what procedure is to be followed, when comments are to be made, and whether to ask questions. I recommend having the speaker give the presentation without interruption, either in full or one segment at a time. Much time is typically wasted during dry runs with continual interruptions. Hold comments to the end of a segment or of the entire presentation.

◆ *Distribute materials to reviewers.* Distribute evaluation forms and copies of visual aids.

◆ *Make the presentation.* Often presenters show the visuals and merely state, "Here, I intend to say . . ." This process exercises only the visuals, not the speaker.

◆ *Conduct the evaluation.* The key to success is maintaining a positive environment, not always easy when one's best efforts are being dissected. Presenters and evaluators both must work to keep the environment productive. Use of a moderator to conduct this part of the dry run may be helpful.

◆ *Give an overview evaluation as well as an evaluation of specific parts.* With extensive feedback, the speaker may wrongly conclude that the whole presentation is a disaster and needs to be redone completely. An overview helps keep the proper perspective.

◆ *Comment on strengths as well as deficiencies.* If the emphasis is almost exclusively on the negative side, the presenter may overcorrect and discard useful material or practices.

◆ *Offer specific observations, not vague generalities.* This greatly facilitates communication among the parties. "The organization needs work" is not particularly useful to the presenter. "I was confused by your first two points. I think there is some duplication there," gives the presenter something specific to look at.

♦ *Offer alternatives wherever possible.* One of the strengths of evaluators is that they offer a different perspective from the speaker's. It is much more helpful to a speaker to see a quick sketch of an alternative to the concept presented than just to hear, "I thought chart four was too busy." This places a greater burden on evaluators, but it is a justifiable one.

♦ *Address the minor but focus on the major.* In the process of detailed analysis, it is easy to spend a disproportionate amount of time on relatively minor flaws. If all the attention is given to improving the speaker's eye contact and reducing the number of "uh's," the fact that the presentation completely missed the mark because it was at the wrong level might be overlooked.

In Summary: Pay Attention to Staging, a Major Success Factor

Staging of presentations often gets cavalier treatment as speakers get swept up in developing and preparing presentations. If the arrangements and operations are taken care of, and all aspects are polished with well-done rehearsals, these help get the message across. If not taken care of, they can prevent the message from being heard, and the medium may dominate the message.

For final reinforcement, here is a poem compendium of mostly true snafus that have befallen many colleagues. They laugh about them now. They didn't at the time.

ODE TO MURPHY
It's away to Washington for a major pitch,
A Winning Presentation and they'll all be rich.
They've busted their fannies to lay out their story,
They're loaded for bear, Brand X better worry.

The team of four aces, came together at two,
Was sabotaged early by the Asiatic flu.

Joe arrived looking green and lurched back on the plane,
Anne's charts came up missing, with the luggage again.

But the show must go on, the general won't wait.
So the rest of the team ran for the interstate.
But Avis said "What car?" and Hertz said the same.
"Hey taxi, over here, get us out of this rain."

Finally at the Pentagon, half an hour late,
Mac's clearance had lapsed, he's stuck at the gate.
The team's last two members, polishing their boots
Dashed to Conference Room A, in their power suits.

"Oh no, no one's there! How can that be?"
Simple, they're all waiting in Conference Room C.
To C they then headed, by now a bit whiffy,
"Turn on the projector, we're on in a jiffy."

What projector? There's none to be seen!
"Didn't you?" whispered Anne. "I thought you . . .," said
     Dean.
A projector arrived. "Let's go!" came a shout.
But 'twas not yet to be, the bulb was burned out.

Patience was fading as a new bulb was found.
Now the show did commence—oops, chart upside down.
Dean moved through the data, waving pointer with zest,
One swoop pitched hot coffee on the general's vest.

Anne then took the floor for the final appeal,
One nifty demo the proposal would seal.
First sparks, then much smoke—yep, incorrect power.
The general was drenched by the sprinkler's shower.

Later Anne and Dean, joined once more by Mac,
Cried in their beer, "We'll all get the sack!"
The moral is clear, as in that old saw:
Remember the power of old Murphy's Law.

Deliver and Follow Up

CHAPTER 11

Show Time

Overview and Nonverbal Delivery Skills

R obert E. Levinson said in an article in *Dun's Review*, "In a sense, every executive speechmaker is an actor, giving a performance for the edification, entertainment, and approval of a highly specialized audience. Since the delivery is as important as the content, an executive needs a bit of the ham."[1]

A century earlier, Emily Dickinson described a fellow author: "She has the facts, but not the phosphorescence."[2] That could fit many of today's presenters: knowledgeable, thorough—and boring.

Or it could give a simple guide to winning presenters—those with both the facts and the phosphorescence. On lists identifying characteristics of outstanding speakers, certain phrases keep appearing:

- ◆ Forceful, dynamic
- ◆ Speaks with energy, enthusiasm, conviction
- ◆ A winning presence
- ◆ Commanding
- ◆ Sincere, warm, real, natural
- ◆ Personal—I felt she was speaking right to me

- ◆ Direct—looked us right in the eye
- ◆ Handled himself well
- ◆ Certainly knew what she was talking about
- ◆ Lively, kept us awake, made it fun to listen to

These attributes reveal themselves in the way speakers deliver their messages. They determine whether those messages are listened to, received correctly, believed, and acted upon. All our hard work in preparation may be for naught if we don't deliver well.

This chapter examines how to improve delivery skills in three key areas: overall, apprehension, and nonverbal communication. Tips are summarized in Figure 11-1.

Presenting Successfully: Overall Tips

You've done your homework: carefully analyzed the audience, organized your presentation soundly, gathered solid supporting material, covered the arrangements, rehearsed, and checked out the room. You're ahead of the game as you head into the meeting. Now your degree of success will largely depend on how you deliver.

Figure 11-1. Apply these tips for winning delivery.

- ◆ Dress appropriately, to enhance, not detract.
- ◆ Get there early. Check it out: Know the territory and the gadgetry.
- ◆ Get physically and mentally ready.
- ◆ Let the real you show up.
- ◆ Talk to all; project to all.
- ◆ Talk, don't read, except where required.
- ◆ Don't let visuals displace you.
- ◆ Let your natural body language operate in all its forms (eyes, smile, posture, and gestures).
- ◆ Use your voice to focus, punch up, and dramatize. Avoid monotone.
- ◆ Speak so others can understand you and won't be distracted by your nervous mannerisms.
- ◆ Keep an eye on the clock and your plan.
- ◆ Stay flexible. Gauge responses. Shift gears, cut material, or open discussion.
- ◆ Have your closing down pat and don't shortchange it.

If you've been a bit loose about the preparation and your material is a bit shaky, experience fully that queasy feeling and make a mental note never to put yourself in this position again. That dress-for-success wardrobe and suave delivery will not likely be enough to save you.

Review the Core Essentials

◆ *Have something worthwhile to say.* Fire and technique lacking substance (e.g., all phosphorescence, no facts) are "a tale told by an idiot, full of sound and fury, signifying nothing," as Shakespeare put it.

◆ *Own your material.* If others have prepared material for you, such as graphics or manuscript, go over it carefully. Otherwise confidence and performance suffer.

◆ *Recognize this for the opportunity it is.* Your enthusiasm for communicating will come across and spark your audience.

◆ *Let the real you show up.* Tight nerves, high stakes, rusty skills, thin preparation . . . all can result in a wooden imitation of yourself standing up before that audience

◆ *Believe in yourself and your idea.* "Two very important factors," said Ron Stoneburner, former aerospace vice president. "One—project absolute sincerity, which comes from belief in your topic. Two—project confidence, which comes from your knowing what's in every bit of that sucker. I've watched well-packaged presentations taken on by people who had one or both factors missing, and they fell apart. And yet you know the data was good."[3]

Readiness Starts with Preparation

◆ Dress suitably for a positive impression.

◆ Get there early and make sure the setup and gear are ready.

◆ Loosen up, as if you were an athlete about to perform. Presenting is a physical activity, involving body, mouth, and mind. Stretch, do a few jumping jacks, shadow box, wave your arms in the air, hum, sing.

◆ Step into the restroom (preferably the correct one) for a final physical check.

◆ If the meeting is in progress, slip into the back and case the joint unobtrusively. Observe the speaker, note the setup, and identify any problems. This will ease your entree onto the scene and allow you to change the setup as needed. (At a national conference, I sat in on the presentation given before mine. The presenters kept the room entirely in the dark, so you couldn't see them, only their slides. I didn't like that setup and during the transition was able to change it so room lights could be kept partly on, a much better arrangement.)

Show Time! You're On and in Charge

Here are several tasks often overlooked or poorly done:

◆ Make sure the first visual aid is ready, whether on screen or for you to activate.

◆ Let the room come to order, look people in the eyes, and begin. Don't start speaking until you and audience are ready, though in many meetings you may have to call them to order.

◆ Have your opening well polished to get the presentation off in good fashion (review organization tips), then transition smoothly into the body of the presentation.

◆ Connect with your audience. Talk with them, not at them.

◆ Give lots of focusing clues—transitions, verbal and vocal emphasis and body language—to help the audience track your story flow and get information.

◆ Enjoy. When you enjoy something, you're less tight and more yourself. Audiences respond positively, which adds to your own confidence.

◆ Keep reading the sensors—the verbal and nonverbal signals that come from each audience member, especially key people. Are they fidgeting, daydreaming, or inspecting fingernails? If so, these are strong signals to change—fast.

◆ Adapt to what is happening. According to Anteon's former COO Mike Cogburn: "Be attuned to your audience. Watch how they listen and respond, then adapt as you watch. Those who can do that tend to be more successful."[4] If it's clear that your listeners have grasped something faster than you thought they would, cut the rest of the material on that subject and go on to something they'd rather hear. If you guessed wrong and assumed the audience knew more than it does, you may need to dwell a bit longer on some material.

◆ Respond to the comments and questions of the audience. How you conduct yourself under fire is a strong factor in acceptance or rejection of your ideas.

◆ Check the clock to stay on track (a common shortcoming in presentations).

◆ Do not shortchange the summary. If you find yourself running out of time, cut material and visuals, but save enough time to give the summary a good treatment. Make a clear transition to the next phase—questions, break, or next speaker.

◆ Wrap it up. Distributions? Action items understood? Your contact info? Next action?

What About Notes?

During the dry run for a recent proposal presentation, the program manager insisted on using a plethora of notes. He would be the key person on the contract, so a strong presentation was vital. But by constantly referring to notes, he created a poor impression. When he viewed himself on video—the first time he'd ever seen himself—he heartily concurred, and with some effort got rid of most of the notes and came through in good style.

According to Department of Energy executive Michael Bayer:

> Nothing is so unnerving as the guy giving a presentation and reading a script. This is an instant, "Hey, this guy doesn't know what he's talking about. Where's the guy who wrote the script, and why aren't we talking to *him*?"[5]

In an earlier chapter I recommended that speakers prepare talking notes or delivery scripts for their presentations. These are to help during preparation and practice; use them long enough to get the points clear and then put them aside. Use them minimally, if at all, during delivery. Assuming you know your material and have prepared well, the brain and visuals should provide all the thought triggers you need.

Notes can be beneficial for some materials or when graphics don't provide clues. Use them to help you stay on course (and in case your brain quits) and get key points addressed. Use notes for specific information that needs to be accurately conveyed, such as notices, procedures, quotes, or examples.

One of the keys to using notes well is to quickly grab the thought with little distraction. Index cards are usually more manageable than papers. Number each card, write large, and use only key information. Sketches or flow diagrams may be preferable to words only. Place the notes on the lectern or table so you can see them easily and handle them smoothly.

What About a Manuscript?

Manuscripts are required for some formal speeches, as when invited to give a eulogy, speaking at a major conference, giving the bad news to stockholders, giving a university graduation speech, or testifying before a congressional investigation committee.

Some read speeches are well done, others are poorly done and sometimes an embarrassment to the organization and the speaker, such as when the speaker is clearly unprepared, uses poor technique when reading, or has had too many cocktails to relax before the meeting. At an expensive, all-day conference, I watched a nationally-known TV commentator deliver the worst speech of the day, from a manuscript, because of admittedly poor preparation and fumbling delivery.

If you must use a manuscript or TelePrompter, be involved in content preparation, listen to the technical advisors, practice and polish. Even though you're reading, communicate with your audience. Go over your material, marking places for emphasis or pauses. Work toward a conversational delivery style, watch the monotone tendency, and engage your audience by looking up after appropriate phrases or during pauses. During one commencement speaker's entire talk all we in the audience saw were flipping pages and the top of his head.

Managing Anxiety Successfully

Tight nerves and speaking anxiety are not unusual, even among experienced speakers, but excessive stage fright can lead to stage flight, sapping your confidence and preventing the real you from shining through (Figure 11-2). It's vital to know how to keep the butterflies at a manageable level, or, as one speaker put it, "to get them to fly in formation."

Apprehension stifles people in many situations. It can deter people from asking questions, making valuable input during discussions, assuming leadership in organizations, even showing up at events that might expose them to uncomfortable speaking situations.

Mary Mandeville, a speech communication professor at Oklahoma State University, works with many students to help them become more comfortable and proficient at public speaking. She cites studies showing that 20 percent of the population are terrified when faced with the prospect of public speaking, and 10 percent fear it worse than a great catastrophe or death. "The physical effects are real, with pulse rate for the terrified ones going from a normal 70 beats per minute to 190 when they stand up to speak."

She applies a three-step ABC process "to avoid the problems of beating yourself up."

Figure 11-2. For many people, excessive anxiety impedes opportunity.

1. *Affective* is the process of desensitizing. "People hear the word 'speaking' and they hear 'anxiety' or 'terrified.' Relaxation techniques help them hear 'relaxation' instead."

2. *Behavioral* means learning how to prepare for presentations.

3. *Cognitive* works on the mind. "Lots of self-talk gets us off course. We make a mistake and it triggers to old fears and doubts. A valuable technique is visualization, to develop in your mind positive images of success."[6]

I frequently hear seminar participants admit to a long pattern of speaking anxiety and avoidance from stress-inducing situations. They've ducked attending company seminars before—you can almost see the fingernail tracks on the floor as if they've been dragged into this seminar against their will. Most stick around and quickly make progress toward more confidence, plus realize the rewards from continuing their progress. A few others have looked for the first opportunity to exit and unfortunately missed an opportunity to overcome that career-damaging pattern.

Look at the rewards that come with speaking up: increased participation and influence, the good feeling that comes from having your ideas and opinions listened to, increased ability to organize and express your thoughts, growth from exposure to new people and situations, and improvement in relationships because each party knows better where the other stands. I have seen many examples where a change in pattern has brought dramatic career moves, increased self-esteem, and a lot more fun.

Speaking success is also self-fulfilling. Each success makes the next step easier, particularly if positive feedback goes with the successes and excessive self-flagellation is avoided with the flops.

If you have severe apprehension or a speech impediment, seek expert help. Self-help attempts to change may be met with setbacks and leave you worse off than before you started. A professional can help prevent this and probably speed up the process.

"'Tis the mind that makes the body rich." Shakespeare's comment serves as a valuable reminder of both a major cause of anxiety and a major cure. What you say to yourself and how you perceive this event can greatly affect your confidence. Look at it as a feeding frenzy about to occur, and down goes your zeal. Instead, consider it a golden opportunity, with the audience there to hear you, the most knowledgeable person in the room (which is true). Make "I can't wait to get in there" your credo.

Get an Advance Plan Going

- ◆ Join your local Toastmasters club. Their friendly environment, many modest speaking situations, and caring feedback make for quick confidence building.
- ◆ Start small. Then add on progressively.
- ◆ Loosen up in general. Do activities that lessen inhibitions. Play charades; read *Dr. Seuss* and *Harry Potter* aloud to the kids, and ham it up outrageously; spout off more in discussions; write letters to the editor; initiate conversations; speak to strangers; let the child in you come out.
- ◆ Give yourself lots of reasons to feel good about yourself. Since reticence is strongly influenced by how you feel about yourself, a high evaluation of your self-worth is important.
- ◆ Look for opportunities to speak in public: teach kids at church or colleagues at work; ask the boss to let you give a short presentation; speak for your favorite community cause, take on a leadership role with your professional association. It gets easier the more you do it.
- ◆ Take advice from one of the great writers, Goethe: "One ought, every day at least, to hear a little song, read a good poem, see a fine picture, and, if it were possible, to speak a few reasonable words."[7]

Take the Time to Prepare

- ◆ Know the territory. Unfamiliar environments and people can heighten reluctance to speak.
- ◆ Start with a message of importance to you.
- ◆ Know your material.
- ◆ Have your opening down pat. This is when the nerves are tightest, and getting off to a good start is a great confidence builder.

◆ Rehearse, preferably with people who can both simulate the situation ahead and give you helpful feedback. Try it again.

◆ Prepare for contingencies. Uncertainties and problems that unexpectedly pop up are real confidence sappers.

◆ Visualize and assume success is ahead. It has been well documented that envisioning doing something successfully has a positive effect on actually doing it.

◆ Try isometric exercises. Force your muscles to work against each other; tense strongly, then relax. Take a few giant, drawn-out yawns (quietly, if the meeting is in process). Exhaling long and slowly helps you relax and gets your breathing under control

You're Up

◆ Don't be a wallflower. Start talking to people informally before the meeting, if that is possible. This breaks the ice and lessens the barriers. It also gets you interacting, as a warmup to the real thing.

◆ Talk one-to-one with the friendly faces. Anxious speakers often tell me this one tip helps them the most. Speak to one person. Would you be nervous if only the two of you were talking? Not likely. Now move on to a different person. Look for the smiling, responsive faces; as you get warmed up, work on the dour ones.

◆ Focus on the message, not what they might be thinking about you. Realize right now you are the most knowledgeable person about what you're speaking about. The audience wants information from you that can help them. Get into the subject and truly work to communicate your ideas and information to them.

Post-Session

◆ Having concluded, stick around if appropriate. Contribute to the rest of the session, be available for further discussion after the meeting. Don't be surprised if some plaudits come your way. Do a post-meeting review, and identify lessons-learned and further needs.

◆ Give yourself some "attaboys/attagirls" for having done it. Watch the tendency to be overcritical of your performance. So it wasn't perfect—remember hardly anybody else's is either.

◆ Get ready to tackle the next one. Take specific action to make that happen.

Those All-Important Nonverbal Messages

The nonverbal messages may prevent the spoken and graphic message from being heard or given proper attention. A presenter's appearance, posture, style, or mannerisms can be so strongly sensed and interpreted as poor by audience members that the true intended message—the ideas, arguments, substantiating material, visual aids—will be seen through clouded eyes (or their eyes may even be closed!). The contrary is true as well; audience members may become better inclined to listen to what a speaker has to say because his or her nonverbal messages are pleasing to them.

Psychologist Albert Mehrabian underscores the importance of nonverbal communication.[8] His studies show that when two people communicate, less than 10 percent of a key measure of communication success—total liking—comes from the words that are spoken. Over 50 percent of the message comes from facial expressions and nearly 40 percent from vocal tone or expression, called paralanguage (how something is said).

This especially comes into play when the spoken and unspoken messages don't match. When a speaker says "We have a wonderful idea" in a dull voice while looking nervously at the ceiling, would you believe her?

In fact, this is what happens to many presenters. They grip the lectern tightly with both hands. They adopt a rigid position and stare straight ahead, thus stifling their natural facial and body expressions. Then they speak in a monotone, particularly if they are reading material. There goes the bulk of their positive nonverbal value, while the audience picks up negatives of apprehension, unpreparedness, and possibly deception, probably not a true picture of the speaker.

Nonverbal Messages: Basis for Many Listener Judgments

I do not much dislike the matter, but the manner of his speech.
—SHAKESPEARE, *ANTONY & CLEOPATRA*

Nonverbal messages can be door openers or door closers. We often immediately accept someone whose appearance we are comfortable with and reject another because we don't like his or her looks. We turn on to speakers for reasons that have less to do with their words than with their style. We turn off to speakers for reasons we ourselves are not entirely clear about: "There's something about that person I don't like. Can't exactly put my finger on it, but he's just not my cup of tea."

Often we *can* "put our finger on it" and are clear about it: "I won't do business with a guy who wears a beard." "I don't trust a person who won't look me in the eye." "I don't like that woman— she's always smiling."

Other times we know what it is but are reluctant to put it into words, because it makes us uncomfortable or reveals our own prejudices: "Why does he keep telling those vulgar jokes?" or "They expect us to listen to a woman?" or "Why doesn't somebody tell that guy to use a deodorant?"

Nonverbal messages are also tricky, and may lead to mistaken judgments. The person in the sloppy jeans and sweatshirt turns out to be the vice president. We say, "Aha, you're being defensive," to a person with her arms folded, and it turns out she has a bad back and feels more comfortable with her arms folded.

The cover photo for *San Diego Magazine* showed a group of motorcyclists, relaxing near their bikes in typical riding garb. Scary crowd. Made you nervous. Are these Hells Angels or what? Inside the cover was duplicated with each person in their daily work garb: a doctor, scientist, attorney, teacher, etc. Be careful about those first judgments.

Keeping an open mind can quickly change receptivity. At a conference on future lifestyles, the speaker shuffled forward. He wore a frayed suit coat with rumpled and badly matched pants. His hair was long overdue for trimming. He looked a bit hung over, and he slouched. All the things speakers are cautioned to avoid in the power/ success books, he displayed.

Several people near me snickered when they saw him. My first thought was, "Where did they dig up this character?" The snickers quickly stopped, however, as he began to speak. It was immediately evident that this was a person to listen to, and everyone did, intently. His talk was the hit of the conference and the subject of much discussion afterward. No one cared anymore that he needed a haircut and a shoeshine.

Given a choice, I would much rather be a speaker in a rumpled suit to whom people listened intently because of the power of my words than one perfectly tailored without substance!

Sending Positive Body-Related Messages

First, we'll examine what the body does to create positive or negative impressions for presenters.

First Impressions

◆ *Watch your nonverbal behavior while you're in the wings.* Often a presentation is part of other activities, such as other presentations, group discussions, or preliminaries. Audience members may already have formed their impressions of you even before the meeting, based on your bio, title, reputation, etc.

◆ *You're on.* Stride with assurance and eagerness to the podium or proper place in the room and take command.

Posture and Movement

Adopt a comfortable stance, with weight evenly balanced on both feet. Directly face the audience, and stand as close to it as makes sense (if not speaking from a lectern). Strive for a natural posture. Watch the slouch, the most common flaw. An erect posture, with all parts in alignment, projects an image of assurance and is better for voice production than one that is slouching or cockeyed.

Here are three easy checks on posture:

1. Stand against a wall, with fanny, back, and head against the wall. Now walk away holding this position. If your normal position isn't close to this, you're probably slouching.

2. To reduce the shoulder-slumping tendency, force your elbows backward several times to loosen your chest and shoulder area. Then, with elbows extended to the rear, drop your arms.

3. As a check of posture, look at where your hands rest along your legs. If they are either in front of or to the rear of your pants or skirt seams, you are probably slouching.

You need not be cemented to one place. You can speak from different locations (e.g., at the screen) or close to specific audience members. Move deliberately, stop, and talk. Do not pace back and forth, bounce, or fidget, as these are distracting.

Hands and Arms

"What do I do with my hands?" is probably the most common question I hear. When presenting, many people cut their hands out of the action by adopting one of several common wooden-speaker positions (Figure 11-3). These become the "home base" for their hands as they

Figure 11-3. What do I do with my hands? "Wooden speaker" positions are not uncommon.

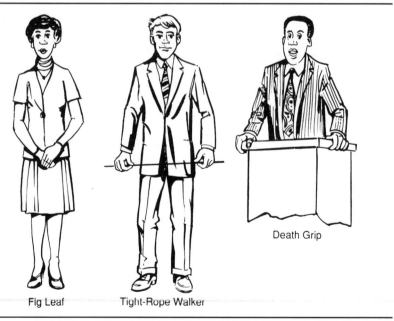

Death Grip

Fig Leaf   Tight-Rope Walker

may gesture a bit or point to the screen, and each time return to the same position:

Fig leaf	Both hands gripped together and covering the groin
Reverse fig leaf	Hands gripped behind the back (like the military at-ease position)
Mortician or concert singer	Hands gripped together at the navel
Gunfighter or gorilla	Both arms hanging stiffly away from both sides
Casual	Hands in pockets
Challenger	Hands on both hips
Death grip	Hands firmly holding onto a lectern, chair, pointer, or papers
Tightrope walker	Both hands on the pointer, which is held across the waist

To let your hands operate naturally and forcefully:

◆ Check your personal style by watching a video of yourself as you present. Note whether you are adopting any of these counterproductive patterns, with arm movement stifled. Compare that to your typical gesturing during regular conversations.

◆ Don't let both hands grip things or each other. If you start to go to one of these wooden positions, break from it. It takes a conscious awareness, then an action to break the pattern.

◆ Once the hands get ungripped, let them do what they would do as you normally talk to someone at a gabfest. Most people have a reasonable amount of hand movement. Some people can hardly talk without it.

◆ Now work on refinements. Broaden gestures—away from limited hand-only gestures or short movements of the forearm—toward broader, more sweeping movements involving one or both arms. Develop more forceful gestures, with increased vigor going into them.

◆ If you're among the small group that is too wild in their gesturing to the point of distraction, put some discipline into it by toning down excessive movement.

◆ Eliminate irritating mannerisms. Coin and key jangling head the list.

One division general manager was advised by the corporation's CEO that he was paying one of his top executives too much money. This was just after the executive had given them a presentation. The GM asked why. "Because," came the answer, "he doesn't know enough not to jangle the change in his pockets when he is giving a presentation." Do CEOs pay attention to the little things?

The distraction can come either from the presenter or from a non-speaking team member. Says consultant Denny Krenz, who chaired many governmental review boards: "A twitch, a nervous mannerism distracts more than the speaker thinks. We had one guy on a team who sat there and kept bouncing on his feet. Terrible distraction."[9]

Here are a few more side-tracking irritants: ball point pen clicking, pointer fumbling, crossed leg bouncing up and down, facial grimacing, head scratching, chin rubbing, beard-scratching, and my all-time favorite: dip-spitting.

Facial and Eye-to-Eye Communication.

What the face and eyes say is tremendously important for communication, though to different degrees depending on the receivers' culture. In the United States, when people avoid eye contact we wonder about them. Talking far more to the screen than the audience is the most common example of this.

◆ As you present, connect with your audience, one person at a time. Establish eye contact and truly engage that person with you. A guideline is to complete a phrase with person A, then move to person B.

◆ Be sensitive to proper duration of eye contact. Research says that three to five seconds works, less than that gives a fluttering impression. Gaze intently at a person too long, and he may become uncomfortable.

◆ Look at and face people directly. Side glances do not instill confidence.

◆ If using visuals on a screen, position your feet so you can easily look to the audience. Many people face the screen excessively, creating an over-the-shoulder glance at the audience.

◆ Speak to everyone. Many presenters direct their attention solely to the highest-ranking person, irritating the lesser folks. Definitely talk to that person but also to the others. Even when answering a question, keep the whole group in the dialogue.

◆ Don't shift your gaze from left to right and back as though watching a Ping-Pong game.

◆ Even when using notes or visuals, remember to talk to your audience, not the screen, projector, ceiling, or lectern.

◆ It's O.K. to smile. Tightness and excessive concentration on the material may prevent a natural smile from shining through. The key again is to be yourself, letting your personality and warmth come through. The audience warms up and often smiles back, adding to the speaker's confidence. A smile is linked to a more pleasant voice too.

◆ Become aware of negative facial expressions. It is hard to be enthusiastic about information coming from a person who looks sour or downcast. Confidence will be low in a person with a frightened-rabbit or bewildered look. A person who speaks out of the side of his mouth may come across as secretive.

Style and Manner Speak Volumes

A variety of nonverbal behaviors in the area of presenter style and manner interplay to communicate strong messages. Competence, trust, maturity, sensitivity, sophistication, and strength of character are all measured to a great extent by nonverbal factors. So are arrogance, boorishness, evasiveness, nonprofessionalism, and weakness.

Much of this is sensed from tone of voice; sensitivity to space, time, protocol, and touch; and operation under fire.

The following suggestions apply not just to presenters but also to accompanying team members.

◆ *Understand rank and protocol.* With any audience, powerful unspoken rules function regarding showing up late or wasting time, being excessive familiar, failing to know or use military ranks, or violating space "bubbles."

◆ *Respect your audience.* Wasting the time of others by poor preparation, insulting the local facilities, badmouthing the competition, using profane language, or telling ethnic or sexist jokes can cause the audience to walk out, literally and figuratively.

◆ *Be and stay positive.* With their opening words, many presenters doom their purpose. "I really didn't have much time to prepare these visuals, so I hope you'll bear with me." Apologizing for an upcoming performance loses points immediately. This applies to problems during the talk too. When Murphy's Law prevails, speakers often go to pieces or apologize profusely, focusing attention on something the audience had perhaps barely noticed. When a mishap occurs, fix it and get on with the business.

◆ *When you are subjected to opposing viewpoints, keep your cool and your perspective.* When answering tough or even hostile questions, be careful about several undesirable tendencies that may surface, such as ignoring the questioner, becoming defensive, attacking the questioner, or caving in. You will lose if you give in to any of these options.

◆ *Let your human side show.* A characteristic shared by several outstanding speakers I know is that they are comfortable with their audiences. They come across as real human beings, with humor, vitality, feelings, and even occasional goofs.

◆ *Be considerate of others besides the audience.* A program director became irritated at one of his own speakers, and proceeded to berate him for his deficiencies in front of the audience. "Isn't he a big man," a colleague said. You don't win by being domineering to others, especially those not in a position to fight back.

◆ *Polish your business etiquette.* One after-dinner speaker had already lost many of his audience by loudly slurping his soup and belching during the dinner. Another speaker failed to shake the hand that was extended to him by a listener as they were introduced before program. While waiting his turn to talk, the same speaker put his feet on the walnut conference table.

◆ *Be professional.* This final aspect of the speaker's style encompasses all the previous ones. The way you prepare for and conduct yourself during a business presentation says much about the type of manager, professional, or person you are.

◆ *Know the local rules about smoking and follow them.* Tobacco smoke has become a major issue, including being banned entirely in most indoor facilities in the United States. If you're a smoker, absolutely don't smoke when you're presenting, and ask for permission as a meeting participant or in another's office.

Dress and Grooming Do Matter

Like it or not—some people don't—dress is important in business. Listeners are sizing you up long before you open your mouth, and probably the first "sizing" factor is your outward appearance—wardrobe, neatness, haircut, and shoe shine.

Speakers whose motto is "I'll do it my way" often overlook that as presenters they are representing their organization, not just themselves. The impression they create will carry into other business activities with their organization.

Dress is more important in some settings than in others (Figure 11-4). An audience of engineers at a technical seminar is less likely to be concerned about dress than a banker's loan approval committee hearing a pitch for a $10 million loan, or a review board hearing a proposal for a major new contract.

Presenters talking outside the organization need to be particularly aware of their appearance. Wearing casual or flashy clothing may be acceptable when speaking to some internal groups, but all speakers should keep in mind that they are representing the organization as well as themselves. A talk may be part of a broad marketing campaign or a team presentation, and the presenter's image can help or hamper achieving the main objective.

Figure 11-4. Take a business wardrobe tip from the Wizard.

THE WIZARD OF ID By Brant Parker and Johnny Hart

SOURCE: By permission of John L. Hart FLP, and Creators Syndicate, Inc.

Yet it is a mistake to assume that dress is not also important for internal presentations. The sloppy presenter may never get the chance to speak externally and may miss out on opportunities.

Finally, if you look good, your clothes fit well, and you know you are perfectly in tune with the situation, you will perform better. Your confidence will zoom, you will stand straighter, and you will move and speak with more assurance.

Six months after I conducted a training seminar in the Midwest, one of the participants called. She had been an articulate presenter, an independent sort based on her wardrobe, which was follow-on hippie. Her message was: "I wanted to let you know the effect of the seminar. From seeing myself on the video and getting helpful feedback, I changed a few things. I lost twenty pounds, updated my hairstyle and wardrobe. Since then I've received comments from several higher-ups that I seem to have a more business-like approach to the job. I'm in line for a promotion."

Wardrobe

Here are three general guidelines that will serve you well.

1. *Be comfortable.* Presentations can be stressful. Your clothing should do nothing to add to that stress. If your shirt is too tight, your underwear grabs, or your pants hang wrong, you'll be aware of this discomfort during the presentation. So when you choose your clothing for a presentation, make sure all the pieces feel good and fit well.

   When speaking, many presenters perspire more than normally.

Choose your wardrobe so you will stay cool. Undershirts, vests, polyester shirts, and heavy suits can make you sweat.

2. *Dress appropriately for the occasion.* As has so often been stated in this book, know your audience and situation. Different professions, industries, and geographic areas have different standards for what is appropriate. The key for any situation is to know your audience and select your wardrobe so that it will (a) not call attention in a negative way and (b) enhance your impression.

   When in doubt, dress toward the conservative side. If you are the presenter, it is better to be at least as conservatively dressed as principal audience members. For inexpensive guidance, follow the lead of executives pictured in *Fortune, Savvy,* and local business publications. Or just look upward about two to three levels in your organization. (That sometimes works.)

   In recent years business wardrobe has tended toward more casual. Executives are now seen in publications, especially those covering techie industries, with open collars, without jackets, etc.—very different from years back. However, for anyone pursuing contracts or capital, the standard is still coat and tie for men and counterparts for women. Dress rehearsals are conducted to check wardrobes and give speakers the experience of the actual wardrobe (useful considering that some of them have not worn a tie in years).

   Bill Gates epitomizes the relaxed techie culture, with most photos showing him with an open shirt. What did he wear when speaking to Congress? Suit and tie. At an important presentation in Hawaii, the team members showed up wearing dark business suits. The audience members, however were in local garb. "We felt very awkward and they never warmed up to us," said one of the speakers. So for a later meeting, they all wore Hawaiian shirts (with the local rep insisting he buy the shirts to avoid a carnival-hawker look.)

   In assessing appropriate dress, consider the wardrobe choices in Figure 11-5. For a major audience a conservative look (Level 1) may be the right choice; for an internal meeting, Level 3 or 4 might be fine.

3. *Be yourself.* I recently watched a group of businessmen departing from a conference. All wore the approved plain gray or dark-blue

Figure 11-5. Wardrobe hierarchy, from conservative to casual.

♦ **Level 1** is for the major presentation, such as for a proposal, a top-level board meeting, or a pitch to venture capitalists. The senior executive team will often have this look, typically a business suit for men or women.

♦ **Level 2** is a slightly-relaxed wardrobe, such as a suit in lighter color or fabric for summer; also tuned in to your working world, such as western wear. For women, a less formal look but still a jacket.

♦ **Level 3** is the blazer or non-flashy sport jacket, with matching pants. For women a shirt dress or blouse/skirt or pants. Quality fabric, not shiny, no golf outfits.

♦ **Level 4** is represented by today's casual Friday look, upscale, not jeans.

---

suits; it was depressing. Similarly, a colleague who had attended a meeting of women executives said that all the women wore variations of the men's suits, vests, and ties, and all looked nice but a bit boring.

We don't all have to become automatons, turned out from a factory so we all look alike to be acceptable in business. Every personality and shape is different, so why do the suits all have to come from the identical mold? Within the hierarchy suggested here, there is plenty of room for diversity that is still appropriate.

When buying new clothing, first do your homework. Go to a quality shop that carries traditional clothing and test out a variety of appropriate suits. Talk to a competent salesperson about what styles and colors might complement you best. Find the wardrobe that can add to your overall impression, not just allow you to fit in.

Completing the Package

At a dress rehearsal for a major competition, several speakers were in the decreed Level 1 suits. However, the impressions were marred by the appearance of the well-worn Level 10 jogging shoes, the huge Coors Beer belt buckle, and the stunning chartreuse, yellow and purple patterned tie, hanging crookedly. (I don't have to make these up, I just observe.)

Proper fit of clothing and well-selected accessories complete the image of professionalism. And they convey strong messages. As an example, I was in an audience of 300 for a presentation that represented important exposure for the speaker and his organization. The audience was high level, military and civilian, and definitely conservatively attired. The speaker wore no coat or tie and looked about right for going to a ball game, not for giving a major presentation.

Suggestions for Men Presenters

◆ *Coat.* Many jackets are obviously ill fitting, often because the wearer recently gained or lost weight. If it's under a strain when buttoned or hangs sloppily, get it to a tailor (or Goodwill). The collar should be smooth along the neck, the back also smooth, and the sleeves long enough to allow a half-inch of shirt cuff to show. Button the coat when standing unless you want to direct attention to your belly or be less formal.

◆ *Pants.* The standard chuckle is the "high-water" look—pants three inches above shoes (especially with red socks). Length should touch shoes with a slight break. Color should complement, not clash with, the jacket. Avoid loud patterns—the classic used-car salesman look.

◆ *Shirt.* Collars too tight or too loose are common; shirts should fit comfortably and smoothly. Long sleeves (short sleeves may be acceptable for informal situations, hot summer days, or in Honolulu) should end at the intersection of hand and wrist.

◆ *Tie.* The tie is the major focus of audience nudges and grins when the length is too short or too long or the pattern outrageous. It should touch the belt—Dilbert's always sticks out in front at mid-chest—and not show under the shirt collar. Choose colors and patterns with care; silk ties look and tie the best. Make sure the knot is compact and straight (often an obvious distraction during TV close-ups), and use a Windsor or half-Windsor knot.

◆ *Belt.* Closely match pant color, without ornate buckles or studs.

◆ *Suspenders.* They add a certain flair, but know your audience.

◆ *Shoes and socks.* Colors should match pants. Shoes should be shined, and socks not drooping.

◆ *Distractions.* It is often said that you can always spot an engineer because of the plastic pocket protector with six pencils in it and the Palm Pilot hooked to the belt. (In ancient times, it was a slide rule.) When up before the group, get rid of distractions (cell phones, company badges, keys in pockets (Figure 11-6).

Figure 11-6. Watch thoses distracting coins and ties.

Source: DILBERT reprinted by permission of United Feature Syndicate, Inc.

Suggestions for Women Presenters

◆ *Styles.* Temper "stylish" with good business sense. Floor-length dresses, flowery and frilly blouses, and swirly skirts are best left out of the boardroom. An executive cautions, "Don't look like a stoplight. It can be dangerous to be too 'fashionable' in a hard-core business environment."

◆ *Colors.* Be aware of what's appropriate and current for your industry and profession. A woman systems specialist observed after attending a business women's dress seminar, "Magenta, fuschia, and jade may be O.K. for a bank, but they're definitely not O.K. for aerospace."

◆ *Distractions.* Low-cut blouses and bare backs are fine for the cocktail party but not for the conference room. Regarding skirt lengths, one woman executive said, "Make sure you can sit and not have the skirt ride up another six inches, especially if you're seated at the front table. When the audience members look at you as you speak, you want them looking above the table." Four-inch heels and platform shoes, bulky purses, soft sweaters, and high-fashion hats may detract from the main purpose. Flashing rings, dangling earrings, or multiple necklaces can distract and create an impression of ostentation or frivolity.

Personal Grooming

"Little things mean a lot," says a once-popular song. This is certainly true with personal grooming and cleanliness. A long-overdue haircut or overpowering body odor can prevent a sale in spite of beautiful clothes and a marvelous presentation.

♦ Always have your hair combed and shoes shined. Hairstyle and grooming are high on the list of examinables. I don't recommend you try out your new Mohawk haircut or purple highlight in a serious business meeting. If your style is not somewhat in tune with the times, it may get a negative reaction. Whatever the style, it should be neatly combed and under control.

♦ Makeup should enhance the appearance while creating no undue attention.

♦ Astute presenters ensure that breath and body odors don't leave the wrong lasting impression. Fragrances can cause problems either by being too dominant or by causing allergic reactions.

♦ Oh yes. Also for both genders: Many young people love nose, tongue, and eyebrow rings, multiple earrings, and visible tattoos. If you're planning a serious career, understand that these will limit your opportunities.

In Summary: Sound Ideas and Good Delivery Make a Strong Team

Having diligently prepared for your presentation, make sure your delivery only adds to the acceptance and responsiveness from your audience. At show time, you—not the graphics—are the most important part of the presentation. Remember these key points:

♦ *Overall Skills.* Prepare well so your delivery conveys credibility and professionalism.

♦ *Anxiety.* If excessive anxiety about public speaking is interfering with your success, take action to make it manageable.

♦ *Nonverbal Communication.* How you look and act can weigh more heavily than what you say.

In case you're still not convinced that nonverbal factors can affect your success and career, consider this anecdote from Ben Bradlee, former executive editor of the *Washington Post,* and formerly of *Newsweek.* In his book, *A Good Life,* he described how appearance foiled his desire to add a reporter he rated as a comer: "David Broder, of the *New York Times,* [was] well on his way to being the greatest pure political reporter of his generation. I had tried to hire him for *Newsweek,* but [our executive editor] Malcolm Muir, Jr. was put off by David's wardrobe: brown shoes with blue slacks."[10]

CHAPTER 12

The Spoken Word

Language and Voice

A few well-chosen words are worth a thousand pictures, de-spite what the Chinese philosopher said. I want to know what the man can do with the English language. Our great presidents were able to write well. I don't think a man can lead the nation without a grasp of the language.[1]

Thinis observation from the late news commentator Eric Sevareid fits business leaders as well as political leaders.

A common lament about many business executives, scientists, lawyers, government officials, and educators is that either they do not know how to speak in plain language or they deliberately use language to deceive.

Phillip Dunne, a movie screenwriter and director, in an essay titled "Just Between You and I," put it this way: "In particular, one may protest the misuse of our language by those who should know better: businessmen, educators, holders of high offices, and representatives of the news media. If happy illiterates can enrich a language, the pompous half-educated only succeed in impoverishing it."[2]

While language is a primary vehicle to further communication, it may also be a major interference: inadvertent when we misjudge an audience and use words that listeners will not understand or to which they will react negatively, and deliberate when we use words to impress, deceive, or cover up rather than to communicate.

Effective Language Is Appropriate

One of the fastest ways to lose an audience is to offend it. Few speakers are so foolish as to offend listeners deliberately, but many have innocently done so. Knowing your audience is fundamental to using language wisely. Here are two primary offenders:

1. *Profanity.* Be wary of telling dirty jokes, flashing pictures of naked models on the screen to wake people up, or using locker room language. I have seen this backfire on many speakers who used profanity excessively for shock effect or because they hadn't given a thought to doing otherwise.

2. *Affiliation-Offensive Language.* This means language that will turn off members of the audience because of who they are. It's surprisingly easy to fall into that trap. Just tell a Polish joke to an audience containing some Poles. Or start an answer to a woman questioner with "Well, honey. . . ." Or to a Navy audience, praise the way the Air Force managed a program better than the Navy did. These all occurred during actual presentations, and the predictable effects also occurred.

Effective Language Is Directive and Involving

Speakers can use language to help direct audience attention and encourage involvement. Combined with vocal stress and timing, directive language is a powerful tool for the speaker. Words and phrasing can shift an audience from purely passive to active listeners. Here are some ways to do that:

Enumerate	"The first point is . . ."
Emphasize/Focus	"A particularly important factor . . ."

Repeat	"Sixteen casualties. Sixteen."
Restate	"Let's look at that another way."
Bridge	"We've seen the causes: Let's examine the possible solutions."
Question	"So what is the best choice?"
Invite	"Put yourselves in their position."

With many speakers it seems the audience is irrelevant to the presentations. An example is: "And the customer then takes our program and uses it as is." And to whom is the presentation being given? The customer. Rewording this to include them simply adds the word "you": "And you then take our program and use it as is." Some typical phrases:

"Visibility is improved." (Whose?)

"We've listened to complaints from users. (You mean, ours?)

Effective Language Is Understandable

"Now as you all know, the contract had been set to be cost-plus at 150K, but we were OBE'd. Then getting a firm MA on the RFQ has been like going through max q. We're in the same bind as on our MRQT program, where NAVFLIBTOB pulled the plug as we'd gotten the QZKT-2 on line and our realization in 257 up to viable levels." Now take out your pencils, as we're going to have a little quiz later.

The spoken word in business and government is abundant with jargon, acronyms, abbreviations, and technical terminology that frequently baffle members of the audience. Such professional shortcuts are useful in communicating with peers but become traps when not everyone knows them nor acts to clarify what has been said.

In interviews for this book, many top executives said that speakers frequently subjected them to acronyms they did not know. SAIC Venture's group president Kevin Werner: "Lots of times presenters assume you know too much. They use lots of acronyms and terms particular to their field. With many presenters, I've had to stop them ten minutes into it and say "I have no idea what you're talking about."[3]

I was on the sending end of a terminology gap that made me forever cautious about using acronyms. My report was to a half-dozen members of the company's human resources staff: ". . . and STS is proceeding well. STS is causing some overtime, but milestones are being met."

At about the third mention of STS, an audience member, the company doctor, asked me what STS meant. "Oops, sorry, Doctor," I said. "That's the Space Transportation System."

"Thank goodness," he said, "because in my business STS is well known as the Serological Test for Syphilis" (see Figure 12-1). (I've often wondered whether General Motors was aware of that when they picked the name for one of their models surely targeted to doctors— the Cadillac STS.)

Fortunately, many presentations are interactive, so befuddled listeners have the option of asking for clarification. Listeners may do that, under some conditions, but many won't, for a variety of reasons.

Figure 12-1. Are you sure your audience is following you?

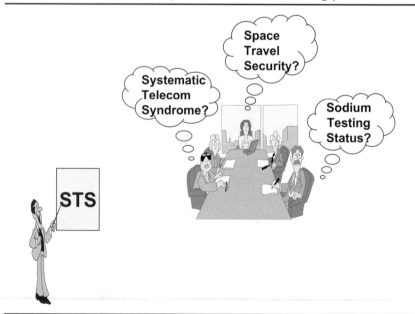

A risk is often associated with asking questions in general, but in particular of the type: "Maybe I'm stupid, but what does that mean?"

Here are some tips for making your language understandable:

◆ *Be careful with acronyms and abbreviations.* These do speed up communication if all parties know what the terms mean and if they understand them to mean the same things. Explain in full any acronym or abbreviation the first time it is used, unless you are certain the audience knows the term.

◆ *Speak a language the audience can understand.* Watch the jargon, trade lingo, and slang. For a guideline, consider how you would speak to be understood if your audience were the senior class from your local high school.

◆ *Explain ambiguous terms.* Check to see if mutual understanding exists. Words and expressions do not necessarily mean the same to all people. The word "contract," for example, comes in different forms, and when a speaker says, "We have a cost-plus contract," she may mean cost-plus-fixed-fee. A listener with a different frame of reference may interpret the comment to mean cost-plus-incentive-fee, which is definitely not the same. Many people are vague about commonly used words, such as productivity, cash flow, disintermediation, hegemony, or robustness.

◆ *Avoid foggy phraseology.* "I want ten delivered on the eighteenth." What he wanted were ten pieces delivered on March 18. What he got was ten dozen delivered on April 18. (Or did they go to the eighteenth green?)

◆ *Be specific.* Does "next to" mean east or west of? Is "several" three, five, or fifteen? Does "50K" mean $50,000 or 50 kilometers? As a kid out on the farm, my uncle Ralph loved to tease us with his requests to go get something. We'd bite and ask where? His standard answer "Over yonder" was never much help.

◆ *Distinguish assumptions from observations, probabilities from certainties, theory from established fact.* "Flight failure was due to a pyrotechnic malfunction, caused by a faulty part received from the vendor." You may be certain about the malfunction but guessing about the cause. Not making that clear could cause problems immediately or later.

◆ *Clear up loose sentence connections.* Fix improper antecedents, dangling participles, and disjointed clauses. Here's a sample from an introduction: "Being a corporate executive and a prominent community leader as well, one might assume Miss Wilson can present us with a unique insight."

◆ *Avoid scrambled metaphors.* Said the harried congressman, "We've got to stop milking that dead horse!" Metaphors and other figures of speech add color and insight to expression; they can also add confusion. Make sure yours are correct and clear.

◆ *Fight obfuscation.* Gobbledygook or bafflegab means using large words, euphemisms, or indirect and lengthy phrases. This technique is often intended to impress or dodge rather than to communicate. Some examples:

Energetic disassembly	Nuclear explosion?
Reduction in force	Layoff?
Correspondence review clerk	Mail sorter?
Vertical transportation facilitator	Elevator operator?

Effective Language Is Nondistracting

"Uh, y'know, this stuff about, y'know, how you . . . uh . . . sound seems . . . uh' a bit, y'know, overdone, like y' know what I'm saying?" Not only choice of words but the way we say them can seriously affect a presentation. Effective language does not distract listeners away from the message or cause them to make negative judgments (Figure 12-2).

The "uh, y'know" problems are especially distracting. I counted them for one speaker and quit at forty-five "uhs" after only three minutes. When asked for his own estimate of the number, the speaker guessed three to four. The Toastmasters have excellent success at eliminating "uhs" quickly. They ring a bell or make some other obvious noise at every "uh," and it takes only a few short speeches for this problem to fade.

Rough delivery—excessive pauses, stops and starts, fragmentary sentences, uncertainties, and fillers—all add up to a poor impression.

Poor grammar, mispronunciations, and word misuse will be in-

Figure 12-2. Language fillers and errors focus attention the wrong way.

stantly noted by astute listeners. When national politicians refer in their speeches to "newcewlar weapons," many listeners cringe. I have heard speakers in the energy business make that same error. In a poll by *Public Eye Magazine*, mispronunciation of the word "nuclear" was voted the worst crime against the English language by most readers.[4]

Language misuse has stymied advancement for several bright businesspeople, and often they don't even know the reason, as others may avoid telling them. A common comment about such speakers: "Isn't it a shame? If it weren't for his language . . ." (and not referring to profanity).

Here are some tips to reduce language distractions:

◆ Read aloud often to improve fluency, reduce faulty grammar, and sharpen lazy language.

◆ Listen to yourself as you read aloud or give presentations by using an audio or video recorder. Compare yourself to good speakers in your area, such as the top local newscasters.

- Learn a foreign language. This helps clear up subject/verb mismatches and double negatives.

- Have a knowledgeable friend or speaking coach listen to the way you use language in formal and informal situations, looking for errors in pronunciation, grammar, and word use. Have them try the Toastmaster technique of ringing a bell when "uhs", "y'knows," or other distractions occur (in practice settings only, of course).

- Watch overuse of one word, such as "okay," "basically," or "next slide please."

Grammar Flaws

Double negatives	"I didn't never say that."
Subject/verb mismatches	"We wasn't told. Who done it?"
Nonstandard contractions	"ain't," "warn't," 'his'n."
Confused tenses	"He drunk his coffee already."
Confused pronouns	"With who am I speaking?"
Adjective/adverb confusion	"She spoke good."
Verb confusion	"I'll learn you.

Pronunciation Flaws

Extra consonant	"staStistics," "colYumn"
Extra vowel	"athAlete," "grievious"
Confused letters	"substantUate," "eKcetera"
Lazy or colloquial term	"bidness"
Misplaced emphasis	"DIrect your attention"
Vowel mispronunciation	"Aaa-rab," "Eyetalian," "theAter"
Erroneously sounded silent letter	"poiGnant," "suBtle"
Erroneous consonant sound	"gesture" (with hard g)
Foreign terms	"coop day grass"

Selection or Usage Confusion

Confused words	"irreverant data, "effluent society," "jet entrails"
Nonexistent words	"irregardless"
Singular/plural confusion	"the first criteria," "a rare phenomena"

Mannerisms

Informal slang	"yeah," "ya," "yep," "nope," "uh huh," "huh?"
Overused expressions	"for sure," "fantastic," "wow," "dude," "hey," "Not!"
Insidious fillers	"like," "y'know," "I mean," "uh," "okay"
Runtogethers	"gonna," "woncha," "hadda."

Effective Language Is Forceful

The great speakers, the ones to whom we listen and by whom we are moved, almost always use language well. Susan B. Anthony, Winston Churchill, John F. Kennedy, and Martin Luther King were acclaimed as outstanding speakers because their ideas met the needs of their times and their messages were spoken in words and phrasing that were stirring and memorable. Their speeches are often quoted.

The business conference room is not the same as the political platform, yet the speakers discussing lasers or cash flows who are effective generally have the ability to use the language well. Conversely, the speakers who bore us or leave us unimpressed often do so, in large part, because of bland or murky language, such as "At this point in time, and commensurate with the mitigating circumstances with which we now find ourselves, it seems advisable to shift to a different paradigm and interface with the really good liquid refreshments made available to us, that, I am assured by the cognizant personnel, are not too shabby." [Or, if you prefer, "Let's take a coffee break."]

Here are some ways to turn drab language into forceful, colorful expression that is more likely to be listened to, understood, and re-called.

◆ *Start with a subject you are excited about and want to com-municate.* Sparkling language will rarely be present if conviction is absent.

◆ *Avoid clichés like the plague,* such as:
  ◆ "Not too shabby."
  ◆ "This whole subject blows my mind."
  ◆ "We've got to get our act together, bite the bullet, pull out all the stops, get with the program, Charlie, and win one for the Gipper."

◆ *Minimize use of "in" terminology (vogue words).* When "bid-ness" people verbalize, it seems imperative that they legitimize their words, messagewise, by optimizing the application of current buzz words, lexiconwise. Thus, they facilitate instead of build, strategize instead of plan, or grow peoplewise instead of add jobs.

◆ *Delete and cut out unnecessary redundancies.* Cut out words or expressions that add nothing to the meaning:

"Full to capacity."	How about just "full"?
"At this point in time."	Now.
"Obviously."	Not to me. And if it is, why say it?
"Consensus of opinion."	Is there any other form of consensus?
"A somewhat unique proposal."	It's either unique or it isn't.

◆ *Don't use qualifiers very much, hopefully:* "Real good . . . pretty complicated system . . . quite sophisticated."

◆ *Use the simple word rather than the pretentious.*

utilize	or	use
terminate	or	end
fabricate	or	make
paradigm	or	model

◆ *Make use of verbs in their simplest forms.*

"render inoperative"	"shut off"
"take into consideration"	"consider"
"exhibits a tendency"	"tends to"
"make use of"	"use" (but you spotted that already, right?)

◆ *Use active over passive tense.*

"Inflation is increased by oil imports."	"Oil imports increase inflation."
"Programs were reviewed by Jan."	"Jan reviewed programs."

◆ *Choose words that stir the senses.* These are words with bite, color, pungency, flavor, and snap. One of the best ways to get people to listen intently is to use language that stimulates their active mental or sensory participation. Three ways help do this.

1. *Replace abstract with explicit.* The more specific the example, the clearer the concept becomes and the more strongly listeners identify with it, assuming they are familiar with the specific example. Adding detail increases the association. Which is more distinctive?

An automobile	A 1936 silver Dusenberg
Injuries	Punctured eyeballs
Drugs	Crack, speed, ecstacy

2. *Choose the vivid over the bland.* Which has more spark and accuracy?

Move	Shake, tingle, quiver, slink, dash
Speak	Hiss, bellow, drawl
Good	Splendid, savory, impeccable

3. *Choose the imaginative over the commonplace.* Speakers who use metaphors and other figures of speech, colorful expressions, and unusual word arrangements well have powerful tools at their command, as these examples show:

◆ From Martin Luther King's "I have a dream" speech in 1963: "America has given the Negro people a bad check—a check that has come back marked 'insufficient funds.'"

◆ A corporate lawyer, referring to two corporations trying to do business with each other while suing each other: "There's an old saying in the legal profession: thou shalt not litigate by day, and copulate by night."

◆ Because of funding cuts, personnel at Goddard Space Flight Center were hard pressed to keep their programs alive. One director said: "We have one foot over the cliff, the other on a banana peel."[5]

◆ *Let phrasing be dramatic and varied.* Good speakers use clever phrasing, short sentences, dramatic single words, repeated themes, and occasional rhetorical and hypothetical questions to invoke a more active listening process. For example:

◆ John F. Kennedy's 1963 inaugural speech: "Ask not what your country can do for you; ask what you can do for your country."

◆ Sojourner Truth, born a slave, speaking out for all women's rights: "That man over there says that women need to be helped into carriages and lifted over ditches. . . . Nobody ever helps me into carriages, or over mud puddles. . . . And ain't I a woman? Look at me! Look at my arm. I have plowed and planted and gathered into barns, and no man could head me. And ain't I a woman?"[6] (The power of the repeated theme is well-demonstrated by speeches of Mark Antony, Martin Luther King, and many politicians at national conventions.)

◆ Winston Churchill: "I say to the House as I said to ministers who have joined this government, I have nothing to offer but blood, toil, tears, and sweat."[7]

Transmission of Language: The Voice

A good speaking voice is a valuable asset. The vocal deliveries of Oprah Winfrey, Billy Graham, and Paul Harvey make them commanding speakers. "This is CNN," and *Star Wars'* Darth Vader were made memorable by the voice of James Earl Jones.

We have all heard speakers we dislike or distrust, as much because of the way they sound as what they say: the aggressive telemarketer, arrogant bureaucrat, or shifty personnel manager.

Psychologist Albert Mehrabian has shown that we are five times as likely to be influenced by the vocal tone than by the spoken words in developing our feelings and attitudes toward a speaker.[8] Thus both intuition and research indicate the wisdom of developing our ability to use our voices well.

We'll focus on five important attributes for a positive vocal impression (as summarized in Figure 12-3):

1. Quality

Audiences generally have a negative reaction to presenters whose voices are squeaky, harsh, shrill, gushy, guttural, raspy, or weak. A "good" voice either will not be noticed at all or may be acknowledged as pleasing, powerful, or rich. The "poor" voice may or may not be immediately evident to the listener as amusing, irritating, or even painful.

The voice can also be a reliable index of character, according to Lyle Mayer.[9] An unpleasant voice can itself be distracting and lead listeners to form negative judgments, consciously or unconsciously. It behooves a presenter to become aware of and work on vocal characteristics that may be hampering the effectiveness of his or her presentations.

To improve or maintain good vocal quality:

◆ *Don't smoke.* This is at the top of the list of every voice expert. In coaching many speakers I've found two common characteristics of those with harsh voices: they smoke and they rarely sing.

◆ *Drink moderately, if at all.* Alcohol dries out the vocal cords.

◆ *Tone down the screaming.* How many hoarse throats or cases of laryngitis have you witnessed the day after the big game?

◆ *Heed the danger signals; don't overdo it.* If you've been speaking for a long time and you sense your voice is giving out, let it rest. If possible, let a colleague continue the presentation.

Figure 12-3. Tuning up your voice can bring big rewards.

Characteristic	Most Common Problems	Tune-Ups

Quality	Thin
	Tired
	Rough, whiny,
	  irritating
		Don't smoke. Avoid
		  alcohol.
		Check posture and
		  breathing.
		Watch coffee effects.
		Sing often.
		Check attitude. Get
		  upbeat.

Projection	Deficient Spotty Tail-off	Practice better breathing. Talk to person in back. Talk to all. Carry through phrases.

Variety/inflection	Monotone, droning
	Low energy
		Don't read—talk.
		Emphasize key words.
		Change pace. Pause.
		  Repeat.
		Vary language patterns.
		Read poetry aloud
		  often.

Clarity	Poor diction Heavy accents Rapid pace	Read aloud often. Try tongue twisters. Read poetry. Get voice coaching.

Fluency/smoothness	Distractions,
	  mannerisms (ums,
	  okays, throat
	  clearing)
	Jerky patterns
		Be aware &
		  determined.
		Practice, get feedback.
		Use audio, video.
		Read aloud.

◆ *Be kind to your voice—plan ahead.* If you're scheduled to lead a tour of fifty members of the local chamber of commerce through the factory, during working hours, get a portable public address system. It beats shouting and not being heard even then.

◆ *Avoid excessive clearing of the throat.* This can damage the vocal cords. A gentle cough or drinking liquids may alleviate the catch with less potential damage. If you need to clear your throat frequently, see a doctor.

◆ *Lubricate if needed.* A sip of water can help alleviate the dry mouth problem that nervous speakers often have; take a cup to the lectern or the table. Hot tea with lemon and honey is a favorite of many professional singers and broadcasters.

◆ *Work on correct posture.* A major contributor to poor vocal quality and power is poor posture. Proper alignment allows vocal mechanisms to operate properly. Poor alignment leads to straining, poor quality, and damage.

◆ *Improve breath management.* Good sound production must begin with a good air source. Voice experts recommend abdominal or lower-chest breathing over extreme upper-chest and shoulder breathing. The latter is what many people do when told, "Now take a deep breath." Such upper-chest breathing does not provide a deep breath, gives little power for voice production or air management, and may be accompanied by throat tension and poor voice quality. Keep resupplying the air. Particularly nervous presenters often have difficulty breathing as they speak. Panting, gasping, and frequent swallowing are the signs (along with a general appearance of wanting to be anywhere else). Rather than wait until your air is exhausted and you gasp desperately to replenish it, keep breathing in little bits as you speak. Try these exercises:

• Stand in a good posture with your hand over your abdomen. Breathe normally. Then, with an adequate air supply, exhale slowly and evenly while making a hissing sound. Your hand should feel the air slowly being pushed out. Exhale completely. Then let the air pop into the lungs. Your hand should feel that happen. Repeat two more times.

• Lie on your back with your head supported. Place several books on your stomach. Raise the books by inhaling; let the weight cause you to exhale slowly. This develops breathing capability and coordination.

• Purse your lips and very lightly exhale, being totally conscious of the long, steady exhalation. Time how long you can do this. You may be able to double your capability with practice.

◆ *Sing often.* "[Singing is] the best method in my experience to develop the voice per se," said NBC broadcaster Paul Taylor.[10] In addition to singing in the well-known shower venue, get a CD of songs you can actually sing along with, and belt them out while you drive.

◆ *Yawn-sigh.* Imagine it is the end of a full and perfect day. All is well with the world, and now you're satisfyingly tired. You yawn a long "ha-h-h-h-h," starting with a high note and descending to a low one. Make it a clear, light tone, and glide down most of your vocal range. This develops freedom from tension in the larynx and coordination of the breath and sound elements. The yawn-sigh can also be used to warm up the voice or anytime the voice tends to tighten up.

◆ *Use muscle stretchers.* They increase flexibility, extend range, reduce tight-ness in the muscles concerned, and lessen the tendency to induce tension in other parts: (1) Flap your lips as a horse blowing, (2) vocalize "ooo-whyeee" as you move your lips to extreme positions, (3) say bu-bu-bu, and (4) open your mouth slightly and hum while shaking your jaw from side to side.

2. Projection

Requests for Proposals (RFPs) often state that speakers will not be interrupted unless they cannot be heard. In meetings when members are asked to stand up and introduce themselves, clearly a marketing opportunity, generally one out of three cannot be heard clearly. At major conferences it's common for segments of the audience to be left out due to poor projection.

If you're speaking, wouldn't it be useful for everyone to hear the presentation you've so carefully crafted? To make sure consider the following factors:

◆ *Become aware.* Generally, the low-volume speakers are surprised when told they are not speaking loudly enough. "Really? I thought I was shouting," is a standard reply. Project to the farthest person in the room.

◆ *Talk to the audience, not the screen, windows, or computer.* When using graphics, direct audience to a screen topic, then turn and talk.

◆ *Talk so all can hear, not just a selected member, such as the big boss or pal.* A common mistake is when, in response to a question, the speaker directs comments only to the questioner. As a result the other audience members cannot hear and may get highly aggravated. For example, at one large conference, several panelists seated off to the side kept directing their comments to audience members near them, while the rest of the audience could not hear them.

◆ *Watch tail-off.* A very common problem. Many speakers let their sentences fade at the ends of sentences, so audiences miss those parts. Others fail to emphasize key words; these may be heard but not absorbed as significant.

◆ *Repeat questions so others can hear it.* How often do you attend an interactive session where the shouted statement "PLEASE REPEAT THE QUESTION!" is heard repeatedly.

◆ *Use a microphone correctly.* This is one of the most common failures in large conferences. Watch turning away from a fixed mic; it's better to use a lavaliere or clip-on mic. Test ahead so you know where to place it for adequate projection.

3. Variety/Inflection

Presenters may project and be speaking clearly, yet wonder why people don't listen to them. The audiences fall asleep, their eyeballs glaze over, or they keep asking dumb questions, indicating that the clearly delivered message isn't getting through. One of the most common reasons for these results is poor expressiveness.

Attention, impact, and credibility are affected by how the speaker applies pitch, pace, and volume. Say aloud, "Of the people, by the people, for the people" in a monotone and see how little sense it makes.

It is fascinating to watch dull speakers view themselves for the first time on video playback. Often they can't stand to watch themselves. As one speaker commented, "Oh, that's so boring! I'm putting myself to sleep." The ultimate evaluation.

"We are the best contractor to build your new facility for three reasons: Our design is better, our technology is sound, and our production capability is proven." Would you give the business to the presenter who delivered this message in a monotone?

Speakers with strong convictions rarely lack vocal expressiveness. Listen to Tom Peters speak about excellence and you will hear an expressive speaker. The vocal expressiveness of poets Carl Sandburg and Maya Angelou add greatly to their power.

On the other hand, there's the often-imitated voice of monotonic Henry Kissinger, showing that even boring speakers can achieve success. Television host/actor Ben Stein's deliberately drab vocal style has brought him many a paycheck.

Here are some tips to expand vocal variety and expressiveness.

◆ *Start with you.* If you never show your emotions, are always in tight control, or rarely get excited, you may find it hard to become expressive before a group. Many people lack expressiveness because they are watchers, not participants; they aren't informed enough to talk intelligently about pertinent topics; or even when they are they rarely speak up. They become cautious, uninvolved, dull. Why should they be any different in speaking before a group? Get into some lively discussions with informed people. Take some positions and defend them. Write letters to the editor or your congressional representative.

◆ *Look at your material.* If the topics you've been choosing don't inspire you, select ones that do. Are your visual aids all word charts? Is your support or illustrative material mostly dry statistics? Are you using notes that resemble the morning newspaper? These are all common characteristics of low-key, lackluster speakers. The material you use can take you to its level, up or down.

◆ *Emphasize important words or phrases with varying stress, volume, or pace.* Increased volume on word groups or expressions places significance on them ("Cost credibility," or "We must bid this contract now!"). Softening of words occurs naturally and to good effect in the end of this expression: "That is our greatest strength; it is our competitor's major deficiency." With graphics, especially bullet charts, do not read each word, a major irritant, but select a key word or phrase.

◆ *Watch tentative patterns.* It is common for the speaker to state a series of topics, with vocal inflection rising at the end of each topic. Speaking it with a downward ending adds variety and a firmer emphasis.

◆ *Vary your pace.* Pick it up for mundane material, slow it down for more important topics.

◆ *Repeat key words.* Listen to the "Music Man" describe trouble in River City.

◆ *Change sentence phrasing from only declarative.* Throw in some rhetorical questions: "Have you ever had this problem?" or "And what was our solution?" Or use some actual questions intended for response topics.

◆ *Apply pause power.* Mark Twain was a famed lecturer as well as a writer. He knew well the power of the pause: "That impressive silence, that eloquent silence, that geometrically progressive silence which often achieves a desired effect where no combination of words howsoever felicitous could accomplish it."[11]

◆ *Stretch that vocal system.* The following suggestions should help:

1. Sing often, in the shower, in the car, at work around the house.

2. Speak aloud the ABCs or count to 100. Vary pitch, volume, and rate. Whisper, shout, race, slow to a crawl, speak in sonorous tones.

3. Read magazine or newspaper advertisements. Imagine you are on television delivering a commercial for your favorite product.

4. Obtain an anthology of great speeches and read aloud the words of Patrick Henry, Winston Churchill, Martin Luther King, and contemporary speakers.

5. Read aloud to your children or to yourself. Choose material with high emotional content and ham it up. Voice authorities rate poetry reading as one of the most worthwhile exercises. Read bedtime stories, the poems of Dr. Seuss or Shel Silverstein, or story poems, such as *The Shooting of Dangerous Dan McGrew* by Robert Service, or *Casey at the Bat* by Ernest Lawrence Thayer.

Casey at the Bat
It looked extremely rocky for the Mudville nine that day;
The score stood two to four, with but one inning left to play.
So, when Cooney died at second, and Burrows did the same.
A pallor wreathed the features of the patrons of the game.

A straggling few got up to go, leaving there the rest,

With that hope which springs eternal within the human breast.
For they thought: "If only Casey could get a whack at that,"
They'd put even money now, with Casey at the bat.

But Flynn preceded Casey, and likewise so did Blake,
And the former was a pudd'n and the latter was a fake.
So on that stricken multitude a deathlike silence sat;
For there seemed but little chance of Casey's getting to the bat.

But Flynn let drive a single, to the wonderment of all.
And the much-despised Blakey "tore the cover off the ball."
And when the dust had lifted, and they saw what had occurred,
There was Blakey safe at second, and Flynn a' huggin' third.

Then from the gladdened multitude went up a joyous yell—
It rumbled in the mountaintops, it rattled in the dell;
It struck upon the hillside and rebounded on the flat;
For Casey, mighty Casey, was advancing to the bat.

There was ease in Casey's manner as he stepped into his place.
There was pride in Casey's bearing and a smile on Casey's face;
And when responding to the cheers he lightly doffed his hat,
No stranger in the crowd could doubt 'twas Casey at the bat.

Ten thousand eyes were on him as he rubbed his hands with dirt,
Five thousand tongues applauded when he wiped them on his
      shirt;
Then when the writhing pitcher ground the ball into his hip,
Defiance glanced in Casey's eye, a sneer curled Casey's lip.

And now the leather-covered sphere came hurtling through the
      air,
And Casey stood a-watching it in haughty grandeur there.
Close by the sturdy batsman the ball unheeded sped;
"That ain't my style," said Casey. "Strike one," the umpire said.

From the benches, black with people, there went up a muffled
      roar,
Like the beating of the storm waves on the stern and distant
      shore.

"Kill him! kill the umpire!" shouted someone in the stand;
And it's likely they'd have killed him had not Casey raised his
    hand.

With a smile of Christian charity great Casey's visage shone,
He stilled the rising tumult, he made the game go on;
He signaled to the pitcher, and once more the spheroid flew;
But Casey still ignored it, and the umpire said, "Strike two."

"Fraud!" cried the maddened thousands, and the echo
    answered "Fraud!"
But one scornful look from Casey and the audience was awed;
They saw his face grow stern and cold, they saw his muscles
    strain,
And they knew that Casey wouldn't let the ball go by again.

The sneer is gone from Casey's lips, his teeth are clenched in
    hate,
He pounds with cruel vengeance his bat upon the plate;
And now the pitcher holds the ball, and now he lets it go,
And now the air is shattered by the force of Casey's blow.

Oh, somewhere in this favored land the sun is shining bright,
The band is playing somewhere, and somewhere hearts are light;
And somewhere men are laughing, and somewhere children
    shout,
But there is no joy in Mudville—mighty Casey has struck out.

4. Clarity

Many speakers talk loudly enough, but their message fails to get across because they are hard to understand. "Wadizzitchurtrynagit ucross? Thas th'prolemwitmosofyou expurts, youspeckmirculs." Some speak so fast people can't absorb the information.

    It is a rare speaker who cannot stand some degree of improvement in making speech more understandable. Lyle Mayer cites a survey that found that more than one-third of speakers talk so indistinctly that they are in need of special help. He adds: "Of all the problems involved with voice and speech, poor articulation is the most common."[12]

How does a speaker know if he or she is hard to understand? Few people are unintelligible on purpose. Recording your voice in a speaking situation and listening to it may help. Most people, unfortunately, do not listen to their own voices critically, according to Hilda Fisher in her book *Improving Voice and Articulation*. Yet, she says, "auditory feedback is of prime importance in changing speech habits." She recommends listening extensively to other speakers, identifying what distinguishes good voices from bad, and comparing your own criticisms with those of experts so as to "awaken your hearing."[13]

You can also ask for an evaluation by people in your business whom you recognize for their presentation skill. Your chums may lack objectivity: "Ya soun fine—you tawk jist like us."

Some regional accents can be detrimental to speakers. New Yawkers and good ole boys from the South have often found their accents to be professional liabilities outside their native areas. Accents that come across as affectations, such as Hahvad accents, can also alienate some listeners. Heavy "street" vocal styles can hugely hamper speakers' job opportunities.

Having an accent can sometimes be an advantage rather than a detriment. Would you change the accents of Sean Connery? Zsa Zsa Gabor? Antonio Banderas? Nelson Mandela? Speech expert Gloria Goforth advises: "If a musical lilt or charming brogue *adds* to the positive atmosphere of the conversation, keep it. If your accent *hampers* communication because listeners can't understand your words or develop adverse impressions due to associations your accent creates, run and get help from your nearest speech coach. Don't let an easily correctable speech problem keep your true capability from showing."[14]

To improve clarity, here are some tips:

◆ *Listen to your audiences.* Do they frequently ask you to repeat something you just said, perhaps to the point of becoming irritating to you? (What do you think it is to *them*?) The acid test is to speak to someone with a limited knowledge of English. If that person can understand your peers but not you, that's a strong sign your understandability is low.

◆ *Read aloud often.* Take advantage of opportunities to practice sharpness in speaking aloud. An easy way is to speak the names of freeway exits or advertising slogans as you drive. To practice sharpening your diction, lower your voice to a bare whisper. To be understood at a distance, you will need to speak more precisely.

 Do vocal diction exercises. To work on consonants, read this aloud:

> Amidst the mists and coldest frosts,
> With barest wrists and stoutest boasts
> He thrusts his fists against the posts
> And still insists he sees the ghosts.

Or pronounce clearly:

Lecture, humanist, important, restrict, productive, facts, explicit, right, correct, most, just, had to, next week.

 Try tongue twisters. They can help improve fluency, and they're fun.

Peter Piper picked a peck of pickled peppers.

Betty Botter bought a bit of better butter, but she said this butter's bitter.

Theopholis Thistle, the thistle sifter, sifted a sieve of unsifted thistles.

A box of biscuits, a box of mixed biscuits, a biscuit mixer.

The seething sea ceaseth seething.

 Work on simple, yet tricky phrases. Say "toy boat" rapidly ten times. If you make it past two or three times, you're unusual. Mastered that one? Try "Peggy Babcock." (Say it ten times rapidly.)

5. Fluency/Smoothness

Recognize any of these?

      The stumbler, who says "Well . . . um . . Er . . We . . y'know . . . need to really, like, get moving . . . uh, y'know . . . uh . . ." These resemble the last words of an actor in the dying scene.

Which is close to what the speakers are doing (not in a literal sense).

◆ *The drawler,* who speaks so-o-o de-lib-er-ate-ly that audiences want to use a cattle prod on the speaker.

◆ *The syncopator,* who speaks five words, pauses, speaks five words, pauses . . . This one quickly drives audiences out of the room.

◆ *The agitator,* whose vocal style includes a lot of hesitations, throat clearing, nervous coughing, and false starts and stops. Audiences start getting twitchy themselves, and reaching for the gong.

These are all examples of how sharp people damage their effectiveness by creating their own serious distractions, to which they are generally oblivious.

Here are two diction and fluency exercises. Read them aloud until you can speak them crisply and smoothly.

1. The first exercise features commonly difficult vocal sounds. Read it aloud slowly to pronounce distinctly each sound, then gradually pick up the pace, making sure you don't slur the words.

> A percolating, perambulating parakeet
> Eyed a beer-battered halibut bit.
> A rubbernecking, redundant rodent
> Started a statistically-supported scheme
> To connect, direct, select, and protect
> Their hundred business pursuits.
> Despite fictitious fractional fluctuations
> The perennially populist pipsqueaks
> Began fixing, matriculating, and speculating,
> Then thinking, thanking, and thoroughly mirthful
> Their valiant victory was verified.

2. This second exercise is a challenge even for native English speakers (except Hawaiians). All the words are real places in and around Honolulu. *Tip*: Pronounce each syllable and you'll get there.

On the Road in Oahu
By Tom Leech

Head out from Honolulu, along Likelike Circle.
Look up to Puu Kanehoalani, around on Kamekameha.

Look for menehunes at Puuomahuka, and big kahunas
Gazing toward Healeakala and Kialakahua.

Pass the famous beaches of Kahanamaku, Makapu'u
And Nahonani. Come back onto Liliuahulani.

Shop at Ala Moana, pay homage to Duke Kamahameha.
Relax at Kahaloa and you're back in Waikiki.

In Summary: Winning Presenters Need the Whole Package: Content and Delivery

Remember these key points:

◆ *Language.* In striving for splendor, use language that is directive, appropriate, clear, distraction-free, and forceful.
◆ *Voice.* For many presenters, the voice is a barely tapped resource. Improving your vocal techniques can have a dramatic impact on your presentation's effectiveness.

As Ralph Waldo Emerson said, "I learn immediately from any speaker how much he has already lived through the poverty or splendor of his speech."

CHAPTER 13

Interact

Successfully Managing Q&A

S uccess at Questions and Answers (Q&A) takes special effort, preparation, and on-the-spot skill—all often lightly considered. Audience questions can throw speakers off course and damage presentations irreparably, or they can be the speaker's best friend and become the key factor in success (Figure 13-1). According to Denny Krenz, who headed many review boards for Department of

Figure 13-1. Q&A is standard for most presentations.

Energy proposals: "If you're an expert on finance, then be ready to answer questions on that specialty. The board will pulse you with questions to see if you know your subject. If not, you're in trouble. Once you blow your credibility, it doesn't matter what you say."[1]

How important is the ability to handle the Q&A? Here are some highly-publicized examples of significant Q&A:

- ◆ During the 1988 Presidential debates, candidate Michael Dukakis was asked what he would do in the event of a family member being attacked. His logical but tepid response was widely noted as an indicator of lack of passion and cost him votes.

- ◆ During the 1984 campaign a serious issue was raised about President Reagan's age. His team had prepared him well for the answer when challenged by candidate Walter Mondale, and his strong response eliminated his age as a campaign issue. (When Reagan came down with Alzheimer's disease, the issue surfaced again about his capability in the later years of his Presidency.)

- ◆ In the 1976 Presidential campaign debates, the incumbent Gerald Ford was asked about the status of Iron Curtain countries, such as Poland. Ford's response that these countries were not under the aegis of the Soviet Union was regarded as a huge fluff.

A contractor team was bidding on a major construction contract. During the final interview, an audience member asked a question about the team's specific commitment to a specific activity. The responsible team member waffled. The questioner asked again, and again more indecision. With that single question, poorly answered, the team's program director believes they lost that contract.

Another person was having a poor time with the presentation. He was clearly uncomfortable speaking, especially to a high-level audience. His hands were shaking, his voice quavering, and his words coming out hesitantly. Then his boss asked him a question. The presenter paused a moment while he collected his thoughts and then answered the question well. This gentle nudging shifted him from being clearly uncomfortable to a more relaxed style.

Here are some techniques for achieving productive Q&A (as summarized in Figure 13-2).

First, Understand the Critical Role Q&A Can Play and Commit to Doing it Well

According to Kevin Werner of SAIC Venture Capital Corporation, "The best interchanges are when we can just sit across the table and converse. I don't especially care about a presenter's dress or accent. The biggest need is to be open and receptive to questions."[2]

In coaching executives and teams, a major challenge is getting them to even commit to preparing for Q&A as well as the formal presentations. Presenters will spend hours getting the right graphic layout and the precise language, yet ignore what is likely to be far more important: How to work with the audience in the interactive part. I've long included Q&A in training seminars, and most people come up short on what makes for good or poor responses.

When the team commits to Q&A preparation, the first rehearsal is almost always poor. Shaky answers, fumbling teamwork, defensive or challenging body language are among the standard results. Video

Figure 13-2. Apply these keys for a productive Q&A session.

◆ Assume audience input is something to look forward to, not dread.

◆ Have solid content, clear organization, solid reinforcement, good graphics.

◆ Do your homework. Be prepared for questions that are likely to come up.

◆ Practice Q&A as well as the formal presentation.

◆ Be ready with backup data or graphics.

◆ Make the room layout conducive to dialogue, not intimidating.

◆ Set Q&A procedures at the start.

◆ If warranted, repeat all questions or comments so all can hear.

◆ Go to a specific visual under discussion.

◆ Listen carefully and think before responding.

◆ Answer all questions courteously and accurately, without sarcasm or dodging.

◆ Watch that your nonverbal communication doesn't conflict with your spoken presentation.

◆ If you don't know the answer, say so and commit to provide the answer later.

feedback is a powerful nudger toward taking this seriously, followed by advance training about the process, a critique of the Q&A session, another Q&A practice session.

Now, Do Your Homework

At a corporation's quarterly review, the general manager from one division began his planned one-hour presentation. He put the first graphic on the screen, and one hour later it was still there as the presentation had immediately switched to an intensive dialogue mode. Could this have been averted, perhaps with better pre-meeting activity? For many presentations, effective advance preparation is a key factor in achieving productive Q&A.

Planning

Understand the rules: Be aware of any time constraints. Are questions expected throughout or is there a separate Q&A period? Will questions be supplied in advance? For example, in a competitive procurement situation, all questions supplied in advance must be addressed or your bid may be deemed nonresponsive.

Many Q&A problems arise because audience analysis and approach are faulty. The speaker may be using unfamiliar terminology or assuming background that isn't there.

Organization

Many questions in the irritant, low-value class can be averted by the simple expedient of an agenda chart, a clearly-stated purpose, periodic summaries, and strong transitions. Tighten your organization, and prune out anything not directly contributing toward the main objective. Allocate time for Q&A, depending on the likely dialogue mode. For a thirty-minute presentation, save five to ten minutes for potential Q&A, either during or after the presentation.

Support

Have solid substantiation ready to back up your claims; data should be current, complete, and accurate. The design and content of visual aids are major factors in expediting or disrupting the presentation flow.

◆ *KISS your graphics.* (Keep It Simple, Sam.) Busy charts invite nitpicking, as has been demonstrated in many conference rooms, to the dismay of speakers who find themselves having to address minor topics in great detail. They created their own disruption. Simple, readable charts with clear messages will do much to calm the potentially troubled waters.

◆ *Put numbers on all your charts.* It's easier for both audience and presenter to go back to chart #12 rather than to "that chart about logistics."

◆ *Be ready with backup charts.* Backup charts are often called Just-In-Case (JIC) charts. When a question hits, it's impressive to be able to immediately provide a visual that may quickly put the issue to rest and head off a possible ten-minute discussion. Financial executive Brook Byers notes the importance of backup visuals support: "Comes the question and the speaker reaches into the briefcase and has the perfect overhead transparency. Having that shows they've anticipated the question. It can be more impressive than forty or fifty slides."[3]

◆ *Identify questions provided in advance.* Clearly identify each specific question that was provided in advance. Leave no doubt that you have responded to their requests.

Staging

If the audience realizes you are poorly prepared, they might give you the same treatment you are giving them: cavalier. Readiness is taking care of arrangements, having equipment in place, and having all details covered.

Room quality, comfort, and layout can affect the meeting process; a disorderly room invites a disorderly crowd. Where people sit can help or hinder. To facilitate dialogue, reduce barriers between you and audience members. This is often a problem with computer-driven presentations, where speakers may operate from a lectern or even behind a computer. For these presentations, audience contact is improved by wireless remote controllers. Keep room lights up to facilitate face-to-face contact. With current projectors, that's more feasible than with earlier models, which needed a totally dark room.

Include Q&A in your rehearsals, a common deficiency. Develop a list of potential questions (and suitable answers). Simulate the upcoming meeting by having colleagues ask questions and see how well you do. Videotape the Q&A practice session and review it for quality of answers, body language, and teamwork. Learn and repeat.

Clarify the Process

The first few minutes of your presentation are critical. They can do much to set a positive pattern for the presentation:

◆ *Explain your agenda including Q&A.* Let them know what you plan to address and what others will address. This can avert questions not in your knowledge area.

◆ *Capsulize your talk at the start.* High-level listeners particularly value hearing the essence of the talk immediately.

◆ *Agree on procedures.* Often audience members will ask questions at any time, in spite of requests to "Please hold the questions until the end." If you intend to make that request, have a good reason why, other than that you don't want to be bothered. Mutual understanding of the agenda and time will help keep questions from sidetracking the presentation.

Field and Clarify Questions

DOE's Denny Krenz tells of how one team's Q&A performance cost them heavily: "We were reviewing the proposal presentation of a contractor's management team. One member was an arrogant SOB. When our reviewer would pose a question, the guy would challenge it. Our side would ask another question, he'd challenge it. What a turnoff! In our evaluation, he got zero. For God's sake, don't talk down to the board."[4]

◆ *Listen to the entire question.* A common urge is for the presenter to start answering before the questioner completes the question. Often this results in the wrong question being answered and irritation to the questioner.

◆ *Make sure you understand it.* Even if you listen to the total question, you may not understand it the same way the questioner does. Audience members don't necessarily put into words exactly what they mean and often don't clearly know what they want to ask. Some checking and restating may help clarify ambiguities and get at the real question.

◆ *When appropriate, repeat the question.* In large meetings especially, before answering make sure that all can hear. How often in meetings do you hear the irritated shout, "PLEASE REPEAT THE QUESTION!!!" Sometimes it takes three or four of these shouts before the speaker gets the message.

◆ *When using graphics, consider putting that graphic up on the screen.* For computer-based presentations, learn the software method for locating a given visual. If the discussion is not connected to the on-screen image, blank it to eliminate the distraction. With an overhead projector, locate the specific transparency, which is easy if you've (a) numbered each one, and (b) kept old ones in a neat stack for easy recovery.

◆ *Treat each question seriously and respond professionally.* Avoid verbally or nonverbally rebutting with, "Boy, is that a dumb question!" or "I just told you that." It's possible that you may not have communicated as clearly as you thought. Before answering, explore and develop the question so that you understand it. Above all, don't embarrass the questioner.

◆ *Resolve factual errors or misunderstandings quickly.* Often the question arises from incorrectly stated or understood facts.

◆ *Defuse the loaded question.* Audience members have been known to ask no-win or trick questions—the "When did you stop beating your spouse?" type. Questions asked in a way that prevents a fair answer need skilled but decisive treatment. "Is it A or B?" can be expanded to include C and D before answering. Shaky premises should be tactfully challenged. For example, the statement "Since oil companies caused the so-called fuel shortage, why shouldn't they be nationalized?" should not be answered with "What a dumb statement."

◆ *Determine whether you or a colleague should answer.* If the question can be better answered by someone else, direct it to her. Caution: First look at your colleagues to see if they're eager to help or have gone into hiding.

◆ *Give all audience members a chance to ask questions.* As the person in front, you may have control over who asks questions by where you stand and look. Listen for interruption points in a monologue to divert the discussion to another audience member who seems anxious to talk. State that you would like a variety of inputs, to encourage others.

Answer with Tact and Skill

The questions have been sorted out. The next key is how they get answered.

◆ *Talk to the whole audience, not just the questioner.* This is a common mistake. People don't like to be left out. Eye contact is important to maintaining control and not letting side discussions develop. It may also be more important that someone other than the questioner hear the answer to the question.

◆ *Answer positively, without apology.* Saying, "Oh, I'm sorry, I forgot to cover that," is immaterial, time-consuming, and self-deprecating.

◆ *Be careful with humor, sarcasm, criticism, or arrogance.* You can make an enemy for life by making a "witty" answer to the wrong person. Innuendoes about the questioner's motivation or intelligence generally backfire. Even if the questioner's manner is negative, resist the urge to reply in kind. While you may succeed in "putting down" the questioner, you may lose other key people.

◆ *Hold your temper.* Often the intelligence section of the brain gets short-circuited when temper flares. Losing control can act as bait for an audience that doesn't think much of your ideas anyway.

◆ *Let your sense of humor show.* Speakers sometimes lose points by not loosening up and enjoying the humor that often is a part of Q&A. Humor can be an effective vehicle for breaking down barriers between presenter and audience.

◆ *Expand the answer when appropriate.* Elaborating may give the audience time to formulate another question on the same topic. A quick "no" may be the correct answer, but if perceived as abrupt, it may cut off further communication.

◆ *Yet, don't get carried away with your answer.* Mark Twain is reported to have observed about a rambling answer to a straight-forward question, "We just heard a lot more about penguins than we really wanted to know." You may have answered the question with your first statement, then led them into a progressively deeper state of boredom with your next dozen. (At a large conference the keynote speaker bungled the Q&A badly, in one case rambling on for twelve minutes about a question most had never even heard.)

◆ *Don't be afraid to say "I don't know."* You may want to acknowledge that you really should know, or have the right person there who does know. Let the questioner know you will get the answer.

◆ *Don't be afraid to defer some questions.* Depending on the situation, ask to defer a question that requires a lengthy answer or that will take up more time than it's worth. It's often wise to give a capsule version of the answer and then offer to discuss it more fully later.

◆ *Let the audience give you valuable input and support.* They can be a valuable resource, helping you out of sticky spots by providing information or perspectives you may be lacking (and might find valuable). Be careful not to put people on the spot, however.

◆ *Measure feedback and test for the quality of your answer.* How is your answer being received? Is the questioner obviously attempting to interrupt or shaking his head in disagreement? Has the question been answered satisfactorily?

◆ *Maintain perspective.* Keep your eye on the goal and the clock. You want to let the dialogue flow freely but productively: You also want to achieve specific goals with this presentation. Questions that are excessive, of marginal usefulness, or that require detailed answers, can sidetrack from the main goals of the presentation.

Follow Up

Remember those questions you didn't have answers for? And the ones you said you'd get back to the questioner about? Well, don't forget to do it. Quickly. They may be withholding commitment or approval until you take care of the open issues. Coming back with the answers is generally well received.

Facilitate Reluctant Audiences

With some audiences, such as subordinates, getting a question period started is difficult.

◆ *Adopt a positive attitude that shows you truly do welcome questions.* One speaker at the conclusion of his talk folded his arms, raised his chin so he could look down at the audience, turned the corners of his mouth down, and said in a flat tone, "Are there any questions." All aspects of his nonverbal message conflicted with his verbal "invitation." In that situation, listeners generally believe the nonverbal over the verbal (and usually they are right).

◆ *Choose transition statements that encourage feedback:* "We've covered a lot of territory. I'll be pleased to go into detail on any points you choose" works better than "Any questions?" (often accurately interpreted as "There'd better not be").

◆ *Offer an exit opportunity for those who want to leave.* Rank or protocol may deter some from leaving, so your explicit invitation may be well appreciated. This will also let anyone with more urgent business elsewhere leave without disrupting the session.

If they don't ask questions, here are some ways you might stimulate them:

◆ *Suggest potential topics.* "One area we had to skim over was our planned test program. I'll be happy to elaborate on that, if you like."

◆ *Refer to a probable question.* "A question that came up with another group was how many of these systems have we delivered. The answer is forty-two, which includes twenty to other governmental agencies."

◆ *Invite their contributions.* "Something I'm interested in hearing more about is experience any of you have had with this type of program." Ask questions that stimulate contributions without putting people on the spot: "We've suggested this new procedure. Have we overlooked anything?"

◆ *Use humor.* "Let's see. This could mean that my presentation was so outstanding it answered all your questions or else so confusing you don't know where to start."

End the Q&A with a Final Summary

The end of the Q&A can be an important opportunity for you to retake control of the session and drive home once more the key message of the presentation. It lends a professional touch and ends the show on a positive note. Take action to end the talk when the productivity of the Q&A session has waned rather than letting it drag on while participants drift away. If the allotted time is up, call this to the attention of the group and prepare to wrap it up, unless key participants choose to extend the time.

Your summary comments might go like this: "We've run out of time, and I'm pleased that so many of you are interested in further discussion. Let me summarize by saying that our proposal offers the government a low-risk, low-cost alternative that promises a major technical advance toward practical solar energy. Our team is ready to get started."

In Summary: You Will Help Your Cause with Well-Managed Q&A

In many presentations, how well the Q&A is handled can help or hurt your success. Ability to perform well under fire is a definite asset for a presenter.

In a lengthy British libel trial, the fast-food giant McDonald's was battling groups opposed to some of the company's practices. During the trial the head of purchasing was asked why it was environmentally friendly for McDonald's to produce mountains of throwaway packaging. His answer, "Otherwise you'd end up with lots of vast, empty gravel pits all over the country," was reported with glee on the opposition Web site as not especially helpful to the company's case.[5]

CHAPTER 14

Switching Hats

Becoming a Sharper Listener

Presenters put forth considerable effort to help listeners get the message more quickly and better. Yet messages don't get across, interruptions abound, and much time is spent explaining and repeating material. While many of these common presentation characteristics can be attributed to the speaker, many result because most of us are lousy listeners. Few of us are willing to admit it, but we all know plenty of others who are poor listeners: the entire audience for our last presentations.

Studies have shown that as much as 75 percent of presentation content typically is not absorbed by listeners.[1] For presentations using graphics this may differ—better comprehension with good visuals, worse with poor—but the point is that we don't listen so well.

Success and efficiency of a presentation have almost as much to do with the audience as with the speaker. Audiences can set a speaker at ease or be intimidating. They can be facilitative or disruptive, courteous or antagonistic. The results of a presentation are vastly different with positive or negative audience behaviors. Another aspect of listening concerns what we do with whatever little information we've absorbed. I think the evidence is ample to show that too often we don't do anything with it. We don't challenge it, evaluate it, or even think about it. We just accept it. Here's a comment by Leonard A. Stevens in his important book, *The Ill-Spoken Word: The Decline of Speech in America*:

> There is unsettling evidence of speakers and listeners in positions of wealth and power who use the modern techniques of spoken language without regard to the intellectual integrity that "is one of man's necessities" in a democracy. . . . At the same time we suffer an oversupply of poor listeners who do not have the critical sense to demand good speech ethically committed to issues of importance.[2]

A key premise of Stevens' book is that a society that does not concern itself with the proper use of the spoken word is headed for trouble. He offers the example of Hitler, who rose to power in large part by skill in oratory in a country that had limited experience with orators. Since almost all their great leaders and thinkers had communicated through the written word, the German people were unsophisticated in dealing with the spoken word. Hitler recognized and used the power of speech incredibly well and mobilized a speakers' bureau of thousands of party members. Technique, enthusiasm, and careful staging were key elements, not the message that was put forth.

Unfortunately, reasoned speaking and listening have declined since the first printing of this book. Radio talk shows, TV expert panels, and confrontation interviews all seem to be talk competitions: people often talking at the same time with little true dialogue, analysis, and listening to others' viewpoints.

From my experience in many speaking situations, I think that the audiences in most business and technical presentations demand more of presenters than the general public does of public speakers. Top management and government proposal evaluation teams are trained in and charged with analytical thinking. They expect that presenters will be clear about propositions, that their claims will have been thoroughly investigated and backed up, and that they will satisfactorily stand up to penetrating questions.

These requirements are often not expected of, or assumed by, speakers to general audiences. Political candidates, media preachers, and, yes, businesspeople, when communicating with general groups, often get by with messages that would be shot full of holes by the average proposal evaluation team.

In an article entitled "Bafflegab Pays," J. Scott Armstrong, marketing professor at the Wharton School of Business, notes the evidence that we professionals have provided that says we are more impressed with complex communication than we are what is more easily understood. He offers this advice: "If you can't convince them, confuse them."

Armstrong was digging deeper into the celebrated "Dr. Fox" experiment done during the early 1970s, in which groups of learned people passed highly favorable judgment on presentations by a Dr. Fox, a complete phony who pitched made-up data and theories using double-talk, though in the style of the professionals. Professor Armstrong's tests, using written material with management professors, found that competence of sources was rated high if the material was harder to read than if the same material was written in simpler style. We apparently may not understand the complex stuff, but we sure seem to be more impressed by it.[3]

What receivers do has a great effect on the presenter, for better or worse. By constant interruptions or poor listening, they can seriously disrupt the presentation and meeting productivity. As a "coaching" listener, they can greatly aid the quality of presentations and benefit themselves as well (Figure 14-1). Finally, astute listeners can keep speakers straight by ensuring that the information and techniques used meet legitimate standards of fact and ethics.

Figure 14-1. Audience members can help presenters by applying these guidelines for good listening.

- Be prepared for meetings.
- Get there on time and stay there.
- Help keep the environment safe rather than intimidating.
- Truly pay attention to what the speaker is saying.
- Be part of the dialogue, not a stone face.
- Give the speaker a chance; don't constantly interrupt or divert your attention.
- Be a coach, helping rather than intimidating speakers.
- Sharpen and apply critical listening skills to keep from being bamboozled.

Facilitative Listening: How Audience Members Can Help Presentations

At San Diego's Scripps Institution of Oceanography, a vital presentation is the Ph.D. dissertation. One such presentation was covered in a *San Diego Union-Tribune* article:

> When the candidate-advisor opened the floor to questions, generally a tense time for students, his mother tried to help by lobbing what she thought was a puffball about meteorites becoming contaminated when they enter Earth's atmosphere. "He bluffed his way through, but it was a good question and she kind of stumped him," explains a professor who was there. "And the guy goes, 'Awwh, mom!'—which you could hear throughout the room."[4]

A common term in many organizations is the "Murder Board," describing the group they have to face in an upcoming presentation review. I strongly discourage that term for what it indicates: a humiliating experience, with reviewers ripping presenters to shreds. How about making that a meeting with the "Coaching or Review Team," for a truly constructive session that adds to success while keeping the presenter's person strong.

Commit to Being a Good Meeting Contributor

Isn't it in your own best interests to have a good meeting: to get what you need from the presentation, to get your input into the discussion, and to get it done efficiently? Here are some guidelines for meeting attendees:

- ◆ *Examine your style.* Are you a positive contributor or notorious for ripping speakers apart? Would some style adjustments possibly be beneficial?
- ◆ *Come prepared to meetings.* A major flaw of meeting attendees is that they haven't done their homework.

◆ *Get there on time, and stay there.* A major disrupter of meetings is key people coming and going or frequently having their attention diverted and then asking for an update.

◆ *Buy into the process.* What are the rules, objectives, timetable? If they're poorly defined, get them cleared up. If they are reasonable, commit to doing your part to see these are met. It's in both your interests to get this meeting over with expeditiously.

◆ *Shut off the cell phone.* If waiting for a vital call, step out of the room to take it. Make your contributions additive.

◆ *Important tip: Shhhhh.* Give presenters a chance. Some executives interrupt early and often. Giving speakers just a bit more leeway may return a big dividend. Concentrate on what the speaker is saying. Keep an open mind and avoid drawing hasty conclusions, particularly if the speaker's views are different from yours.

◆ *Be a responsive listener.* Entertainers and public speakers say they perform better for a "good" audience. The worst audience is that which does nothing—no facial expression (unless a blank stare is an expression), no verbal response, no smiles, cheers, not even boos. It is disconcerting to presenters not to know whether they have established satisfactory rapport or even whether the audience is alive. Better to be responsive, with eye contact, a head nod or smile, writing down an important point, even with a puzzled look. And remember, if you don't laugh at the joke, the speaker may assume you didn't understand it and tell it again.

◆ *Be a team player.* Sometimes a nervous presenter needs a little help to get unstuck, especially in the early phases of the presentation. By asking a stumbling colleague a helpful question, you can gently help the presenter relax and come across more naturally and confidently.

◆ *Request clarification of unclear material.* Complex concepts, special terminology and acronyms, references to events and people, and inadequately covered material offer possibilities for misunderstanding. The speaker assumes everyone is following, and often listeners sit quietly even though they are confused. No one wants to be the one to say, "I don't know what you're talking about." When someone does ask the "dumb" question, generally others are grateful, because they don't know either.

◆ *Think before asking questions or making comments.* Keep your input brief and to the point. Frequently audience members make lengthy and circuitous comments before getting to the point, if ever. Or they sidetrack, bog down, or take over the presentation. This may meet their particular needs (or be good for their egos) but probably does little to meet the needs of the rest of the people, who came to hear the presentation. A facilitative listener will choose a good breaking spot rather than interrupt others, make queries or inputs that are relevant to the immediate topic, and speak loudly and clearly so that all, not just the speaker, can hear.

◆ *Work with the speaker toward mutual understanding.* Communication snags are common in presentations. Help the speaker resolve these by suggesting specific examples, paraphrasing statements, stating points in different terms, and offering insights or additional information from a different perspective.

◆ *Resist side conversations or other distractions.* Another severe handicap to a presentation is when six conversations go on simultaneously.

Apply a Coach's Methods

◆ *Balance your feedback.* As Ken Blanchard and Spencer Johnson said in *The One Minute Manager*, "Try and catch them doing something right."[5] Many presenters hear nothing but negatives about their presentations. An occasional pat on the back might be appreciated by your presenters, though they might look warily at something so out of character.

◆ *Give feedback tactfully.* In the heat of the action, it's easy to come down on the speaker with "hobnailed boots," to beat him or her into the ground. Humiliating and clobbering the speaker may be momentarily satisfying but may backfire as conflicts erupt, personalities clash, issues get clouded, and other audience members turn on the caustic critic.

◆ *Keep the environment safe.* Group leaders particularly influence the style in which a meeting is conducted. Lower-level speakers may be intimidated by the presence of higher-level managers. Abrasive behavior by leaders can stifle presenters and set a pattern that others may follow. Ensure that all parties feel free to participate regardless of rank and without intimidation by others.

◆ *Listen with perspective.* Keep main ideas and priorities in mind and limit nitpicking. Separate valid from shaky material and hear out a speaker rather than discount all of what is said because of minor flaws or disagreement with some part.

Critical Listening: Shaping Up the Flim-Flam

As a member of the group to which the presentation is being given, you do not want to be bamboozled. As a member of the presenter's team, you want to be able to help upgrade the presentation and advance your team's cause. As a presenter you want to be able to present arguments that will stand up to critical assessment, that will not be shot down by the sharp critics who abound in the business world, especially when it is their dollars that are being spent or their business success that is at stake.

For any of these purposes, knowing what makes sense or doesn't, being able to spot the flaws or flim-flam, and cutting through the razzle-dazzle to get at the crucial stuff require that *attentive* listening be backed up with *smart* listening. The sophisticated listener knows what to look for to understand and appreciate sound thinking and to challenge or discount faulty thinking. Here are some tips.

◆ *Look beyond technique to substance.* It's easy to be dazzled by flamboyant speakers, resonant voices, or full-color multimedia displays. Hitler's audiences certainly were. Many listeners walk away from such shows saying, "Wasn't that great!" and even fork over ten dollars or twenty dollars for the snake oil. When asked what the speaker said, they're hard pressed to come up with anything. "But," they say, "wasn't he wonderful, and so dynamic!"

◆ *Look for strength and even greatness in ideas.* Many people talk a lot and say little, following the strategy: Tell lots of stories, overwhelm them with data, stay on safe ground, and don't get into trouble. If ideas and opinions are stated, they fit into the motherhood category: rehashing of old ideas or parroting of commonly held views with little deliberation given to them. The critical listener looks for ideas with something behind them—ideas that show reasonable thinking, insight, and imagination. Some useful questions to ask are:

What is the point of all this?

What do you propose we do?

What are you offering that is unique or better, or has more promise than anything else we've been hearing about?

- ◆ *Insist on specifics, not generalities.* If a speaker says, "I can stop inflation," the critical listener asks, "How?" Unfortunately, political campaigns are built on generalities; candidates are advised to forget issues and not to get into specifics, because that can cause trouble.

- ◆ *Don't blindly accept clichés.* "In foreign affairs," a major Presidential candidate once said, "it's time we got our act together." No more than that. And we let that person get away with that and cheered mightily. The easy clichés can be heard by the thousands during political campaigns, and few people seem to ask, "Just what do you mean by that?"

- ◆ *Demand evidence and verify that it meets acceptable standards.* Speakers of all types often get loose with "facts": "Nuclear power plants are unsafe," or "Nuclear power plants are safe," or "300,000 people die every year from air pollution," or "Illegal immigrants are sapping our resources." These may or may not be "facts." The critical listener listens to the claim and says: "Prove it." That's step one, which too many listeners don't bother to take. Astute speakers are ready for that rare request, however, and out comes the "proof"—the figures, the expert witnesses, the examples. Now the critical listener applies step two, subjecting that "proof" to reasonable tests to see if it indeed backs up the claim.

- ◆ *Scrutinize the assumptions.* Results and conclusions can be greatly influenced by the choice of ground rules. In the continuing debate in California over freeways versus rapid transit, one advocate for freeways compared the number of people a trolley car would carry versus four people per automobile. He made a pretty good case that autos would do the job, except his assumption of four people per car was not close to reality. By my own test on a very slow LA freeway, there were about twenty single-occupant cars for each dual passenger one, and that magic number of four people per car was even rarer.

◆ *Make sure apples are being compared to apples, not potatoes.* The glib salesperson asserts that the Hapmobile Special is a better buy than the competition's 560L, because it costs less and gives better mileage. ("Particularly, heh, heh, when I leave off the Hapmobile $2,000 accessories costs, and compare the Hapmobile's highway mileage to the 560L's city mileage. Just sign on the dotted line.")

◆ *Be alert for sidetracking ploys.* In lieu of reasoned arguments, and particularly when their case is weak, speakers often resort to subterfuge to throw listeners off the trail. As the minister wrote on his sermon manuscript: "Weak point—*shout.*" Here are some methods used by speakers to divert listeners' thinking:

- Inserting a few loaded words. A fiery young speaker calls businesspeople "bloated parasites," and the crowd roars its approval of whichever cause the speaker is touting. A politician calls for patriotism and blasts lazy bureaucrats, and the crowd roars its approval (different crowd).

- Slinging a little mud. This is one of the most commonly used methods to avoid discussing issues and evidence. Attacking an opponent's associations, appearance, and life-style is much simpler than legitimate debate.

- Blowing a minor flaw out of proportion. "This so-called expert admits he knows nothing about the Murchison Co. case, back in 1947. Obviously his case won't hold up, so we can dismiss his testimony immediately." Almost any presentation has some areas that are weaker than others. The side-tracker tries to focus all attention on those areas, aiming to discredit the entirety. The astute listener examines the weak areas but keeps them in perspective.

- Tossing in a red herring. This can be a subversion technique by the presenter: "We're a little vulnerable in the quality-procedures area. So let's overwhelm them with data and busy charts. They'll be either so impressed or bewildered that we should be able to slip by."

- Bringing out the handkerchief. When all else fails, who can help but be enchanted with the speaker who storms back and forth across the stage, delivers lines in hushed tones and exuberant shrieks, and pounds the table furiously. As the audience leaves, obviously moved, someone may say, "But he never did answer the real question."

◆ *Shoot holes in faulty thinking.* "On the basis of what you have heard, there should be no doubt that my proposal is the only way to go." Maybe. The critical listener looks carefully at how the presenter got from A to B to see whether that path will hold up to rigorous inspection. Fallacious arguments often succeed, much as a shell game does. It all seemed so easy and logical, except that the con artist now has your money. Here are some examples.

- "Inflation is caused entirely by excessive government spending. Therefore the cure is simple—cut government spending." The premise has to be examined carefully before the conclusion is accepted.

- "Battleships were instrumental in winning World War II. Therefore we should go back to battleships today." Perhaps this is a valid analogy. The critical listener doesn't accept it on assertion alone but tests the validity of the first "fact," the true similarity between the two situations, and the existence of other factors that might lead to the opposite conclusion.

In Summary: Listening Well Can Add Much to Communication

The listener can do much to advance or disrupt a presentation. The facilitative listener is a positive force and beneficial to the speaker and meeting productivity. Then, by examining presentations with a demanding ear, eye, and brain, the critical listener keeps the speaker straight and helps maintain the discussion at a level where it truly addresses the issues at hand.

A presentation built on solid ideas and support gains from a good listener. In the words of Samuel Hoffenstein's poem "Rag Bag II," a presentation with a shaky foundation and supported mostly by flamboyance crumbles before a good listener, as:

> Little by little we subtract
> Faith and Fallacy from Fact,
> The Illusory from the True,
> And starve upon the residue.

CHAPTER 15

Follow Up

It Ain't Over 'Til It's Over

T he party's over. The guests have departed. The room is dark and empty. The projector has been returned. You've made your presentation. There's nothing more to do.

Or is there? It may be a poor assumption to conclude that all the work is done when the presentation is completed.

- ◆ Your team just concluded a presentation to a company with which you want to establish a mutual relationship for product development and marketing. It went over mostly O.K., though there were some tough questions.

- ◆ The company's financial manager said it would be good if her VP could see the presentation. The technical specialist said he'd like to give that presentation to the next meeting of the company's technical committee.

- ◆ During the presentation, issue was taken with some of the conclusions stated because certain assumptions were no longer valid. No one from your team could state with certainty how the new data would affect the projections.

◆   Presentation preparation had meant a lot of last-minute work. Some graphics inputs never got in, a valuable video clip wouldn't work, hard copies were dashed off at 2 A.M. at Kinkos, and the budget was overrun.

So, is it all over? Sounds as if there is some more work yet to be done. What goes on after the presentation may be as important as the presentation itself.

Next Steps

The presentation may have just been a door opener or one part of an overall marketing program. You made it past hurdle #1. What's #2, #3, etc.? Further meetings as separate working groups or one-to-one meetings with key people are common.

The customer may have indicated that a presentation elsewhere would be useful, or other presentations may make sense as well. Someone else wants to borrow the presentation to show to another group. Do you want to fix the flaws and perhaps delete some confidential information before loaning it out?

The oral presentation may be followed by a formal written proposal or report. The work that went into making the presentation may be extremely useful in preparing the written document.

Take Care of Action Items

Questions raised may require further study and feedback to audience members. Any open items or commitments made during the presentation should be followed up.

Gather and Assess Intelligence

A presentation is an excellent opportunity for picking up information of a variety of types. The audience members may offer their opinions, objections, and concerns about your approach or proposals. They may provide corrected, updated, or additional data. They may share some of their plans and concerns, as well as what your competitors have been doing.

As much information may be gleaned from what was not said—the nonverbal messages—as from what was said. These include facial expressions or other reactions to your statements, the presence or absence of key people, people coming late or leaving early, congeniality or aloofness of listeners, glances exchanged or side discussions, and the tone of voice in comments or questions.

All this can be valuable information for you, but it has to be observed, documented, and evaluated to be useful. Getting the players together afterward to process these data and incorporate them into future activities is an important post-delivery function.

Keep Communicating

Send a note of appreciation to each person who was instrumental in bringing the presentation about and helping with it. This might be the contact person who coordinated the meeting, a host who provided a tour, or team members. Don't forget them. A "thank you" costs almost nothing, is well appreciated, and may be conspicuous by its absence.

Keep on Team-Building.

For an arduous exercise, how about a team lunch or, my favorite, a victory party?

Assessment and Feedback

Review Your Score Sheet

Something that happens too often in presentations is that the same mistakes keep occurring. It's helpful to prepare a scorecard after the presentation. For example, why did the preparation have so many problems, and why couldn't we get in that excellent video clip? What can be learned from that exercise to improve the process?

When, on the other hand, the presentation seems to have been successful on many counts, was that by accident? Not likely. What made it successful? It helps to know what worked, because you may want to use those things again or even make greater use of them the next time.

Provide Feedback

Presenters often overlook providing feedback to the behind-the-scenes people who contributed to the presentation. Rarely do the people who helped generate data, edit material, and prepare visuals get to see the finished product or get feedback that tells them how it went. To keep getting better work, fresh ideas, and improved turnaround, it is well worth the time to conduct a debriefing.

In Summary: Complete the Staff Work

What goes on after a presentation may be just as important as what went on before or during. Carrying out the next step, following up the loose ends, integrating what was learned from the audience, capitalizing on strengths, and learning from mistakes are all important post-delivery functions.

Here's an example where the follow-up actions were the key to success. During a proposal presentation, the presenting team had received a batch of questions about certain approaches. In fact, they received so many questions that they were terribly discouraged. They did have the opportunity to make changes in a BAFO (Best and Final Offer), so the next day they met to go over the nature of the questions. They gave them serious attention and returned their responses, which in some cases involved changes in their proposal.

The result? They won the contract, knocking off the incumbent. Later they were told by the review board that they won because of their paying attention to the problem issues. Much later, the head of the losing team told me that they also had received extensive board interaction, but had not taken it seriously. "We did not follow up, made no changes, and we lost."

Special
Presentation
Situations

CHAPTER 16

Not Just One but a Winning Team

Teams play a major part of history:

Ben Franklin: "We must all hang together or assuredly we shall all hang separately."

The Three Musketeers: "All for one and one for all."

Shakespeare's Henry V: "We few, we happy few. We band of brothers . . ."

Team presentations play a major role in business:

◆ To get money, the CEO and top team members pitch to potential financial sources.

◆ To win business, teams deliver proposal orals and short-list interviews to customer selection evaluation boards.

◆ Once business is won, a whole series of presentations occur through the life of the program, reviewing design, readiness, product introduction, and investigation.

◆ An organization has its annual conference to update franchisees or users of their products.

◆ A city's convention and visitor team goes on the road to persuade a major convention to select their city.

Team Presentations: Varied and Important

Team presentations are important; the stakes are often high. There generally has to be a significant reason to gather a diverse, highly paid, and often influential group together to hear a team of presenters. And whether the presentation involves the company president or a junior designer, the presenting team generally must put forth a great deal of time and money in getting ready, reflecting the importance an organization places on team presentations.

The team presentation gives an audience a first-hand preview of the ability of this team to work together. If the team looks more like the Three Stooges than the Three Tenors, the audience has just been given Exhibit A in favor of giving the business to someone else.

Preparing a Winning Team Presentation

Several factors seem to be consistently associated with efficiently produced and effective team presentations:

◆ *Understanding How the Presentation Fits into the Overall Communication Scheme.* Is the presentation paramount, with the expectation that it stands alone, or does it work in conjunction with written reports that provide most of the detail?

◆ *Recognition of the Importance of the Presentation and the Energy That Will Be Required to Put It Together.* A last-minute or poorly budgeted effort may cost more in the long run than adequate attention from the start.

◆ *Getting a Head Start by Considering What It's Going to Take to Win.* Among the items to be considered are identification of likely speakers, assessment of their availability and presentation skills, and possible early training and team building. A common expression is "If you've waited for the RFP (Request for Proposal) before starting, you're too late."

One approach is to provide a training seminar months in advance, including trial run presentations by the likely speakers. This gives all players an awareness of what would be required, gets concerns out in the open, and identifies possible deficiencies in the key speakers. Doing this in advance gives the team time to work on the problems and makes it more likely that the presentation will be successful.

◆ *Early Direction and Frequent Review by Leadership.* Too often the working troops are left to flounder in several directions. Weak or absentee leadership generally guarantees poor team spirit, massive last-minute changes, and shaky presentations.

◆ *Selection of a Committed Team Program Manager.* This is a critical decision as this person has primary responsibility for running the show, from preparation through execution, and sets the pattern the team will follow. A program manager (PM) could be the designated project head (often required), perhaps the CEO, or, for a financial presentation, the CFO (chief financial officer). Having worked with over 200 teams, I've seen how a PM can enhance or hamper the process:

• PM Joe Cheerleader recognizes the importance of team-building, clear communication, adherence to schedules, and support of colleagues during an arduous process. He seeks out and listens to others' expertise, works hard on his own segments as well as coaches others. He is a team builder.

• PM Oscar Grimm knows it all, except he doesn't. He operates as a solo player, with little linkage with other team members. He refuses suggestions, doesn't meet milestones himself, and doesn't enforce them with others. He belittles the process, giving only lip service to practice or review teams.

◆ *Support by Upper Management of the Program Manager.* The PM must wear many hats and often is running an ongoing program while leading the team toward winning a new one.

◆ *Recognition by everyone of the team focus.* Whether in sports or in business, team efforts generally come through best. All contributions are significant.

◆ *Treatment of Content that Recognizes That the Audience Is Probably a Team Too.* Team presentations often draw audiences more diverse in both level and discipline than do single-speaker presentations.

◆ *Getting to Know Each Other.* The keys to team cohesion may rely as much on group dynamics as on specific procedures. For proposal presentations, teams are often pulled together for the project and may be barely acquainted. Getting that vital team flavor may take some working or socializing together. For example, when I was coaching such a team and it was clear they were uptight, we scheduled a highly informal dinner. Relaxing over pizza and beer brought everyone close together, which paid off during the next day's rehearsals.

◆ *Careful Attention to Operational Detail.* Plenty can go wrong in a single twenty-minute presentation. Add in several players and segments, and the potential problems are compounded.

Here are some specific techniques that can help bring winning team presentations about (summarized in Figure 16-1).

Plan Thoroughly

Careful up-front planning gets it all started in the right direction (revisit Chapter 5).

◆ *Identify requirements.* Foremost in planning are specific directions from the audience, whether external or internal. For a proposal or review, this may be explicitly stated, or the customer may have provided specific topics or questions to be discussed.

◆ *Identify audience members.* Be aware especially of key decision makers and their familiarity with your team and history, their biases, and their expectations.

◆ *Make sure you know the key issues and hot buttons, whether identified overtly or subtly.* Team members close to the situation can provide important input about these.

◆ *Develop analysis, strategy, and your plan.* Make sure your plan is understood by all participants. Failure to establish and communicate this leads to individuals misdirecting their emphases.

Figure 16-1. Apply these tips for successful team presentations.

◆ Determine and provide the needed priority and resources.

◆ Size up team capabilities and provide advance training as warranted.

◆ Avoid wasted efforts and excessive rework by getting early and continuous input from top management.

◆ Clearly communicate and stick to win plan, requirements, assignments, and schedules.

◆ Communicate overall team theme and strategy and make sure all speakers support them.

◆ Stress organizational clarity and consistency.

◆ Use storyboards and delivery scripts to aid cross-communication, review, and practice.

◆ Tailor visuals to a mixed audience, with ample use of message titles and clear layouts.

◆ Have all visuals adhere to a standard style for a team impression.

◆ Practice, practice, practice.

◆ Include team-building as you go.

◆ Present as a cohesive, competent team, with PM clearly demonstrating effective leadership.

◆ Track and meet time targets.

◆ Be fully responsive to audience questions and adjustments, within bounds of meeting requirements.

◆ *Assign a presentation coordinator to take the load off the PM and to manage all the details.* This will help to keep everything on course. I've heard PMs say, "Well, I'm going to do that myself." Sure—and land in the hospital's critical-care ward at the end of the job.

◆ *Set team members and topics.* This may be specifically requested or inferred from the customer's requests, or there may be considerable latitude. For proposals or financing meetings, the customer will want to hear from certain key individuals. Will those people be available? What are the presentation abilities of potential speakers? What strengths or deficiencies do candidates bring?

Steve Aliment, who coordinated many major presentations for the Boeing Services Division, said: "You must let the team know early who the actual presenters will be. For one presentation the PM didn't identify speakers until late in development. Then they got up at our dry run and stumbled badly as they hadn't prepared the material."[1]

◆ *Commit resources.* Recognize this is not going to get done with-out the people and budgets to make it happen. Besides speakers, what else is needed to get the job done: content support, graphics, coaches, reviewers, equipment, production?

◆ *Lay out and stick to a realistic schedule.* Scheduling is a frequent trouble area. Let milestones slip by and soon you need a last-min-ute crash effort. I once worked with one large team that waited too long to get going. The result was speakers who are over-stressed, graphics people working until 3 A.M., and production at Kinkos at 4 A.M. Rehearsals?

◆ *Provide strong direction and clear communication.* Make sure all players are onboard, understand the plan, and are committed to it. Alert them to expect an iterative process.

Get Organized

With multiple presenters, clear and coordinated organization is vital.

◆ *Set the agenda and time targets for each speaker.* Be prepared for howls from the speakers, stoutly proclaiming that can't be done in seven minutes. At a venture capital conference, teams each had thirty minutes in which to make their case. A consistent failing was poor time balance, most due to allowing too much time for product features and then having to race to end on time, short-changing vital topics. Either the time budget or time tracking were faulty.

◆ *Consider likely audience interaction.* Will they ask questions and when? Make sure your agenda allows for this.

◆ *Develop section outlines and review them.* Shortchanging this step may be tempting but may surface later as a bad move. In a six-person team, five (with some nudging) did outlines; one re-fused ("I've never done that and got through just fine"). His seg-ment was clearly the only one needing major structural surgery.

◆ *Give the audience lots of road signs.* With most team presenta-tions, an up-front summary is wise. Use the repeated agenda as you move from one speaker to the next. Strive for organizational consistency. For example, if three segments have summary charts and the fourth does not, it jars the sense of order and leads to listeners wondering whether these speakers have met before.

◆ *Develop storyboards.* These give an early sense of each segment's length, message, and visual content, plus compatibility with other sections. They also aid review by management and colleagues (Figure 16-2). Even in the computer era, many teams find posting paper copies on the wall is a useful method.

◆ *Get management review and redirection.* This is a key time for management to give its input again. Changes beyond this point become more costly and difficult as artwork gets developed and time is shortened.

Build Effective Support Material

Fit the level to the audience specialties and levels. Consider what will keep them tuned in, made aware, and won over. That may be less because of the hard data—extensive studies, voluminous statistics, detailed information—and more because of personal experiences, lessons learned, clear interpretations, and portrayals of data.

Figure 16-2. Storyboards facilitate graphics development and cohesion across sections.

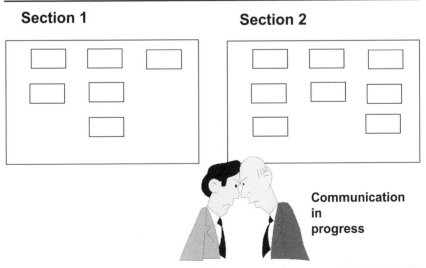

◆ *Design in variety.* These audiences often will hear from four to five teams, all covering much the same material. Give them some changes of pace. An example: After two presenters had spoken with heavy use of projected graphics, the third stood up, shut off the projector, and opened his segment with a personal story. The renewed audience interest was obvious.

◆ *If this is a selling situation, look for support that will win over the audience.* Remind speakers that this is not a tutorial, but a selling situation. Identify what will help enhance the case, such as items often overlooked: personal success stories, testimonials, awards, or success measures. These are often difficult to locate from somewhere in the system.

◆ *Make sure graphics quality is suitable for the audience and situation.* Also make sure that graphics have a team look. With multiple presenters and organizations, a variety of styles can appear. Two keys are:

1. Set a template to be used by all presenters.
2. Make sure one person (coordinator, graphics guru) has responsibility for integrating all visuals.

◆ *Put extra effort into the clarity and message of your visual aids.* All presenters should put forth extra effort to come up with punchy visuals whose messages can be quickly grasped. Valuable are interpretive titles, focused information, more visual aspects—pictures, graphs, relationships—than words, and color. Hardware, models, displays, and videotapes can provide high audience interest and an appreciated change of pace.

◆ *Have speakers prepare delivery scripts.* This helps to focus material, meet times, and develop transitions (both between slides and between speakers).

◆ *Ensure necessary supplementary material.* Some material, such as visual aid brochures, will be in a revision state along with the visuals themselves, and the publication requirements must be rigorously observed to be available when needed.

Stage It Carefully

◆ *Check out the facility—early.* Horror stories abound of extensive rework required due to faulty information about the facility. If it's your facility choose a conference room that will not alienate the audience. (For an upcoming critical meeting, the room was good but the chairs weren't. We changed them to "Admiral-level"— chairs of significantly better quality.) Visit the customers' facility if possible. If using their A/V gear, check it out. Switch to your own gear when your advance tests show the mediocre graphics quality of the customers' equipment, but check with them first.

◆ *Make a comprehensive checklist.* With many speakers and divided responsibilities, it's easy to have important details slip through the cracks. Hello Murphy (see Chapter 8).

◆ *Draw up a set of operational procedures, clearly communicated to participants.* Set computer and slide advancement procedures. To prevent the old "Didn't you? I thought you . . . ?" routine from occurring, rigorously plan procedures and assignments for rehearsals, travel, clearances, distributions, and anything else.

◆ *Review in steps.* For speakers with limited experience or high anxiety, have them rehearse their sections in a low-pressure mode. Give them constructive feedback, with video review. Then practice in sections and finally with all speakers. Have speakers observe others' presentations and offer input.

◆ *Use a review team productively.* Select reviewers or coaches (Red Teams) to provide a suitable variety of backgrounds. Provide requirements and strategy plan in advance. Set process for timely and helpful good feedback. Include a graphics coordinator for faster graphics repair.

◆ *Simulate all aspects of the presentation.* Include interaction, scenarios, or other required elements. Use actual equipment and room layouts. Try out seating and transitions. Practice transitions and coordinated activities. Conduct a final complete dress rehearsal. Test your backup (you do have one, right?).

Deliver with Precision

Individual and team competence will be sensed strongly from how this team now performs under pressure.

◆ *Demonstrate a cohesive team.* Denny Krenz, a former Department of Energy official who has headed many proposal review boards, talks about that important team situation: "When the team comes in, it's very important that the lead person runs the show. Fifty percent of the score is based on that senior manager, so it's important to show leadership. If a deputy or another person runs it, that's not so good."[2]

Former CEO and venture capital (VC) partner Martha Dennis concurs: "Listeners are trying to evaluate the team and its interactions. They're judging your presentation on several levels, as an indicator of how you'll relate to customers. If the CEO or CTO does all the talking, that can be a problem. Generally it's better to bring in other team members as appropriate."[3]

The PM should thus demonstrate good leadership qualities during the presentation, and all presenters should show they can work smoothly together (Figure 16-3).

◆ *Make smooth transitions between speakers.* The PM may introduce each upcoming speaker, the current presenter may introduce the next one, or each person does his own. The key is to do these well, and they often are not. One PM didn't know the name of two of his teammates, an instant negative signal.

To avoid having speakers pop up to often, consider having two speakers up at the same time. For example, the presentation by the

Figure 16-3. Showtime: Look and function as a team.

SO - WHO WILL SHOW UP?

The Bumbler Brigade
or A Winning Team?

winning team for a major library design was done by two speakers, standing and working together for the full forty-five minutes.

◆ *Add credibility.* Weave in examples of how individuals will work (or already have worked) with colleagues or with the customer in executing the tasks.

◆ *Adhere closely to allocated times.* The speaker who gets carried away can wreak havoc with upcoming speakers, who then have to shorten their presentations. (*Tip*: Make sure all know the signals and that your timer stays awake. A speaker told me with great hilarity of a presentation where he, as the timer, signaled his colleague to move faster. The signal was a discrete tug on the ear. His colleague thought that meant "You're right on course," and continued at his steady pace. Soon the timer was almost ripping his ear off, to no avail.)

◆ *But be flexible as warranted.* Team leaders need a strong sense of perspective coupled with the ability to adjust the program where it clearly is not meeting audience needs or team objectives. The leader may opt to extend or shorten segments if it makes sense. For one presentation, the PM showed the agenda to the principal listener, who didn't like it, and it was adjusted on the spot.

◆ *Support each other.* Team members are all on stage during the entire presentation. They should be attentive and alert to assist other speakers and not create distractions. They should look, think, and act like a team. Some examples (all true) of what to avoid:

- Crunching ice while a colleague is speaking, especially if you're the PM
- Creating irresistible (to audience attentions) diversions, such as chatting with your seatmate, toying with your laptop, fidgeting continually, or reacting derisively to audience questions or comments
- Challenging your teammates as they present (Whew!)
- Using a cell phone in the room, or stepping just outside the door and loudly talking while your colleague is trying to make a point

◆ *Coordinated Q&A response is vital.* This is often more important than the formal presentation. The PM is in charge, clarifying, transferring, or answering questions. Others need to be ready to pitch in when needed but should resist the urge to jump in. One PM hurt his team's success by answering all questions himself, some of which would have been better handled by colleagues.

VC partner Martha Dennis, who has reviewed many presentations, says: "Listeners will probe to figure out the relationship. The last thing you want to do is to have team members contradict each other. It the exec says 'Let's ask my specialist on that,' and that person provides a good answer, that's O.K. If the response is poor, and the exec sits there twiddling, that's a bad sign."[4]

In Summary: Team Presentations Are Too Important to Toy With

Team presentations are often high-stakes events involving many people. They are important factors for influencing decisions and a first-hand measure of likely future performance. Because they use up resources, time, and energy, it's important that they be done right. The keys are careful planning, early top-level support, practice, and teamwork in execution.

As an example, in a major competition, the Department of Energy awarded a $2.2 billion contract for environmental cleanup to a team headed by Fluor Corporation, following "short-list" presentations by Fluor and the runner-up contractor, with two others eliminated earlier. In an article about the contract award, the principal DOE executive said: "All the firms had capabilities, but how the team works as a team in the oral presentations is a key determining factor."[5]

CHAPTER 17

Making Sure
It's Not Greek to Them

International Presentations

We really appreciate the chance to talk to you folks from (Japan). We have some new ideas we want to bounce off you that we think will really blow your minds. Our new Widget has been cutting through our competitors like Joe Schmucko going through the line. Speaking of Joe, there's a funny story about a hot romance, ha, ha, ha. . . . Our Widget has had great success in CONUS, especially on DoD spook programs such as HTSM and FRGM. . . . I know you'll want to put in an order today, so we've got our sales manager here and we can get to that right after we take a coffee break. Let's take ten and hit the john.

G iven today's high degree of business and governmental linkages, presenters often may find themselves speaking to audiences from countries other than their own. Language and culture differences make this a vastly different presentation situation from what the speaker is used to. The stakes can be high and the

299

pitfalls many, so wise presenters will consider these differences in preparation and delivery.

The monologue at the start of the chapter encompasses many of the problems U.S. presenters give themselves and their foreign audiences. While it is a fictional example, it is not entirely a product of my imagination. I have heard presenters make comments that are not much different from the ones printed here in that they have been incomprehensible, confusing, and sometimes offensive to listeners. An early lesson for me was while conducting a seminar in Canada, I cited as an example of powerful language that used by "the great patriot, Patrick Henry." During the break a chap came over and enlightened me that while Patrick Henry might be a patriot in the United States, he was regarded as a traitor in Canada. Oops.

When presenting internationally, the fundamental requirement is to recognize that business as usual is dangerous business. "They" are not the same as "we." We speak different languages, even if we both speak English; we act differently; and we view things from different perspectives. These differences set the stage for communication difficulties and potential misunderstandings.

We particularly misread messages from people of different age groups, economic levels, religious or racial backgrounds, or nations. The use of time, need for "space bubbles," and gestures all differ greatly among different groups. Sidney Jourard observed touch frequencies between people in ordinary conversation in coffee shops around the world. In Paris, people touched each other 110 times per hour. In London and the United States the numbers were zero and two.[1] So what happens when a Frenchman and an American get together to do business? The Frenchman keeps touching, the American keeps recoiling, and each one thinks the other one is nuts.

The concept of presentations differs for different cultures. In the United States, full-blown graphic presentations are a standard part of business. We value the efficiency, the conciseness, and the potential rapid response that come with presentations.

U.S-type presentations may not apply in countries where business proceeds in a much less structured, less rapid manner, and often on a one-to-one basis rather than in the group format that is common for our presentations. Without knowing your audience, you can easily head down the wrong track. In Japan, presentations—and plenty of them—are expected to be given to the whole range of departments involved in the decisions. Cateoria and Hess point out that a business-person needs to use a soft-sell approach in Great Britain and the hard sell in Germany, to emphasize price in Mexico and quality in Venezuela.[2]

According to Paul Sullivan, managing director of Global Partners, Inc., who has worked with organizations in forty different countries:

> Americans are probably some of the worst at conducting themselves in the international business world, with the result they often turn off their audiences. One poor practice is unknowingly putting down the local people. Another is using American colloquialisms and slang, or overuse of examples from their home experience: "hitting home runs, or throwing the long bomb." This is particularly unwelcome language now that Americans are seen as gun-toting aggressors. The use of sarcasm is another mistake. It seldom goes over well abroad. And generally they talk too fast. Although more and more people around the world speak English, it is hard to remember that it is a second, third or fourth language for many in the audience.[3]

Actually, it's not just Americans who have difficulty understanding international no-no's. Toronto was in the running to be host city for the 2008 Olympic games. The mayor and his team were to make a presentation to the Association of National Olympic Committees of Africa, meeting in Kenya. Right before the trip he said, "What the hell would I want to go to a place like Mombasa for? I just see myself in a pot of boiling water with all these natives dancing around me."[4] Can you picture his reception upon arriving at the Kenya meeting? (He later apologized for his comment.)

Then there was that cross-border brouhaha in summer of 2003, kicked off with a derogatory comment in a speech at the European Parliament by the Italian Prime Minister comparing a German lawmaker to a Nazi prison guard. It was not well received. This was followed by the Italian Minister of Tourism's description of German tourists (Italy's largest market) as beer-swilling, chauvinistic boors. He resigned shortly thereafter.

Well, dudes, with that heads-up litany of caution flags, let's charge full-bore down the yellow brick road into that tricky turf of presentation to non-U.S. audiences (summarized in Figure 17-1.) Go Bears.

Plan Carefully, Drawing on Experts and Experience

For presentation success across cultures and in foreign environments, the importance of careful planning cannot be overemphasized.

◆ *Learn all you can about your listeners and how they do business.* Use the experts, such as the Department of Commerce, who know the specific country well. Consulates and embassies located in the United States can provide helpful background on their countries, as can U.S. government offices located overseas. AMA

Figure 17-1. Apply these tips for winning international presentations, whether in your location or theirs. All are subject to tailoring for the specific group.

◆ Know your audience, and consider cultural as well as business backgrounds in planning your presentation.
◆ Consult experts to understand the audience better and to prevent faux pas.
◆ Communicate with the host contact about any aspects to be aware of. Sort out the plan for the entire event, such as social meetings outside the conference room.
◆ Understand details of shipping, travel, on-site arrangements, etc.
◆ Clarify specific goals and the agenda.
◆ Organize your talk so it can be easily followed, with moving agendas and mini-summaries.
◆ Allow for extensive two-way communication (though it may not occur).
◆ Emphasize simplicity and visualization in visual aids.
◆ Prepare speakers to consider language and cultural problem areas.
◆ Rehearse with someone familiar with the audience's culture and language.
◆ Know how to pronounce key words.
◆ Speak clearly and probably slower than your standard. Gauge understanding.
◆ Make sure the spoken word closely follows the visual aids.
◆ Be careful with acronyms, jargon, and colloquial references.
◆ Use standard international business terminology.
◆ Be aware of body language differences, both yours and theirs.

International, headquartered in New York and with centers in Europe, Canada, South America, and Mexico, can be an important contact as well.

The "do" list could identify protocol requirements, often more significant in other countries than in the United States; considerations related to timing and form of presentation, even including giving no presentation; meeting procedures; and probable desires of the audience.

Use the "no-no" list to surface taboos. Talking about "boiling pots of water" will not get your presentation off to a good start in Africa. Making reference to Montezuma's revenge is not the way to endear oneself to a Mexican, as President Carter discovered during a well-publicized visit to that country. Referring to women or animals is not wise when speaking to Arabs. And knowing that many Asians have strong feelings about lucky and unlucky colors may prevent some serious mistakes on visuals or brochures.

◆ *Give special attention to how cultural differences might affect style of presentation and strategy.* Howard Van Zandt provides this example about doing business in Japan:

> In making a presentation, it should be remembered that Japanese and Americans have different objectives in doing business. The former continually stress growth, steady jobs for their own employees, full employment in the nation as a whole, and superiority over competitors. Profit, as a motive, falls behind these needs. But U.S. executives are motivated only by profit—or, at least, that is the way Japanese businessmen see it. . . . Since the Japanese prefer a low- pressure sales approach and value sincerity so highly, Westerners are advised to build up their case a step at a time, using modest language rather than making extravagant claims.[5]

◆ *Be rigorous and precise in your arrangements planning.* If you do not have previous experience with the country in which you are presenting, or an established, reliable base there, call in the experts early. Organizations specializing in international meetings or meeting managers of international hotel chains can provide valuable consulting and handle arrangements in other countries. The experience of other businesspeople in the country may be of value. Many countries today have sophisticated facilities and considerable experience in audiovisual presentations. The main thing to remember, however, is that paperwork, power requirements, terminology, equipment, and common practices may all be different there.

Schedule all elements carefully, including support needs such as delivery of gadgetry or slide brochures. Do not take anything for granted that has to be provided, delivered, shipped, or carried. Customs delays can be unpredictable and often lengthy.

♦ *Discuss fully with the key contact person at the other end the main aspects of the meeting.* Be sure to cover the following: purpose; desires of both parties; incidentals, such as arrival times and hotels; agenda for the day, such as tours or private visits; and the presentation itself. Identify as fully as possible the exact names, titles, and backgrounds of the audience members. Obtain phonetic spellings of the names. Maintain a dialogue with your key contact to stay abreast of current information and to ensure that both parties are clear and in agreement on the purpose of the meeting and the presentations.

♦ *Provide as much assistance and information as possible to smooth the way for the other parties.* If they are in your environment, it will be strange to them, and they will probably appreciate any help to make them comfortable and to avert gaffes. They will have as much trouble with your names as you will have with theirs. You may want to provide a list of attendees' names (speakers plus audience) and their titles, which are often used, as well as name place markers.

♦ *Consider differences in hospitality.* Do not overlook the simple things, such as refreshments during breaks or lunch. For example, for an important competition, my firm had linked with two major European companies. The kickoff meeting included morning fare typical for an important meeting. Later the head of the Dutch company asked me: "Did you notice no one from our team ate anything?" I had not. "In the Netherlands sweet rolls and donuts are not something we would ever eat for a morning meeting."

- ◆ *Allow private time and space.* In planning agendas and facilities, consider that the audience members may wish some time to meet separately.

- ◆ *Select your speakers carefully.* Be aware of potential problems certain types of speakers may present. A hard-charging, fender-slapping salesperson may not go over well with some audiences. A person with too many rough edges may create a poor impression with sophisticated listeners. If the listeners have a limited knowledge of English, it may be wise to screen out speakers who are hard to understand.

- ◆ *Prepare your speakers.* They should know how to pronounce any foreign names that are in the presentation. If you're trying to get business in Saudi Arabia, all your team members should know where Riyadh is located, that it is the capital city, and how to pronounce it. They should know key people and agencies involved. As an example, after about fifteen minutes into the presentation by a team seeking to win a contract in Hawaii, one reviewer stood up and emphatically said she'd heard enough. The team's program manager was startled and asked her why. "Because if you don't even know how to pronounce the name of our town, I'm certainly not going to give you our business."

- ◆ *Orient presenters to audience culture and style.* Many speakers are heading into an environment with which they may have little experience. Jay Carson has had many technical and managerial assignments in several mid-East countries. For one program, he said, the U.S. prime contractor hurt itself badly on customer presentations in Saudi Arabia: "They would come in with arrogant attitudes, assuming they were experts. They'd want to get right to the heart of the matter and tell them what to do versus persuading them. After they left, they would be cut apart within an hour. Over there, if you're prideful and arrogant, you won't get anywhere."[6]

Paul Sullivan is no stranger to the international environment. "When I travel I make a point of staying in the hotel of the country (versus the large chains with the same hotels in the United States). I want to understand the culture, the nature, the thinking of the people. You won't get that so well in the other hotels." Here is his favorite example:

> On my first trip to Korea, I came across an article noting there were fifty-eight universities there. The night before my meeting, I sat down to dinner. At the next table was an American who'd come over on the same plane as I did. He was having dinner with a Korean client, and I heard him ask, "Are there any universities in Korea?" Can you imagine that? The Korean client responded politely.[7]

◆ *Try to find nuances.* Business executive and professional speaker Somers White has spoken widely to audiences around the world. He says it can be valuable to learn about local events and interests, such as government, population makeup, policies, and local hot issues. "In the Philippines, I spoke to a group about various financial topics. A man asked a question about investing in Philippine art. I was able to answer knowledgeably about the current status of why Philippine art has not been a good investment for the last six months. What did that do for my credibility?"[8]

◆ *Consider how other attendees can be of help.* One company has employees who are natives of the audience country attend its international presentations. Being familiar with both the company and the visitor's country and language, they have helped make the audience comfortable as well as assisted with explanations.

Develop Appropriate Material

Presentation content must be understandable, accurate, and received positively. One need not look far for blatant language mistakes; they often are the source of humor or frustration, just like those easy-to-assemble instructions found in some manuals. It also pays to be aware of local sensitivities. For example, a team pursuing business in Saudi Arabia displayed on the repeated agenda chart a map showing the Persian Gulf. A consultant immediately spotted it as not real smart, noting that to the Saudis it's the Arabian Gulf.

◆ *Cover less material.* I once coached a presenter heading for Japan. It was obvious he was trying to cover too much. Reporting back later, he said he'd cut a lot out, but he definitely should have cut more, since he failed to allow adequate time for questions, comments, and repetition.

♦ *Aim toward greater organizational simplicity than for standard presentations.* Use plenty of direction signs and reiterations. Provide moving agenda charts to introduce each section, with names of all speakers spelled out in full. Summarize frequently.

♦ *Provide an up-front summary unless not appropriate for the culture.* This enables both parties to see at the start just what the objectives and essence of this presentation are.

♦ *Eliminate references that will mean little to non-Americans.* Avoid referring to game plans, *Sixty Minutes*, and Lone Star Beer (unless you're selling Lone Star Beer), and so forth.

♦ *Design visual aids with simplicity.* Use photographs and relationship diagrams instead of busy word charts. Make them readable. Hold acronyms to a minimum, and spell out those that you do use. Use message titles to increase the ease of grasping the points.

♦ *Translate visuals if warranted.* Graphics layouts may need to be changed. For example, English-language graph axes and flowcharts don't directly transform into Arabic, which moves from right to left. Where the audience is not familiar with English, translation of visual aids may be wise, but keep in mind that translating is tricky business. In the same language, many terms differ across dialects (e.g., Madrid Spanish versus Guadalajara Spanish; Hong Kong Cantonese versus Beijing Mandarin).

Although native speakers can be helpful, there are potential risks. For example, a Puerto Rican doing a Spanish translation for an audience in Caracas may make serious mistakes (and vice versa). A person away from his or her native country for more than a few years can quickly lose touch with the language. A native speaker may be fluent in everyday usage but not proficient in technical language.

Some words don't translate so well. Boeing discovered that its slogan for the 747—"the Queen of the Sky"—was precluded from use in several languages because it translated as the Virgin Mary.[9] Also be wary of literal translations, since some terms may have different meanings in different languages. For example, "short-term debt" is defined differently in the United States and Germany, so translating the term literally might create more confusion. If it is left in English, the Germans probably will know which definition to apply.

♦ *Provide paper copies of visual aids to start, but check first as to appropriateness.* Executive Thomas Kurtz has given many international presentations. "I always gave them copies of my slides at the start so they could make notes on them in their own language as I talked. This worked out very well."[10] Howard Van Zandt recommends distributing copies of presentation material in Japan because this provides a test of sincerity, which Japanese value highly. "They feel that when a man is willing to put his case in print, where all may challenge what he has said, it is likely that he will be accurate so as not to lose face." He also advises this because oral statements are often misunderstood due to the heavy use of homonyms (words that sound the same but don't mean the same) in Japanese. He also suggests that presenters in Japan lend copies of visual aids to the Japanese for their use with other groups.[11]

♦ *Test out your presentation and all your speakers.* This works best when the listeners are knowledgeable about the target country.

♦ *Rework your spoken message so it flows better.* In coaching an executive for whom English was a second language, we identified several phrases he kept stumbling over. We replaced those phrases with words that were simpler to pronounce.

♦ *Allow time to meet with interpreters.* Often interpreters are essential to conducting international business. According to advertising executive Robert Smith, who has had ample experience with interpreters, both in international marketing and as a conference leader for AMA International:

> The important thing is to go over the presentation in advance with the interpreter. Review the handouts, visuals, and anecdotes. Then remember to pace yourself so the interpreter can do his job, so the two of you can work as a team. This is especially critical for simultaneous translations.[12]

◆ *Learn a few words of the language.* Cross-cultural expert Dr. Sondra Thiederman says that nothing else will win trust more. "And don't worry about doing it right—do the best you can. You show a certain leveling and vulnerability by trying to pronounce a few local words and sort of floundering, as long as you're not arrogant about it. You might also learn to say 'That's all I know,' in case they come rushing up and start to talk to you."[13]

Deliver with Courtesy and Caution

During the 2003 war with Iraq, much friction was generated between the United States and some European countries. Although President Bush gave many speeches and press conferences aimed at winning over European support, they only served to harden support against the U.S. position. In an article titled "To Some in Europe, the Major Problem is Bush the Cowboy," the vice chairman of the Foreign Relations Committee in the German Parliament, said, "Much of it is the way he talks, this provocative manner, the jabbing of his finger at you. It's Texas, a culture that is unfamiliar to Germans. And it's the religious tenor of his arguments."[14]

In your own presentations, careful preparation should have already surfaced and corrected such potential delivery problems. Here are some further tips:

◆ When in Rome . . . know what to expect. Your cultural training should have prepared you for your Saudi conference room, where many people may be reclining around the room. You should know about a more formal flavor in Munich or Osaka, where orderly introductions with titles and perhaps passing of business cards and gifts are the rule.

◆ Speak slowly and clearly if you are speaking to people whose native language is not English. Make sure you can be heard easily. This applies as well to non-natives presenting to Americans, who will have difficulty grasping many unfamiliar names.

◆ Speak in simple, single-clause sentences as much as possible.

◆ Do not use slang, colloquialisms, clichés, metaphors, and other expressions that mean nothing to the listeners (Figure 17-2).

Figure 17-2. International presentations can be tricky.

Mornin'. I'm Davy Smith. Call me Smitty. We've got some new ideas about our PQM-3 that will blow your minds. So let's get goin', O.K.?

♦ Limit acronyms and jargon, and then explain those you do use, checking for mutual understanding. "This was one of our biggest problems," said international businessman Meredith Goodwin, who himself speaks English. "As soon as the speakers lapsed into their technical jargon and mnemonics, they lost us. This can be a potentially very serious problem, for example, when terms are not fully explained. In one business relationship, it was months before we realized that when the representatives of the U.S. company said 'cost-plus' and we said 'cost-plus,' we weren't talking about the same thing."[15] To prevent such potentially expensive misunderstandings, use the accepted international business terms.

♦ Be careful with jokes or humor. They often don't translate well and may make a puzzled listener feel he or she is either stupid or being made fun of.

♦ Tie your words closely to the visual aids. Lead your listeners through the aids, using a pointer to help them track you.

♦ Repeat and summarize often. Explain key concepts or data in several ways and allow ample "soak-in" time.

♦ Be expressive. It is generally easier to understand a person who uses gestures, facial expression, and vocal emphasis to add to words. Stiff, monotonic speakers are harder to stay with or understand.

◆ Establish and maintain an open environment. If you know the audience views feedback positively, make it clear at the start that you welcome questions or comments, and maintain a dialogue format rather than a strictly one-way presentation. Be careful not to place anyone in an embarrassing position. Provide ample opportunities for easy audience input, even asking such questions of your own as, "Does this provide the kind of information you were looking for?" or "Have I explained that fully?" However, for an audience not oriented toward questions, little feedback is likely, and overt invitations to respond are better tentatively expressed or left out.

◆ Listen intently to their questions and comments. As appropriate, paraphrase them back before responding to make sure that the question is understood correctly. Be patient if it takes them a while to comprehend your message (and you theirs).

◆ Be aware that nonverbal messages may mean different things from what you think. Facial expression, eye contact, hand movements, touching, use of space and time are all ripe areas for misinterpretation and irritation. Be slow in making assumptions on the basis of nonverbal messages. For example, a U.S. manager was giving his first presentation in Sweden. Halfway into the program several people stood up. He was puzzled until informed that the Swedes like to stand up and stretch often.

◆ Be respectful of their customs, clothing, facilities, history, and world status, and be careful about playing up the United States.

◆ Be cautious about pushing hard for commitment or action, or heavy chest thumping. These great U.S. standbys may backfire overseas.

◆ Recognize that the audience may be observing much more than the presentation. Acting like a clod during the coffee break or lunch may destroy your finely delivered presentation.

◆ In spite of all the previous cautions, be yourself. If you truly want to communicate and you recognize that differences exist that can interfere with that process, you will be well along toward communicating successfully with an audience from another background.

In Summary: Presenting to International Audiences Is Not Business as Usual

It is difficult enough to try to communicate with someone from your own background. Presentations to international audiences are made even more difficult because of differences in culture, language, and business practices.

Closing ceremonies of the 1984 Olympics in Los Angeles included lavish salutes to all the previous Olympic cities. While watching it, I was amazed to see the tribute to Mexico City accompanied by a stirring rendition of "Granada." So was the Mexican consul general, who protested the "unjustifiable ignorance" displayed by the hosts in not knowing that "Granada" is a fine song of Spain, not Mexico.[16]

And lest we leave on the note that Americans need some waking up about potential international snafus, here's another reminder that non-Americans need to check that their good intentions don't backfire. According to Andrew Young, who accompanied Martin Luther King to Norway for the Nobel Prize ceremony in 1964:

> Those few of us from Martin's inner circle who were able to attend had to smile when the Norwegian Broadcasting Symphony broke into selections from Gershwin's Porgy & Bess in an attempt to honor black Americans. Maybe they thought "Summertime, and the livin' is easy," was the perfect music to go with the police lines, barking dogs, and fire hoses of Birmingham, Alabama. But we could only feel amused.[17]

CHAPTER 18

Becoming a Winning Presenter

So here you are, having invested much good energy in absorbing at least some of the winning presentations ideas. Don't let this just be a passive reading activity. Adding to your capability takes commitment and action. Here are some specific ideas.

Keep Adding to Your Presentations Knowledge

◆ *Go back to the classroom.* Sign up for an in-house training seminar. Take a college class after work. Ask the boss to send you to a public seminar. Many people duck these learning opportunities—"Don't have time. . . . Don't need it anyway. . . . I hate to give speeches." They stagnate while their colleagues grab the opportunity and grow.

◆ *Watch and learn from good speakers, and poor ones.* Make every presentation you see—at work, in church, at club meetings, from political campaigners, or from television speakers—a learning opportunity. Determine what keeps you tuned in or nudges you toward sleep.

♦ *Buy another book or several, beyond this one* (unless you're reading a borrowed copy). May I recommend *Say It Like Shakespeare: How to Give a Speech Like Hamlet, Persuade Like Henry V, and Other Secrets from the World's Greatest Communicator?*[1] Buy or rent an audio or video program.

♦ *Learn about available tools and resources.* Keep up with advances in computer programs and audio-visual capabilities to develop presentations better and faster. *Presentations Magazine* is a good resource.

Managers: Do Your Part

A primary role of managers is to encourage, cajole, or even direct their associates to work on skills they need or will need to do their jobs well. Performance reviews often focus on "hard" skills—computers, safety, processes—and pay little attention to "soft" skills, such as interpersonal communication or presentation needs.

"Absolutely the most important thing for a leader," says Anteon Corporation's former COO Mike Cogburn, "is to give their colleagues the opportunity to make presentations, to interact with others in meetings, to succeed or fail. These are critical skills for professionals and managers, and often these are not tested adequately."[2]

Managers who place a high value on presentations and get involved in their development, whether as coaches and catalysts, see those efforts bring about significantly improved results in the conference room and in the capabilities of their people. Some suggestions:

♦ *Provide an environment of presentations excellence.* Cleaning up your own act is a good starting point. Do your own presentations display poor organization, cluttered visuals, and slumber-creating delivery? "Do as I DO" is a stronger force than "do as I SAY." (A common suggestion in presentation seminars is that the person who really needs this is the attendee's supervisor or VP.)

♦ *Acknowledge those who have made good presentations.* Let your team know the importance of good presentations to business goals and to them personally. Include presentations effectiveness in performance reviews and career planning.

◆ *Sign them up for a training program.* Then ask for and be receptive to their lessons-learned.

◆ *Be there for early review and support.* One of the miserable experiences many people speak of is being assigned to a presentation with little information or guidance. The "stuckee" flounders, goes off in too many directions, loses sleep, and comes up with a product that gets lacerated when the boss finally takes time to see it, usually during a dry run. "Gee, thanks for the help. But where were you when I needed you last week?" might be heard from presenters as they stagger out of the conference room.

◆ *Participate in rehearsals.* Give them positive feedback (and insist others do the same) to help enhance their readiness and confidence. Your experience and insights can be beneficial to meeting readiness, such as advising them about personality quirks of key audience members or warning them that their ultra-casual wardrobe might not be wise with this audience.

◆ *Shhh. Be a good listener.* Constant interruptions, poor listening, and diverted attentions interfere with productive communication and set back the speaker's skills and eagerness.

◆ *Following their presentation, give them an attaboy/attagirl.*

Keep on Rolling

Learning to swim or play tennis well takes practice. So does learning to be a better presenter. It is especially important to speak often, get helpful feedback, and grow. You'll get rusty if you don't speak for six months. Here are some ways to get that exposure and keep tuned up.

◆ *Join Toastmasters.* I often ask seminar attendees how many are past or current Toastmasters, and typically only a few hands go up. Yet Toastmasters is an effective and convenient way for novices and experienced people alike to advance speaking skills through frequent safe practice and feedback sessions

◆ *Take on a leadership role in your professional association, management club, or personal interest group.* In this role, you'll usually run meetings, introduce people, and give reports, all opportunities to try out your speaking skills.

◆ *Look for extra speaking opportunities.* Offer to give a five-minute status report at a group meeting. Submit a proposal to deliver a paper at a professional conference. Talk to your training department or local college about teaching a class in your specialty. Volunteer for a speakers' bureau for a favorite cause.

◆ *Keep a scorecard about your own performances.* Keep track of the hits and misses (rephrased as opportunities to improve). Ask colleagues to give you feedback. Above all, apply winning presentation concepts to all your normal work situations. And keep growing.

The Greeks of old laid down many of the rules of speaking, and applied oratory toward achieving success for themselves and their causes. One of the greatest was the general Pericles, who compared his own powerful skills to another: "When Pericles speaks, the people say, 'How well he speaks.' But when Demosthenes speaks, the people say, 'Let us march!' " Now there's a goal for you to ponder.[3]

Notes

Chapter 1

1. Lee Iacocca, *Iacocca, An Autobiography* (Toronto: Bantam, 1984), pp. 16, 54.
2. Interview, October 3, 1991.
3. Interview, June 17, 2003.
4. Interview, June 27, 2003.
5. Greg Jaffe, "What's Your Point, Lieutenant? Please, Just Cut to the Pie Charts," *Wall Street Journal*, April 26, 2002, p. 1.
6. Interview, July 20, 2003.
7. Martha Rader and Alan Wunsch, *Journal of Business Communication*, Summer 1980, p. 35.
8. Interview, June 20, 2003.
9. E-mail, June 30, 2003.
10. Interview, July 15, 2003.
11. Interview, June 23, 2003.
12. U.S. Air Force, *Presenter's Guide*, Document 27-3-72/3000.
13. Robert Levinson, "Executives Can't Communicate," *Dun's Review*, December 1972, p. 119.

Chapter 2

1. Interview, June 20, 2003.
2. Interview, June 18, 2003.
3. Interview, June 23, 2003.
4. Interview, June 27, 2003.
5. Interview, July 25, 2003.
6. Interview, June 23, 2003.

Chapter 3

1. Dwight Kirkpatrick and Alan Berg, "Fears of a Heterogeneous Non-psychiatric Sample: A Factor Analytic Study." Paper delivered at 89th

annual meeting of the American Psychological Association, Los Angeles, 1981.
2. *San Diego Union*, April 21, 1988.
3. Interview, July 28, 2003
4. Steve North, United Stations Radio Network, quoted in *Readers Digest*.
5. Lee Iacocca, *Iacocca, An Autobiography* (Toronto: Bantam, 1984), pp. 16, 53.
6. Interview, January 25, 1980.
7. Andrew Young, *An Easy Burden* (New York: Harper Collins, 1996), p. 43.
8. Interview, June 27, 2003.

Chapter 4

1. *San Diego Union*, February 7, 1978.
2. James Beveridge and Edward J. Yelton, *Creating Superior Proposals* (Talent, Ore.: J.M. Beveridge & Associates, 1978), pp. 21.
3. Gerald M. Phillips and J. Jerome Zolten, *Structuring Speech* (Indianapolis: Bobbs-Merrill, 1976), p. 76.
4. Paul Holtzman, *The Psychology of Speakers' Audiences* (Glenview, Ill.: Scott, Foresman, 1970), p. 42.
5. Interview, July 22, 1991.
6. Interview, July 25, 2003.
7. Stacey Evers, "Gnat 750 May Raise Profile of UAVs," *Aviation Week & Space Technology*, February 7, 1994, p. 54.
8. *Engineering News Record*, November 29, 1991, p. 24.
9. *Engineering News Record*, August 28, 2000, p. 24.
10. Robert E. Miller and Stephen E. Heiman, *Strategic Selling* (New York: Warner Books, 1985), p. 61.
11. Interview, January 15, 1992.
12. Holtzman, *The Psychology of Speakers' Audiences*.
13. Abraham Maslow, *Motivation and Personality*, 2nd edition (New York: Harper & Row, 1970).

Chapter 5

1. Cited in Wayne C. Minnick, *The Art of Persuasion*, 2nd edition (Cambridge, Mass.: Riverside Press, 1968), p. 262.
2. Don Freeman, "Man Bites Tabloid for a Little Taste of the Big Apple," *San Diego Union*, November 1, 1991.
3. Interview, October 31, 1991.
4. Interview, June 18, 2003.
5. Interview, July 14, 2003.
6. Interview, June 22, 2003.
7. Interview, May 20, 1992.

8. George A. Miller, *The Psychology of Communication* (New York: Basic Books, 1967), p. 1443.
9. Bruce Bigelow, "AMCC's Results in Line with Dim Forecast," *San Diego Union-Tribune,* July 11, 2003, p. E1.
10. Interview, July 15, 2003.
11. Interview, July 22, 1991.
12. Interview, July 14, 2003.
13. James Hebert, "Variations on Title Can Get a Little Ugly," *San Diego Union-Tribune,* July 11, 2003, p. E4.
14. Larry A. Samovar and Jack Mills, *Oral Communication, Message, and Response,* 4th edition (Dubuque, Iowa: William C. Brown, 1980), pp. 105–106.
15. Alan Monroe and Douglas Ehninger, *Principles of Speech Communication,* 6th edition (Glenview, Ill.: Scott, Foresman and Co., 1969), p. 258.
16. Ralph Smedley, *Basic Training for Toastmasters* (Santa Ana, Calif.: Toastmasters International, 1964), p. 30.
17. Richard Borden, *Public Speaking as Listeners Like It* (New York: Harper Bros., 1935), p. 3.
18. Dale Carnegie, *The Quick and Easy Way to Effective Speaking* (New York: Pocket Books, 1977), p. 104.
19. June Guncheon, "To Make People Listen," *Nation's Business,* October 1967, pp. 96–102.
20. Interview, January 11, 1980.
21. Gregory Suriano (editor), *Great American Speeches* (New York: Gramercy, 1993), p. 191.

Chapter 6

1. Robert Hillman, "CIA Director Gets Vote of Confidence from Bush," *San Diego Union-Tribune,* July 3, 2003, p. A2.
2. Associated Press news report, July 7, 2003.
3. Steve Bell, ABC-TV, November 20, 1985.
4. Richard Bernstein, New York Times News Service, "Italy and Germany Exchange New Slaps," *San Diego Union-Tribune,* July 10, 2003, p. A18.
5. Interview, July 14, 2003.
6. Robert Alberti and Michael Emmons, *Your Perfect Right: A Guide to Assertive Behavior* (San Luis Obispo, Calif.: Impact Pubs., 1990).
7. Cited in Clifton Fadiman, *The Little Brown Book of Anecdotes* (Boston: Little, Brown, 1985), p. 170.
8. Robert Half Company survey, Sanford Teller Communications press release, December 4, 1985.
9. Amitai Etioni, "Future Angst, Nine Rules for Stumbling into the Future," *Next,* July–August 1980, p. 69.
10. Michael Shnayerson and Jim Whittaker, "Back on Earth," *Adventure Magazine,* May 2003, p 56.

11. Walter Beran, "How to Be Ethical in an Unethical World," *Vital Speeches of the Day*, July 15, 1976, p. 32.
12. *San Diego Union-Tribune*, September 23, 2001.
13. *San Diego Union-Tribune*, June 19, 1989, p. A8.
14. Correspondence, May 20,1980.
15. Author's notes from television broadcast, September 24, 1984.
16. *San Jose Mercury News*, March 2, 1989, p. 12A.
17. *Los Angeles Times*, October 6, 1980.
18. Jerry Tarver, "The First of the Big Shots," supplement to *Los Angeles Times, undated*.
19. Pat Taylor, "The Relationship Between Humor and Retention," Speech Communication Association, 1972.
20. *Public Relations Journal* 35, no.5 (May 1979), p. 6.
21. Malcolm Kushner, *The Light Touch* (New York: Simon & Schuster, 1990), p. 92.
22. Interview, December 18, 1991.
23. Interview, September 6, 1991.
24. *Los Angeles Times*, May 29, 1980.
25. Elbert R. Bowen et al., *Communicative Reading*, 4th edition (New York: Macmillan, 1978), p. 36.
26. J. Myers and W. Reynolds, *Consumer Behavior and Marketing Management* (Boston: Houghton Mifflin, 1967), p. 60.
27. Joe Griffith, *Speaker's Library of Business Stories, Anecdotes and Humor* (Englewood Cliffs, N.J.: Prentice-Hall, 1990).
28. Robert Torricelli and Andrew Carroll, *In Our Own Words* (New York: Kodansha, 1999), p. 239.

Chapter 7

1. From Genigraphics Corporation.
2. Hower J. Hsia, "On Channel Effectiveness," *AV Communication Review*, Fall 1968, pp. 248–250.
3. "A Study of the Effects of Overhead Transparencies on Business Meetings," cited in *How to Run Better Business Meetings: 3M Team Meeting Management* (New York: McGraw-Hill, 1987).
4. Interview, June 19, 2003.
5. Greg Jaffe, "What's Your Point, Lieutenant? Please, Just Cut to the Pie Charts," *Wall Street Journal*, April 26, 2002, p.1.
6. Robert McKim, *Experiences in Visual Thinking* (Belmont, Calif.: Wadsworth, 1972), p.24.
7. "Priestly Prayer Triggers Plea to Turn in Guns," *Los Angeles Times*, April 10, 1982.
8. *San Diego Union*, April 25, 1979.
9. Interview, July 14, 2003.
10. Electro/Wescon Midcom, *Speaker's Handbook* (El Segundo, Calif.: Electronic Conventions, Inc.), p. 6.
11. Interview, June 20, 2003.

12. Carl Hovland, Irving Janis, and Harold Kelley, *Communication and Persuasion* (New Haven, Conn.: Yale University Press, 1953), p. 99.
13. George A. Miller, *The Psychology of Communication* (New York: Basic Books, 1967), p. 1443.
14. Cited in Ronald E. Green, "Communications with Color," *Audio-Visual Communications,* November 1978, p.14.
15. Jan V. White, *Graphic Design for the Electronic Age* (New York: Watson-Guptill, 1988), p. 31.
16. Margaret Rabb, *Presentation Design Book* (Chapel Hill, N.C.: Ventana Press, 1990), p.66.
17. Jerrold E. Kemp, *Planning and Producing Audiovisual Materials*, 3rd edition (New York: Thomas Y. Crowell, 1975), p. 121.

Chapter 8

1. Interview, July 15, 2003.
2. "Practice for Slide and Filmstrip Projection," Publication No. ANSI PH3.41–1972 (New York: National Standards Institute, 1972), p.9.
3. Ibid, p. 8.
4. Interview with Carol DeVinny, media manager for General Telephone Company of California, November 5, 1980.

Chapter 10

1. Michael Shnayerson and Jim Whittaker, "Back on Earth," *Adventure Magazine*, May 2003, p 56.

Chapter 11

1. Robert E. Levinson, "Executives Can't Communicate," *Dun's Review*, December 1972, p. 102.
2. William Luce, *The Belle of Amherst* (Boston: Houghton Mifflin, 1976), p. 8.
3. Interview, June 27,1991.
4. Interview, June 20, 2003.
5. Interview, October 3, 1991.
6. Interview, June 20, 2003.
7. Johann Wolfgang von Goethe, *Wilhelm Meister's Apprenticeship.*
8. Albert Mehrabian, *Silent Messages* (Belmont, Calif.: Wadsworth, 1971), p. 43.
9. Interview, June 17, 2003.
10. Ben Bradlee, *A Good Life* (New York: Simon & Schuster, 1965), p. 279.

Chapter 12

1. *San Diego Union*, July 19,1976.

322

Notes

2. *Newsweek*, February 13, 1978, p. 15.
3. Interview, June 23, 2003.
4. Jim Hebert, "Word Misuse Makes Folks Go 'Nuke-yoo-ler,'" *San Diego Union-Tribune*, March 9, 2001, p. E2.
5. *Aviation Week*, October 31,1977, p. 15.
6. William Safire, *Lend Me Your Ears: Great Speeches in History* (New York: W. Norton, 1992), p. 569.
7. Ibid, p.132.
8. Albert Mehrabian, *Silent Messages* (Belmont, Calif.: Wadsworth, 1971).
9. Lyle Mayer, *Fundamentals of Voice and Diction* (Dubuque, Iowa: William C. Brown, 1974), p. 110.
10. *A Guide to Better Technical Presentations* (New York: IEEE Press, 1975), p. 157.
11. *The Autobiography of Mark Twain* (New York: Harper Brothers, 1959), p. 198.
12. Mayer, *Fundamentals of Voice and Diction*, pp. 4, 131.
13. Hilda Fisher, *Improving Voice and Articulation* (Boston: Houghton Mifflin, 1966), p.53.
14. Interview, June 24, 2003.

Chapter 13

1. Interview, June 17, 2003.
2. Interview, June 23, 2003.
3. Interview, June 16, 2003.
4. Interview, June 17, 2003.
5. Dirk Beveridge, "Cyberspace Is Sizzling as Big Mac Is Attacked." *San Diego Union-Tribune*, March 28, 1996, p. C2.

Chapter 14

1. Ralph Nichols, "Listening Is a 10-part Skill," *Nation's Business,* July 1957.
2. Leonard A. Stevens, *The Ill-Spoken Word: The Decline of Speech in America* (New York: McGraw-Hill, 1966), p. 131.
3. J. Scott Armstrong, "Bafflegab Pays," *Psychology Today*, May 1980, p. 12.
4. Neal Matthews, "Is There a Doctorate in the House?," *San Diego Union-Tribune*, June 4, 2003, p. F1.
5. Kenneth Blanchard and Spencer Johnson, *The One Minute Manager* (New York: Berkley Books, 1981), p. 39.

Chapter 16

1. Interview, October 14, 1991.

2. Interview, June 17, 2003.
3. Interview, July 25, 2003.
4. Ibid.
5. "DOE Picks Fluor for Fernald," *Engineering News Record*, August 24, 1992, p. 9.

Chapter 17

1. Sidney Jourard, *Disclosing Man to Himself* (Princeton, N.J.: Van Nostrand, 1968).
2. Philip Cateoria and John Hess, *International Marketing*, 3rd edition (Homewood, Ill.: Irwin, 1975), p. 178.
3. Interview, June 27, 2003.
4. *Newsweek*, July 2, 2001, p 17.
5. Howard Van Zandt, "How to Negotiate in Japan," in Samovar and Porter, *Intercultural Communication*: A Reader, 2nd edition (Belmont, Calif.: Wadsworth, 1976) p. 315.
6. Interview, November 4, 1991.
7. Interview, June 27, 2003.
8. Interview, December 15, 1979.
9. Interview, April 21, 1981.
10. Interview, December 19, 1979.
11. Van Zandt, "How to Negotiate in Japan."
12. Interview, April 21, 1981.
13. Sondra Thiederman, "The Speaker and Diversity: Tips on Presenting to the Culturally Diverse Audience," audio cassette, National Speakers Association, 1991.
14. David Sanger, *New York Times*, January 24, 2003, p. A1.
15. Interview, December 15, 1979.
16. "Mexico's Consul General Protests 'Granada' Salute," *San Diego Tribune*, August 16,1984, p. A-24.
17. Andrew Young, *An Easy Burden* (New York: HarperCollins, 1996), p. 321.

Chapter 18

1. Thomas Leech, *Say It Like Shakespeare* (New York: McGraw-Hill, 2001).
2. Interview, June 20, 2003.
3. William Safire, *Lend Me Your Ears: Great Speeches in History* (New York: Norton, 1992), p. 25.

Index